Job-Embedded Professional Development

In today's schools, teachers are frequently called on to adapt new curricula and instructional practices in their classrooms. Making sense of the complexities of teaching occurs primarily during the work day, and instead of relying on before or after school, one-size-fits-all professional development activities, schools must support teachers in learning on the job. The latest book from renowned author Sally J. Zepeda is written for teachers, teacher leaders, and school and district leaders who want to support job-embedded learning, a powerful form of professional development characterized by active learning and reflection grounded in the context of a teacher's work environment.

Job-Embedded Professional Development provides a framework for helping teachers stop, take a deep breath, and learn along the way as they engage in their daily work. Through engaging job-embedded learning activities, processes, and cases from the field explored in this book, teachers will immediately be able to:

- Implement what they are learning in the context of their own classrooms

- Work with supportive peers who can coach them along the way

- Get feedback on what's working and what needs to be tweaked

- Develop as adult learners fully capable of making sound professional judgments

- Engage in conversations that allow teachers to dig deeper into their practices

- Focus intently on content knowledge and the linkages to instruction and assessment

- ◆ Capitalize on learning in digital learning environments before, during, and after school
- ◆ Gain confidence in themselves and others through learning together.

Sally J. Zepeda is a professor in the Department of Lifelong Education, Administration, and Policy in the Program of Educational Administration and Policy, and she is a Fellow in the Institute for Interdisciplinary Research in Education and Human Development at the University of Georgia, where she teaches courses in instructional supervision, professional development, teacher evaluation, and school improvement.

Job-Embedded Professional Development: Support, Collaboration, and Learning in Schools

Sally J. Zepeda

Routledge
Taylor & Francis Group

NEW YORK AND LONDON

First published 2015
by Routledge
711 Third Avenue, New York, NY 10017

and by Routledge
2 Park Square, Milton Park, Abingdon, Oxon OX14 4RN

Routledge is an imprint of the Taylor & Francis Group, an informa business

Library of Congress Cataloging-in-Publication Data
Zepeda, Sally J., 1956–
   Job-embedded professional development : support, collaboration, and learning in schools / Sally J. Zepeda.
      pages cm
   Includes bibliographical references and index.
   1. Teachers—In-service training.   2. Reflective teaching.   3. Professional learning communities.   I. Title.
      LB1731.Z46 2014
      370.71'1—dc23
      2014006106

ISBN: 978-0-415-73484-4 (hbk)
ISBN: 978-0-415-73483-7 (pbk)
ISBN: 978-1-315-81969-3 (ebk)

Typeset in Palatino LT Std
by Apex CoVantage, LLC

Printed and bound in the United States of America by Publishers Graphics, LLC on sustainably sourced paper.

Dedication

Wrists by Michael S. Shuler, M.D.—Thanks—Doc

Contents

Acknowledgments

Writing a book on job-embedded professional development has been a collaborative and reflective learning process because of my association with great practitioners in the field who have shared insights, given feedback, asked incessant questions, and essentially made me think beyond the comfort of the ivory tower. These conversations and experiences have been humbling and have served as a reminder that for practices in professional development to have traction, they must be adaptive to the needs of teachers.

During the past three years, I have had the privilege to work as a professor-in-residence with the Clarke County School District in Athens Georgia as part of a School Partnership with the College of Education at the University of Georgia. Through this work, Dr. Philip D. Lanoue, Superintendent of the Clarke County School District, has asked probing questions, modeled life-long learning, and supported system-wide growth by promoting job-embedded learning for all teachers and leaders. Phil, your relentless challenges have humbly reminded me of what the real work in schools is all about—creating the conditions so that *all* students and adults can learn. Thank you for the lively discussions, your candor, the repartee, and the collaborative work environment.

Dr. Noris F. Price, Deputy Superintendent of the Clarke County School District, is a relentless proponent of job-embedded learning who has operationalized numerous programs, processes, and accountability systems to ensure that teachers and leaders are engaged in meaningful learning experiences that increase personal and system capacity. Noris, you are a champion of professional learning and your work epitomizes best practices. Thank you for modeling professional learning in all the work you do.

You will read a great deal about the Clarke County School District as well as other school systems beyond the state of Georgia in the *Cases from the Field* in each of the chapters.

Working behind the scenes were three very capable University of Georgia research assistants who supported my efforts. Thank you, Brigette Adair Herron, Phillip Grant, and Christopher Pinzone.

Lisa M. Wolf helped me ready to push the send button.

The thoughtful and reflective insights provided by reviewers came at the right time, and this manuscript is a stronger one as a result of the critical but constructive feedback of the anonymous reviewers.

A book about job-embedded professional development would not be complete without *Cases from the Field*. I am indebted to the teachers, instructional coaches, principals, central office leaders, and higher education faculty who contributed their practices for inclusion in this book.

Case from the Field Contributors

Cases from the Clarke County School District (Athens, GA)

Dr. Philip D. Lanoue, Superintendent
Dr. Noris F. Price, Deputy Superintendent

Instructional Services and School Performance
Dr. Mark Tavernier, Director of Teaching and Learning
Ms. Glenda Huff, Mathematics Coordinator, 6–12
Mr. David Forker, K–12 ESOL Specialist

Hilsman Middle School
Dr. Selena S. Blankenship, Principal
Ms. Audrey Hughes, 6th Grade Science Teacher
Mr. Nicholas Hussain, 7th Grade Mathematics and Social Studies Teacher
Ms. Teresa Johns, 7th Grade ELA and Science Teacher
Ms. Jessie Wood, 8th Grade Humanities Teacher
Ms. Holley Ziemann, Humanities Content Leader

W. R. Coile Middle School
Mr. Dwight Manzy, Principal

Cedar Shoals High School
Dr. Anthony Price, Principal
Dr. Rick Tatum, Associate Principal
Mr. Gavin Matesich, Social Studies Teacher, Social Studies Department Co-Chair, and Economics Teacher
Ms. Erica Fletcher, 9th Grade Coordinate Algebra Teacher and Freshman Academy Team Leader
Mr. Marc Ginsberg, 9th Grade Literature and Composition Teacher

Clarke Central High School
Ms. Marie Yuran, Special Education Team Leader
Dr. Linda Boza, Instructional Coach
Dr. Robbie Hooker, Principal
Ms. Mary Thielman, Associate Principal

Case from Southfield School (Shreveport, LA)

Southfield School
Mr. Gordon Walker, Headmaster
Mr. Ryan Berens, Director of Instructional Technology
Mrs. Deborah Kiel, 5th Grade Teacher
Mrs. Susan Murrell, 5th Grade Teacher

Case from the Gwinnett County Public Schools (Gwinnett County, GA)

Lilburn Middle School
Stefanie Steele, Ph.D., Assistant Principal
Mr. Michael Richie, 8th Grade Language Arts Teacher
Wisteria Williams, Ed.D., 7th Grade Social Studies Teacher and Content Leader
Ms. Carla D. Clark, Assistant Principal
Mr. Christopher Carter, Assistant Principal

Case from University of South Florida (Tampa, FL)

University of South Florida
Dr. Judith A. Ponticell, Professor, Educational Leadership and Policy Studies
Ms. Shauna Bergwall
Ms. Marissa Story
Ms. Sherida Weaver

Case from Oconee County School District (Watkinsville, GA)

North Oconee High School
Dr. Philip Brown, Principal
Miss Christina Spears, Science Teacher

These practices are exemplary, and they point to what's possible when professionals are committed to job-embedded learning opportunities.

Numerous professional educators and consultants in coaching shared materials for inclusion in this book. These materials were of such high quality that I wanted to share with a larger audience how they could be used to support collaborative and reflective job-embedded learning. Special acknowledgements go to:

Dr. Karin K. Hess for permission to reproduce the © Hess Cognitive Rigor Matrix in *Linking Research with Practice: A Local Assessment Toolkit to Guide School Leaders* (2009, updated, 2013).

Peter Pappas for permission to reproduce © *A taxonomy of reflection Critical thinking for students, teachers, and principals* (Part 1), Copy/Paste: peterpappas.com; and © *The reflective teacher: A taxonomy of reflection* (Part 3), Copy/Paste: peterpappas.com.

The National School Reform Faculty/NSRF. (n.d.) for permission to reproduce the protocol, *ATLAS Learning from Student Work*. This protocol was originally developed by Eric Buchovecky, based on the work of the Leadership for Urban Mathematics Project, the Assessment Communities of Teachers Projects, and Steve Seidel, and Evangeline Harris-Stefanakis of Project Zero of Harvard University, and then was edited further by Gene Thompson-Grove for the NSRF. NSRF website is www.nsrfharmony.org

Mr. Barry Zweibel, founder of LeadershipTraction® for permission to reproduce 1) © The Coaching F.R.A.M.E. of Reference Model; 2) © Coaching Helps People F.O.C.U.S.; and 3) © Questions that Gather Information versus Deepen the Learning all available at www.ldrtr.com

A special heartfelt farewell goes to Bob Sickles who left his "Eye" authors in the most capable hands of Routledge. Enjoy your own writing, Bob. I fondly recall our years of conversations.

Heather Jarrow, Editor with the Routledge/Taylor & Francis Group, is professional in her work, enthusiastic in her approach, and wise in her counsel in making key decisions about this book and getting it to press. I respect these qualities in an editor and look forward to the next book.

Sally J. Zepeda, Ph.D.

Professor:
Department of Lifelong Education,
Administration, and Policy
Fellow:
The Institute for Interdisciplinary Research in
Education and Human Development
University of Georgia

About the Author

Dr. Sally J. Zepeda, a former K–12 administrator and teacher, is a professor in the Department of Lifelong Education, Administration, and Policy, and she is a fellow in the Institute for Interdisciplinary Research in Education and Human Development at the University of Georgia. She teaches courses related to instructional supervision, professional development, learning communities, and teacher evaluation.

Sally has written numerous articles in such publications as the *Journal of Curriculum and Supervision*, *Journal of Staff Development*, *Professional Development in Education*, *Journal of School Leadership*, *International Journal of Mentoring and Coaching in Education*, and *Review of Educational Research*.

Sally Zepeda has also authored and coauthored over 20 books including the highly acclaimed second edition of *Professional Development: What Works*, the third edition of *The Principal as Instructional Leader: A Practical Handbook*, the third edition of *Instructional Supervision: Applying Tools and Concepts*, the third edition of *Informal Classroom Observations On the Go: Feedback, Discussion, and Reflection*, and *Instructional Leadership for School Improvement* with Routledge.

She served for nine years as the book and audio review column editor for the *Journal of Staff Development*. Sally is a member of the Council of Professors of Instructional Supervision (COPIS) and a lifetime fellow in the Foundation for Excellence in Teaching. She also serves on the editorial boards for several scholarly and practitioner journals, including *the International Journal of Mentoring and Coaching in Education* and the *International Journal of Teacher Leadership*.

In 2005, Sally received the inaugural Master Professor Award from the University Council of Educational Administration. Sally received the 2010 Russell H. Yeany, Jr., Research Award that honors outstanding contributions to research, and, in 2011, she received the Distinguished Research Mentor Award from the University of Georgia. Sally has traveled internationally, presenting across the Middle East on peer coaching, instructional supervision, and other areas related to professional development.

As a professor-in-residence with the Clarke County School District (Athens, GA), Dr. Zepeda assisted with the development and rollout of a teacher evaluation system and supported professional development for school leaders as they work with teachers to improve student learning. She is working with a group of Teacher-Coaches and Early-Career Teachers involved in a Race to the Top Initiative with the Clarke County School District.

Job-Embedded Professional Development: An Overview

1

In This Chapter . . .

- ◆ Professional Development Is Learning
- ◆ Job-Embedded Learning—A Brief Overview
- ◆ Collaboration and the New Arrangement of Teachers' Work Days
- ◆ Self-Efficacy, Human Agency, and Teacher Voice
- ◆ Professional Development Loops Back to Student Learning
- ◆ Collaborative Professional Learning—We Know It Works!
- ◆ Organization of the Book—Collaborative Approaches to Job-Embedded Professional Development
- ◆ Case from the Field
- ◆ Chapter Summary
- ◆ Suggested Readings

Teachers grow, evolve, and emerge throughout their careers and the day-to-day work they do, and that is why job-embedded learning opportunities need to be the focal point of our efforts. Teachers need to champion their own professional learning in tandem with collaborative and reflective approaches with colleagues, so that job-embedded professional development becomes part of the work day. Gulamhussein (2013a) makes it clear:

> Professional development can no longer just be about exposing teachers to a concept or providing basic knowledge about a teaching methodology. Instead, professional development in an era of accountability requires a *change in a teacher's practice* that leads to increases in student learning. (p. 6, emphasis in the original)

Learning is about change and as a result of engaging in professional development, it would be a reasonable expectation that regardless of its form, teachers would be "doing something" however big or small differently, that there would be shifts occurring in instructional practices, and that, in turn, there would be shifts in what students would be doing.

Why are collaborative and reflective approaches to job-embedded learning needed? The answer to this question is a clear-cut one—these approaches work! Professional development is learning nestled in the daily arrangements of teaching and the work day, extended beyond the school day, or even across the globe through participation in professional learning networks.

Teachers need to believe that they can be successful, that they can be lifelong learners, and that their students can learn more if they are actively learning alongside them. Teachers need to feel a sense of self and collective efficacy that they can make a difference (Derrington & Angelle, 2013). Teachers also need a voice in determining what they learn, the types of learning activities that will meet their particular needs, and they need to feel a sense of human agency that they can, indeed, make a difference and enact changes in their classroom and perhaps beyond (Bangs & Frost, 2012; Frost 2011).

Teachers need to be part of a community that embraces multiple points of view, the varied experiences, and far-reaching support that can come from colleagues who are willing to engage in collaborative conversations, ask probing questions, and reflect about the impact of such efforts. This chapter examines some important ideas that influence teacher involvement in collaborative and reflective forms of professional development.

Professional Development Is Learning

Professional development is about learning—learning for students, teachers, and other professionals who support children. Learning to teach is a lifelong pursuit, but it is the quality of the professional learning that counts if we want to ensure learning to teach occurs across the career span. A long-term view about the type, intensity, and duration of professional learning is necessary given the link between teacher effectiveness and student achievement. Gulamhussein (2013b) reminds us that:

> traditional forms [of professional development] operate under a faulty theory of teacher learning. They assume that the only challenge facing teachers is a lack of knowledge of effective teaching practices. However, research shows that the greatest challenge for teachers doesn't simply come in acquiring knowledge of new strategies, but in *implementing* those strategies in the classroom. (p. 36, emphasis in the original)

Professional development that does not include ongoing support through such forms as coaching, opportunities to engage in action research, dedicated conversations with colleagues during team meetings, and other forms of collegial support is, according to Sparks (2013), a form of "malpractice."

One can hardly blame the bad rap that professional development gets, where teachers are held as a "captive audience" for an extended time, engaging in "notoriously unproductive" and fragmented activities (Nieto, 2009, p. 10), in which the content of these sessions holds little promise for immediate transfer to improved instructional practices (Joyce & Showers, 2002).

So let's cut to the chase: What do we know about effective professional development? As overview, Creemers, Kyriakides, and Antoniou (2013) share:

> The research findings have revealed that professional development is more effective if the teacher has an active role in constructing knowledge (*teacher*

as action researcher), collaborates with colleagues (*collective critical reflection*), the content relates to, and is situated in, the daily teaching practice (*emphasis on teaching skills*), the content is differentiated to meet individual developmental needs (*linked with formative evaluation results*). (p. 51, emphasis in the original)

Professional development promotes learning if there are opportunities to collaborate with colleagues about such matters as student work and common assessments, and there is follow-up such as coaching (Darling-Hammond & Falk, 2013; Darling-Hammond, Weir, Andree, Richardson, & Orphanus, 2009).

Job-embedded learning is the ticket to supporting teachers as they engage in the complexities of their work. Timperley (2008, pp. 6–7) indicates that activities that support learning for adults include a variety of modalities that span, for example:

- opportunities to listen to or view others who have greater expertise modeling new approaches in the classroom

- being observed and receiving feedback

- sharing strategies and resources

- being coached or mentored to implement new approaches

- discussing beliefs, ideas, and theories of practice and the implications for teaching, learning, and assessment

- engaging with professional readings and discussing these with colleagues.

These activities mirror job-embedded learning as they occur in the context of the work day.

Job-Embedded Learning—A Brief Overview

Chapter 3 is dedicated to job-embedded learning, and each chapter focuses on constructs of job-embedded learning that promote collaboration.

Job-embedded learning occurs in the context of the job setting and is related to what people learn and share about their experiences, reflecting on specific work incidents to uncover newer understandings or changes in practices or beliefs. Job-embedded learning occurs through the ongoing discussions where colleagues listen and learn from each other as they share what does and does not work in a particular setting. Job-embedded learning is about sharing best practices discovered while trying out new programs, planning new programs and practices, and implementing revisions based on the lessons learned from practice.

Gulamhussein (2013b) makes an interesting point related to the types of expectations teachers hold for student learning, and she wonders why teachers do not hold the same learning expectations for themselves. Job-embedded learning resonates with "meaning making," "incorporating prior knowledge," "making learning social with collaboration and discussion," and "fostering inquiry" (Gulamhussein, 2013b, p. 37). What an adept parallel!

Job-embedded learning can only thrive in a culture that embraces collaboration as teachers are engaged in a new type of work.

Collaboration and the New Arrangement of Teachers' Work Days

So what is the new work of teachers? The work has really stayed the same—it's all about the students. New are the arrangements of the work day and how teachers work with one another in and out of the classroom. We are now more focused on students and learning outcomes. We are asking ourselves tough questions: Are students learning, and if they are not, why not, and what can we do to turn things around? Hopefully, we are digging deeper, framing our discussions around students first and then linking our discussions to our practices. These questions and subsequent conversations are occurring in public, collaborative places with peers.

It's interesting to see how one school leadership team at W. R. Coile Middle School in the Clarke County School District (Athens, GA) has rearranged time every day so that teachers in every grade-level team have consistent time during the contract day where they can collaborate. Figure 1.1 illustrates the schedule that Mr. Dwight Manzy, Principal of W. R. Coile Middle School, has massaged to make collaboration possible.

At Coile Middle School, personal planning time is combined with team planning time, doubling the amount of time for teachers to collaborate.

Collaboration is central to improving student learning. Studies show the connection between professional learning, gains in student achievement, and collaboration (Avalos, 2011; Darling-Hammond *et al.*, 2009; Guskey & Yoon, 2009). The 26th annual *MetLife Survey of the American Teacher* (MetLife, 2010) examined levels of collaboration as reported primarily by teachers and principals. C. Robert Hendrickson, Chairman of the Board and President and Chief Executive Officer MetLife, Inc., prefaced, in part, this report with the following message:

> The 21st century workplace teaches that an education is never complete. There are always adaptations to be made, new things to learn, and opportunities for innovation. Collaboration plays a tremendous role in today's work environment. Success depends on commitment to a common purpose and working to accomplish more together than can be achieved individually, whether with colleagues down the hall, across the nation or around the globe. (Hendrickson, 2010, p. 3)

Darling-Hammond and Richardson (2009) report "collaborative and collegial learning environments . . . develop communities of practice able to promote school change beyond individual classrooms" (p. 48).

Collaboration is a long-term strategy much more enduring than workshops offered by external providers who leave once the "job is done." This thought is not to infer that

Figure 1.1. Collaborative Planning and Learning Schedule at W. R. Coile Middle School

Monday	Tuesday	Wednesday	Thursday	Friday
Professional Learning Sessions	RTI/504/IEP Meetings	Data Team Meetings	Collaborative Subject Planning	Grade-Level Planning

collaboration cannot occur as a result of what is learned through external consultants who provide professional learning opportunities. External providers are still valuable, and they can offer much; however, it falls to the system to ensure that there is follow-up support including, for example, coaching, peer observations, modeling, and other mechanisms for teachers to meet and debrief about implementation of new practices.

Systems are getting "smarter" about crafting professional learning opportunities. System and site personnel are well poised to tailor the content and professional learning processes and activities because they know and understand the context of the system, the characteristics of the teachers and students, and the climate and the culture within specific buildings. Here too, systems are responsible to ensure that follow-up supports such as coaching, modeling, feedback, reflection, and other collaborative forms of learning are incorporated after formal professional development is provided.

In the end, it's all about whether teachers apply what has been learned, if they change or modify practices, or if their beliefs begin to shift. As shifts in beliefs, ideas, and practices occur, the support of a colleague in a collaborative environment is "priceless."

Collaboration Supports the Development of a Culture of Social Support for Learning

Fullan (2008a) reminds us that "professional learning" must be seen "as a part of day-to-day work in the school culture" (p. 5), and until "you have a learning culture, you won't achieve breakthrough results" (p. 6) related to student achievement or teacher development. Collaboration is important for another reason. Teachers want to belong; they want to have peers to turn to for support. Pink (2011) tells us that "human beings have an innate inner drive to be autonomous, self-determined, and connected to one another" (p. 73). The social support offered through collaboration carries many benefits for schools and their teachers. According to Learning Forward (2012), collaborative learning occurs in special places, learning communities. Within the overview of the Learning Forward Standard, *Learning Communities*, the following is shared:

> Within learning communities, members exchange feedback about their practice with one another, visit each other's classrooms or work settings, and share resources. Learning community members strive to refine their collaboration, communication, and relationship skills to work within and across both internal and external systems to support student learning. They develop norms of collaboration and relational trust and employ processes and structures that unleash expertise and strengthen capacity to analyze, plan, implement, support, and evaluate their practice. (2012, par. 4 http://learningforward.org/standards/learning-communities#.Up5Gt-Ilhrg)

Schools with collaborative cultures build camaraderie and send a strong, positive message about the serious nature of teaching.

Self-Efficacy, Human Agency, and Teacher Voice

To promote more collaborative and reflective learning opportunities for adults, it is important to have a broad understanding of three interrelated constructs—self-efficacy, human agency, and teacher voice—as these shape how individuals

Figure 1.2. Interrelated Nature of Self-Efficacy, Human Agency, and Teacher Voice

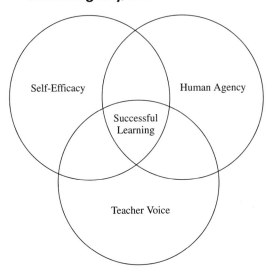

approach, are receptive to, or avoid approaching, persevering, or taking charge of their learning. Figure 1.2 shows the interrelated nature of self-efficacy, human agency, and teacher voice.

Self-Efficacy

Self-efficacy is defined in a variety of ways, with Bandura's work leading our understandings of this construct. Self-efficacy is a person's *belief* about the ability to organize and to carry out to completion a course of action in ways to achieve goals (Bandura, 1977). A self-efficacious person is confident in his/her capacity to achieve goals, to preserve in the face of adversity, and to succeed. In many ways, one's beliefs shape what one considers is possible, which could shape what one pursues—and how.

Linking Self-Efficacy to Professional Learning

Bangs and Frost (2012) link self-efficacy to professional learning in a very important way when they report, "A teacher with strong beliefs in his or her own efficacy will be resilient, able to solve problems and, most importantly, learn from their experience" (p. 8). Given the complexities of teaching and the steep slopes of information teachers have had to master so they can teach with fidelity to national standards (e.g., Common Core), the landscape of teaching is continually changing. The stakes are higher, and the professional learning required to keep pace with the constantly shifting landscape signals a need to be mindful of efficacy and whether or not we are promoting the conditions to support the positive development of attitudes and beliefs about professional learning. Higher teacher efficacy is a significant predictor of teacher change (Parise & Spillane, 2010).

High Teacher Efficacy

According to Pajares (2002):

1. The greater the effort, persistence, and resilience.

2. People with a strong sense of personal competence approach difficult tasks as challenges to be mastered rather than as threats to be avoided.

3. They have greater intrinsic interest and deep engrossment in activities, set themselves challenging goals and maintain strong commitment to them, and heighten and sustain their efforts in the face of failure.

4. Moreover, they more quickly recover their sense of efficacy after failures or setbacks, and attribute failure to insufficient effort or deficient knowledge and skills that are acquirable. (par. 20)

Low Teacher Self-Efficacy

Teachers with low efficacy tend to avoid difficult situations in which they do not believe they will be successful in accomplishing or completing the difficult tasks, and they tend to lack persistence to complete difficult tasks (Pajares, 1992, 2002). Figure 1.3 recaps the importance of self-efficacy related to professional learning for adults.

Figure 1.3. The Importance of Self-Efficacy and Professional Learning for Adults

1. If teachers hold the conviction that they will be effective, they will try to cope with a situation.

2. Teachers will engage in learning, experimenting and doing the work needed to enact personal change when they feel they are capable and not intimidated by their circumstances.

3. Teachers who are more self-efficacious will stay more engaged and persist through difficulties.

Source: Based on Bandura (1977).

Teacher Sense of Human Agency

Professional learning is not a spectator sport. Agency is related to one's ability to shape one's present and future (Bandura, 1977, 2006). According to Bandura (2006) "people are self-organizing, proactive, self-regulating, and self-reflecting. They are not simply onlookers of their behavior. They are contributors to their life circumstances, not just products of them" (p. 164). Bandura's (2006) four properties

Table 1.1. Professional Learning Related to the Properties and Characteristics of Human Agency

Properties of Human Agency	Characteristics	Alignment to Professional Learning
Intentionality	"action plans and strategies for realizing them" (2006, p. 164)	Teachers purposefully engage in planning their professional learning
Forethought	"set goals . . . and anticipate likely outcomes of prospective actions to guide and motivate their efforts" (2006, p. 164)	In like fashion, adults set goals for achieving professional learning objectives, and they set targets
Self-Reactiveness	"self-regulate"; people "construct appropriate courses of action and . . . motivate and regulate their execution" to achieve goals (2006, p. 164)	Because teachers are professionals, they self-monitor goal attainment, work with others as they attain their goals, and are motivated by results
Self-Reflectiveness	"self-examiners"; people "reflect on their personal efficacy, the soundness of their thoughts and actions, and the meaning of their pursuits, and they make corrective adjustments if necessary" (2006, p. 164).	Throughout the process of learning, teachers reflect on their progress toward meeting goals; they regroup based on what they are learning about practice, and they repeat the process of reflecting about practice and the results of their efforts

of human agency are identified in Table 1.1 showing how the characteristics of each align with professional learning.

The relationship between self-efficacy and human agency now turns to teacher voice—the authority to learn and to be heard as they collect and accumulate expertise over their careers.

Teacher Voice

Teachers need to have a tremendous voice—they need to be supported in their learning endeavors. In *The Courage to Teach* (1998), Palmer writes: "The only way to get out of trouble is to go in deeper. We must enter, not evade, the tangles of teaching so we can understand them better and negotiate them with more grace . . . to serve our children well" (p. 2).

Katzenmeyer and Moller (2009) assert "leadership among teachers thrives when they are involved in planning and delivering professional development" (p. 5). The credibility of professional development at the site will yield results that are more positive if teachers are intimately involved in all phases—identifying their own needs, teaching each other new skills, monitoring progress, etc. Self-efficacy, human agency, and teacher voice coalesce around teacher leadership. Professional learning that is

embedded within the work day with collaborative structures that honor adult learners is a prerequisite for the new teaching arrangements that focus on student learning.

Professional Development Loops
Back to Student Learning

The message across the literature and research is that a major factor in improving students' achievement is teacher performance and development. Opfer and Pedder (2011) share, "If student learning is to be improved, then one pathway for doing
so is the provision of more effective professional learning activities for teachers in
schools; where 'effective' activities result in positive change for teachers and their
pupils" (p. 3). To find the elusive "pathway" between professional learning and student learning, there is a need to focus on the types of professional learning teachers
engage, to concentrate our efforts on content, assessment, and to see if we can find
more definitive linkages to student achievement.

Collaborative Professional
Learning—We Know It Works!

Professional development can take many forms, such as engaging in action
research, participating in peer coaching, co-teaching and co-planning, reflecting
with a colleague, being a member of a professional learning network, examining student work, etc.—all covered in this book. A research base supports what we know
about effective professional development. Throughout this text the word "effective"
is used to describe practices that are research-based, tied to standards, and present
a coherent structure for teachers to learn as they collaborate with peers. To this end,
professional development is not an add-on, and is not a series of discrete activities.
Table 1.2 details promising practices learned from key research about professional
development.

**Table 1.2. Promising Practices Learned from Key Research on
Professional Development**

Promising Practices	Illustrative Research and Theory on Professional Development
Professional development extends over time	Darlington-Hammond, Wei, Andree, Richardson, & Orphanos, 2009; Desimone, 2011
Professional development includes planned follow-up activities as part of the process	Darling-Hammond & Falk, 2013; Desimone, 2011; Guskey & Yoon, 2009; Timperley, 2008; Timperley, Wilson, Barrar, & Fung, 2007; Zepeda, 2012a
Professional development is job-embedded, connecting to the work of teaching (relevance)	Croft, Coggshall, Dolan, Powers, & Killion, 2010; Guskey & Yoon, 2009; Yoon, Duncan, Lee, Scarloss, & Shapley, 2007; Wood & McQuarrie, 1999

(Continued)

Table 1.2 **(Continued)**

Promising Practices	Illustrative Research and Theory on Professional Development
Professional development is content-specific (related to subject matter)	Borko, 2004; Darling-Hammond & Richardson, 2009; Desimone, 2011
Professional development promotes ongoing reflection and inquiry	Creemers *et al.*, 2013; Cunningham, 2011; Gulamhussein, 2013b
Professional development includes multiple modalities of learning (active engagement)	Joyce & Showers, 2002; Croft *et al.*, 2010
Professional development is site-based and includes teachers from the same grade level and subject areas	Croft *et al.*, 2010
Professional development focuses on high-yield student outcomes (connects to student achievement)	Avalos, 2011; Darling-Hammond *et al.*, 2009; Guskey & Yoon, 2009; Opfer & Pedder, 2011
Professional development is characterized by coherence by linking to other systems	Desimone, 2011; Guskey & Yoon, 2009; Zepeda, 2012a

Source: Adapted from Zepeda (2012a).

Organization of the Book—Collaborative Approaches to Job-Embedded Professional Development

This book is organized to explore the various models and processes involved with collaborative professional development that can be embedded mostly within the work day; however, technology has expanded learning opportunities for teachers, leaders, and other school personnel. The following chapters are offered:

- ◆ Chapter 2: Adults Learning: What the Research Says

- ◆ Chapter 3: Job-Embedded Professional Development in Action

- ◆ Chapter 4: The Power of Peer Observations

- ◆ Chapter 5: Best Practices in Peer Coaching

- ◆ Chapter 6: Learning from Collaborative and Reflective Professional Development

- ◆ Chapter 7: Authentic Action Research

- ◆ Chapter 8: Studying Student Work and Assessments—Teachers as Change Agents

- ◆ Chapter 9: Innovative Digital Learning Opportunities Support Professional Development

- ◆ Chapter 10: Taking the Fast Track at Your Own Speed

Case from the Field

School Improvement is a Collaborative, Job-Embedded Learning Process

Dr. Selena S. Blankenship, Principal; Ms. Audrey Hughes, 6th Grade Science Teacher; Ms. Teresa Johns, 7th Grade ELA and Science Teacher; Ms. Jessie Wood, 8th Grade Humanities Teacher; Ms. Holley Ziemann, Humanities Content Leader; Hilsman Middle School, Clarke County School District, GA

Case Organizer

Data teams support learning for both students and teachers. The following case illustrates the uses of data not only to monitor student growth and achievement but also as a way for teachers to monitor their own instructional practices through their collaborative work in data teams. Looking more carefully, this case illustrates how learning is embedded in the very work that teachers do through the data team process and beyond, and the new work of collaboration around teaching and learning amid complexities found in schools.

The Context of Hilsman Middle School

Hilsman Middle School, an International Baccalaureate Middle Years Programme Candidate School, is an urban school serving grades 6–8 located in Clarke County, Georgia. Hilsman serves a diverse population of nearly 700 students, and maintains a faculty and staff of over 100 certified and classified professionals. Many ethnicities and cultures are represented within the student body, as Hilsman is 77 percent minority. The major subgroups are: 59 percent Black or African-American, 2 percent Asian, 23 percent White, 11 percent Hispanic/Latino, and 5 percent Two or More Races. The free and reduced lunch rate is 81 percent, qualifying Hilsman as a Title I school. Hilsman is academically diverse as well, with 33 percent of the population receiving either gifted or special education services. Students consistently rank in the top five at the state and/or national levels in MathCounts and Helen Ruffin Reading Bowl. Hilsman is home to a national award-winning Science and Energy Team.

Job-Embedded Learning with Data Teams

Data teams were introduced by the superintendent in 2009 as one way to improve teaching and student performance in the classroom. As a result, teachers have been provided with ongoing, job-embedded learning by being involved in the data team process where the environment offers teachers time to reflect, collaborate, create, and refine their practices. Data teams are work groups made up of teachers teaching a common subject at a given grade level, such as 8th Grade Humanities. Hilsman data teams meet twice per week during common planning periods on Wednesdays and Thursdays. During this time, teachers engage in the data team process to collect and chart student data, analyze strengths and obstacles, establish goals, select instructional strategies, and determine result indicators.

Analysis Builds a Common Lexicon and Shared Practices

As a curriculum data team, teachers monitor student progress through common formative assessments, share instructional strategies, and plan together. Data teams also analyze quarterly district benchmark scores. Digging into benchmark scores involves breaking down scores by standard and school, but then teams go one step further to compare assessment levels by standard and element for *each* teacher. By engaging in this type of analysis, teachers share knowledge, come to a common understanding of this knowledge, and build a common lexicon to talk about instructional practices. Through analysis and common understandings, teachers are more conversant on how to support each other to improve daily instruction. This type of conversation often leads to action such as a peer observation to see the strategy being taught or possibly sharing teacher-developed resources on a common space.

Conversations Matter

While teachers often use common instructional strategies, the delivery can differ. Through data team conversations, if one teacher's students scored much lower than another's, that teacher is able to inquire how their colleague emphasized the material or what additional strategies were used to get results. For example, in 8th Grade Georgia Studies, teachers taught the causes of the Civil War. However, one teacher's students scored better when assessed on that standard during the benchmark. From their conversations, the teachers believed 1) the guided review that the teacher completed with his students provided them with a greater depth of knowledge about the causes of the war; 2) all students struggled with Georgia's first Constitution of 1777; and, 3) students struggled with the concept that the governor's office held a much different structure during Georgia's early statehood. These realizations led to conversations about the misconceptions students had and how we taught the materials. As a result, we were able to make a plan for re-teaching the material to increase student mastery.

What is at the Center of these Conversations?

These conversations are powerful because they help improve teaching and learning in *real time*. Data team conversations also help to improve future practice. When teachers plan for the next year, they use archived data team minutes, blog postings, and benchmark analysis tools to remember their strengths and weaknesses of instruction, ideas they had about changing instruction, and modifications made to instructional materials. After reviewing these materials, data teams begin to plan their common instructional strategies for units. The conversations help teachers to 1) build professional practices as they continue to improve on instructional strategies that worked; 2) reflect collectively on teaching practices; 3) share professional knowledge and expertise; 4) help guide teachers' instruction and improve their professional practice; 5) ensure the continuity of the standards-based curriculum and target the standards with more fidelity.

Increasing Collaboration, Reducing Isolation

A benefit of collaborative data teams is that teachers no longer work in isolation. While the principal's role is to provide the structured time for data teams to meet, some teams have discovered that meeting two times per week is not enough time. The 6th Grade science data team is one such team. They often meet after school hours and on weekends, by choice. They almost always meet for these informal meetings in the data team leader's classroom, which is also the science lab, to have access to the materials that they will need to use. Team members communicate throughout the day by email, blog, and personal phones.

Data Teams Explore "Whatifs"

To say that data teams fosters communication seems to belabor the obvious, but in as mobile a society and fragile an economy as we currently live, this is a significant consideration. Hilsman houses 12 data teams, and in the 7th Grade ELA data team, five members over the past three years have changed. Whether the dynamics in those changes represent a new teacher or simply a new hire, data teams level the playing field and provide a concrete framework—veteran members we can point to and newer members can rely upon for assistance. But most importantly, data teams provide a forum in which contribution by all members is not only encouraged, but it is also expected: "What if we try this . . .?" One teacher stated, "For me it's a great opportunity to bounce ideas off one another and create, augment, and blend ideas together to improve one single idea." Poet Shel Silverstein suggests that the "Whatifs" will get you if you don't watch out, but in data teams, it's those very "Whatifs" that liberate you (Silverstein, 1996).

Many times data teams are seen as a system for assessing skill levels and addressing remediation, and for years the question for remediation used to be "Where are the worksheets that cover this skill?" Data teaming done well raises that energy level and places the focus not only on recouping our weakest students, but also on planning for instruction that reaches them better the first time. Our teams use their team time as a communication forum and to capitalize on the skills of the members. We have learned there is a great deal of expertise, but that everyone at Hilsman Middle School brings talents to the data teams.

Whatifs Lead to Synergistic Learning Opportunities Within and Beyond Data Teams

In the world of analogy, Hilsman data teams can be somewhat akin to a role-playing fantasy game, with a group of disparate characters united by a common quest. There is always the member who is a bit more tech-savvy, blazing the trail to innovation; the dreamer/enthusiast, ready to drop everything at a moment's notice and battle giants or put on a play; and there is even a place for the realist, who brings it all down to the doable realm. But what is important here is that somewhere along the journey, the conversations change from the "Where is . . ." to the "What if . . ." The 7th Grade ELA data team conversations have evolved to "What if we have *the students* design . . . what if *the students* write . . ." There is a synergy that grows as the idea of one is expounded and expanded through collective conversations.

Data Teams Influence School-Wide Learning

A powerful result of this synergy is that the energy moves in all directions. As enthusiasm and innovation builds within the data teams, teachers begin to carry ideas, "forward and up," involving the school-wide, school improvement leadership team (SILT) members to discuss ideas for professional development opportunities and perspectives about innovative classroom practices. Our teams have, at times, moved an entire school toward new initiatives about instruction based on the results at a grade level. The modeling of the "What-If" questions has spread to our SILT meetings. Questions at SILT meetings have included: "What if we get approval to . . . what if we bring in community resources . . . what if we institute service learning . . . what if we partner with the university . . .?" The "What-if" questions have become more commonplace as data teams have grown and evolved since 2009. There is no doubt that data teams help teachers design and present materials in ways that improve learning and foster engagement for the students and teachers at Hilsman Middle School.

The Principal's Role in Facilitating Learning through the School Improvement Process

The principal's role to create the conditions for job-embedded learning is two-fold. First, the principal must provide the time and space for such meetings to occur. At Hilsman, time is protected both after school and during the school day. At the beginning of the school year, a professional learning calendar that includes the meeting dates for all after-school professional learning activities, including school improvement leadership team meetings and vertical and horizontal team meetings is published with the expectation that no other meetings, athletic events, or extracurricular activities are scheduled during these times. Data teams are scheduled during common planning periods, and the master schedule is built so that each grade level has two 57-minute periods per day for planning purposes.

Second, the principal must work to ensure that the structures in place create a network of information and knowledge sharing to benefit the academic growth of students and the professional growth of teachers. The work of the data teams informs the discussion at vertical content meetings, which informs the conversations at the school improvement leadership team (SILT) meetings. The conversations at SILT are captured in the minutes, which are shared with the entire faculty. While the data team is the primary structure through which ongoing job-embedded learning occurs, there is a communication and feedback loop that facilitates job-embedded learning involving data teams, vertical content teams, and the school improvement leadership team (SILT).

Case Summary

Data team structures and the work inherent in these teams aim to produce school improvement by focusing on strategies and approaches that are making the needle on student achievement move; however, for the data teams at Hilsman Middle School, the learning goes deeper as it also focuses on what teachers are learning about their own practices and the practices of their peers. Collaborative, structured, and protected times during the day ensure that teams have the opportunity and the means to learn from one another based on the results they "get in the classroom" as a result of their efforts.

Chapter Summary

Collaborative models of professional learning are multifaceted and include a variety of features including coaching and reflection, for example. Collaborative models of professional learning are social. These models promote the engagement of teachers within grade levels, across grade levels, within subject areas, and across subject areas. With the advent of technology, learning communities are no longer confined to a building or within a school system—Twitter, blogs, YouTube, and other social media have put learning on a global level for adults. Adult Learning is examined in Chapter 2.

Suggested Readings

Creemers, B., Kyriakides, L., & Antoniou, P. (2013). *Teacher professional development for improving quality of teaching.* New York: Springer.

Garmston, R. J., & von Frank, V. A. (2012). *Unlocking group potential to improve schools.* Thousand Oaks, CA: Corwin Press.

Roberts, S. M., & Pruitt, E. Z. (2009). *Schools as professional learning communities: Collaborative activities and strategies for professional development* (2nd ed.). Thousand Oaks, CA: Corwin Press.

Zepeda, S. J. (2012). *Professional development: What works* (2nd ed.). New York, NY: Routledge.

2 Adults Learning: What the Research Says

In This Chapter . . .

- ♦ Principles of Adult Learning
- ♦ The Social Nature of Adult Learning and Collaboration
- ♦ Adult Learners in Digital Environments
- ♦ Reflection = Growth
- ♦ Reflection in a Digital Learning Environment
- ♦ Motivation and the Adult Learner
- ♦ Constructivism and Adult Learning
- ♦ Self-Directed Learning
- ♦ Framework: Individual Professional Development Plan (IPDP)
- ♦ Case from the Field
- ♦ Chapter Summary
- ♦ Suggested Readings

Teachers want to grow professionally; they desire ongoing learning opportunities in spaces nestled within their own schools so that they can improve their practices. The notion of space has changed drastically given the uses of technology and the emergence of professional learning networks (PLNs). Technology has increased opportunities for teachers to engage in learning opportunities that are more self-directed and collaborative connecting with peers, globally (see Chapter 9). Technology has changed some of the ways adults learn, when they learn, and how they learn. With a blink, a new application is available to enhance access to knowledge, to increase efficiency, or to offer a view of a different part of the globe.

To support more collaborative approaches to job-embedded professional development, some ideas about adult learning, reflection, the social nature of how adults learn, motivation, and the relationships of these to professional development are presented. Digital learning environments for the adult learner related to professional learning and reflection are briefly explored. A framework for designing an Individual Professional Development Plan (IPDP) is offered to help support teachers and others interested in charting their own professional learning. This approach to goal development can also be used to help teams or groups of teachers.

Principles of Adult Learning

In an analysis of Knowles' work, Merriam, Caffarella, and Baumgartner (2013) highlight that adult learners are "self-directed, bring a repertoire of experience, they are internally motivated to learn, and they want to apply what they are learning immediately" because learning is "closely related to the developmental tasks of his or her social role" (p. 272). Knowles and Associates (1984, p. 12) indicated that adults learn based on the following principles:

1. Need to Know: Adults need to know the reason—the "why" or the reasons for learning.

2. Experience: Adults rely on and draw from prior experience and knowledge.

3. Self-concept: Adults relate how they learn to their own sense of self.

4. Readiness: The more immediate the need, the higher the readiness to learn.

5. Orientation and Application: As adults learn new knowledge, they want to apply it immediately.

6. Motivation: Adults derive satisfaction and self-motivation to learn as they mature.

We can make the leap from these principles that adults like to solve problems, think critically, engage in work that fills an immediate need and contributes to building self-efficacy (Bandura, 2006; Keay & Lloyd, 2011; Knowles, 1975; Knowles & Associates, 1984).

Linkages between Professional Development and Adult Learning

National (Drago-Severson, 2009) and international perspectives (Keay & Lloyd, 2011) on adult learning are similar and presented in Table 2.1.

Drawing from the early framers in the field of adult learning, Dalellew and Martinez (1988) provide an overview of the principles of adult learning, and Roberts and Pruitt (2009) offer strategies to engage adult learners more appropriately in professional development. Table 2.2 examines the overlap of the principles of adult learning with the strategies that yield richer learning experiences for adults.

Table 2.1. US and International Perspectives on Adult Learning and Professional Development

US Perspectives on Adult Learning	International Perspectives on Adult Learning
♦ Embedded in practice	♦ Self-regulated
♦ Ongoing rather than a one-shot approach	♦ Initiated by the individual

(Continued)

Table 2.1 (Continued)

US Perspectives on Adult Learning	International Perspectives on Adult Learning
◆ On site and school based	◆ Collaborative and collegial
◆ Focused on student learning	◆ Reviewed by the individual through critically reflective practice
◆ Centered around teacher collaboration, and,	◆ Driven by pupil needs
◆ Sensitive to teachers' learning needs (p. 126)	◆ Focused on an inclusive approach to education which builds knowledge and is enquiry driven (pp. 149–150)
Source: Drago-Severson (2009) as cited by Nolan and Hoover (2011).	Source: Keay & Lloyd (2011).

Table 2.2. The Principles of Adult Learning and Strategies to Engage Adult Learners

The Principles of Adult Learning	Strategies to Engage Adult Learners
◆ Adult learning is more "self-directed" and the impetus for learning is to share information, to generate one's own need for learning	◆ Make learning both an active and an interactive process
◆ Adults seek knowledge that applies to their current life situation; they want to know how this new information will help them in their development.	◆ Provide hands-on, concrete experiences and real-life experiences
◆ Life experiences . . . shape their readiness for learning	◆ Employ novelty, but also connect to the adult learners' prior experiences and knowledge
◆ Adults have differing levels of readiness to learn	◆ Give them opportunities to apply the new knowledge to what they already know or have experienced
◆ Staff who voluntarily attend in-services, workshops and seminars usually are those who have determined they want to learn more	◆ Be aware of the diversity in an adult group. Use a variety of approaches to accommodate different styles and experiences and use examples.
	◆ Use small-group activities through which learners have the opportunity to reflect, analyze, and practice what they have learned
	◆ Provide coaching, technical assistance, feedback, or other follow-up support as part of the training

The Principles of Adult Learning	Strategies to Engage Adult Learners
	♦ Give adult learners as much control as possible over what they learn, how they learn, and other aspects of the learning experience

Source: Dalellew and Martinez (1988, pp. 28–29).   Source: Roberts & Pruitt (2009, p. 75).

Learning that is embedded in the work of teaching is strengthened through social and collaborative interactions with peers.

The Social Nature of Adult Learning and Collaboration

People by their general nature are social creatures. With digital learning environments, students, teachers, Wall Street bankers, etc. can connect in nano-seconds. The social aspects of adult learning are important to consider especially since research tells us that feedback, collaboration, group processing, and collaboration punctuate a positive culture of learning.

In a 2013 survey commissioned by Ideapaint™, all generations, not just Millennials are shaped by "community and communication" (p. 1). Moreover, a majority of respondents in this survey indicated that people "prefer to collaborate in small groups to generate big ideas" as a way to "satisfy . . . a sense of community . . . [to] ensure everyone's ideas are heard . . ." (p. 4). Millennials, who make up approximately 25 percent of the workforce, rely on technology to support their work in between meetings, professional learning, and other types of work-related tasks. Communication and collaboration are important for many reasons and, so far, many Millennials are feeling disenfranchised with "outdated collaboration practices" in education, and that academic institutions do not make it "easy for ideas to be shared and take[en] to the next level" (p. 3).

Although adults can learn "on their own," learning in the company of others is a major component of professional development that supports adults. Learning on your own could potentially be a lonely journey, but it does not have to be. Learning is a proactive, collaborative, and reflective process. The journey continues and widens.

Adult Learners in Digital Environments

Technology and broadband width have opened the floodgates for the ever-changing nature of professional learning opportunities for teachers. Given the prevalence of technology and the digital learning environments that schools have created by going beyond one-to-one and using outreach efforts such as "Bring Your own Technology" (BYOT) to augment needs and to engage families and communities, sustained effort now needs to focus on teacher learning.

According to Killion (2013a), technology, like any other component of professional development, provides coherence through its goals and objectives and enhances professional learning in five very specific ways that are congruent with what we know about effective professional learning and the principles of adult learning. According to Killion (2013a), these ways include:

♦ Personalization

♦ Collaboration

♦ Access

♦ Efficiency

♦ Learning designs. (pp. 11–12)

Adult Learners Seek Immediacy of Application. The internet allows adult learners to access information, interact with others, and share knowledge at the speed of their connectivity. Adult learners have a need for immediacy and for application, and the internet can provide for these two conditions (Hanley, 2009). Technologies used to access information can be as small as a smartphone or an ear bud. Teachers can connect with others within the same school, school system, in the same state, or across the globe without leaving their classroom and, in some instances, their own homes or a coffee shop.

Adult Learners Seek Relevance and Choice. There are special interest groups that establish around topics. Teachers share information through blogs, Tweets, and posts on such mediums as Facebook or Pinterest. Teachers demonstrate how to teach concepts on YouTube, they listen to and perhaps watch webinars, enroll in massive open online courses (MOOCs), and participate in other digital learning opportunities.

Adult Learners Seek Flexibility. Learning in a digital world can be synchronous or asynchronous. Professional development that is offered in a synchronous format would include all participants connecting at the same time (regardless of location) to engage in "real-time" conversations, project development, examination of student work, the development of common assessments, etc. Because synchronous professional learning opportunities occur in real time, teachers are able to 1) interact (chat) with one another via instant messaging, Skype, or a phone; 2) work on projects together in small groups; 3) add documents through Google Docs; 4) watch videos together, etc. Synchronous learning environments are highly interactive.

Asynchronous is referred to as "anytime, anywhere" learning because the adult learner can access materials (videos, blog discussions, Tweets, emails) any time of the day or night, including weekends, holidays from any place that has connectivity to the internet. Professional learning opportunities could include such activities as taking virtual tours, following threaded chat room discussions, blogging over a period of time or following the Tweets of a thought leader or even becoming a thought leader on Twitter, Pinterest, or creating a blog.

Because of the flexibility of asynchronous learning opportunities, there is typically no expectation of a response or, if there is, the response is not expected quickly; therefore, asynchronous communities reflect with peers but the reflections are delayed. This delay gives adults the opportunity to use time in between visits to reflect, the flexibility to join in when convenient, or the latitude to just vicariously follow thoughts and ideas without posting.

Adult Learners Seek to Interact with Content. Digital tools can connect teachers to curricular materials through special repositories where they can access instructional resources, self-assess their own skills, find resources to fill gaps, and interact through blogging with other teachers. In many of these repositories, teachers are engaged in sharing and accessing curricular materials, rating curricular materials, and then adapting curricular materials to fit their own needs. Teachers who curate their own materials engage in a variety of higher-order thinking skills (what is archived and why).

Adult Learners Seek Opportunities for Private, Self, and Public Reflection. Through sharing thoughts or resources via online discussion boards or blogs, teachers are able to post, read, and reflect not only on their own practices and experiences but also they can reflect on the practices and experiences of others. By sharing practices on public platforms, teachers can get feedback from a variety of sources (Archambault, Wetzel, Foulger, & Williams, 2010), collecting multiple points of view that can influence the refinement of practice and the development of new content (Williams & Olaniran, 2012). The permanent nature of artifacts, blog entries, Tweets, etc. gives teachers a long-term view of their work, and they can chart their growth and changes in thoughts and beliefs over time (Arnold & Paulus, 2010). Teachers need time to step back and to reflect by themselves and with others.

Reflection = Growth

Bold (2011) shares that reflection occurs through "social construction involving others," so teachers may "interrogate experiences by asking questions and challenging each other's ideas" (p. 192). Reflection signals growth and development and is a fundamental principle of adult learning. Reflection helps teachers to make sense of their practices, and Çimer and Günay (2012) share:

> Reflective practitioners give careful attention to their experiences and how meaning is made and justified. They analyze the influence of context and how they shape human behavior. Teachers who are reflective are responsive to vast array of students' needs in today's classrooms. (p. 52)

Schön (1983, 1987) describes two types of reflection—reflection-in-action and reflection-on-action. *Reflection-in-action* helps us to reshape what we are doing while we are doing it. According to Schön (1983), because we have knowledge in action (KIA) and while we are reflecting-in-action, we are able to make more purposeful decisions. Through reflection "in the moment," teachers are able to make snap judgments based on their reflections while teaching.

Reflection-on-action occurs after an action. In a sense, reflection-on-action allows teachers to look back to think through the lessons learned from their actions. Later in 1991, Killion and Todnem added *reflection-for-action*. Their premise was that through reflection in and on practice, teachers think forward to the future; they reflect to the next steps of action(s) that will support change and improvements in practices. Bold (2011) offers a thoughtful description and visual representation of the relationship of the three forms of reflection. Reflection holds promise for teachers to make sense of their practices, to think more critically about their work, and to examine the impact they are having on students.

However, we must be able to ruminate in a space that is in the center leading to the end result—sense-making. Bold (2011) reminds us that through reflection, it is the hope that teachers will be able to move from critical reflection into sense-making.

Figure 2.1. Cycle of Reflection Leading to Critical Reflection and Sense-Making

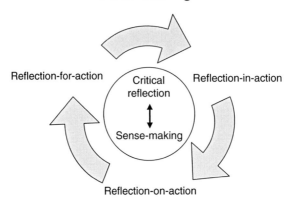

Source: Based on the works of Bold (2011); Schön (1983, 1987); Killion & Todnem (1991).

Through reflection, we are purposefully asking teachers to make critical judgments, ask critical questions of practice, and, then, use judgment to revise methods based on active inquiry over time. Figure 2.1 provides a cycle of reflection that melds the works of Schön (1983, 1987), Killion and Todnem (1991), and Bold (2011) as a way to think about reflection, critical reflection, and sense-making related to adult learning and professional development.

From this model, we see that reflection is not a linear process; instead, it is recursive and cyclical—very much like professional development for adult learners.

Reflection in a Digital Learning Environment

The nature of reflection has been steadily changing along with the tools available to use in digital learning environments. For some, reflection might be supported through the use of digital learning tools and social or private spaces dedicated to individual or collective sharing and reflection.

Digital tools and platforms can provide opportunities for:

1. Teachers to collaborate with one another locally and globally;

2. share resources, develop new resources based on what they are "picking up" on posts;

3. engage in reflective conversations via communication tools within the platforms (message boards, blogs, etc.); and,

4. openly reflect with others.

Table 2.3 offers a view of some digital learning spaces, platforms, and tools that support reflection.

There are more digital tools and platforms that will increase our abilities to connect with others. Motivation is also essential to adult learning as it relates to risk taking, influences self-efficacy, and can support or inhibit group involvement.

**Table 2.3. Digital Learning Tools and Environments
that Support Reflection**

Tools/Spaces	Description	Web Resource
Blogs	A blog can be as simple as a personal journal (diary) or a running discussion across a group of people.	http://en.wikipedia.org/wiki/Blog
Wikis	According to Sandifer (2011), "a wiki is a website that can be edited by anyone or by anyone with appropriate privileges if the wiki is restricted to registered users" (p. 5). Wikis can be used in the development of documents, assessments, for posting documents, etc. People can build knowledge and share knowledge on a wiki.	http://en.wikipedia.org/wiki/Wiki
Twitter	Users Tweet messages up to 140 characters; must be registered to reply to a Tweet but can read only if not registered.	http://en.wikipedia.org/wiki/Twitter
Jaiku	Similar to Twitter using s60 phones. Posts can be public or private.	http://en.wikipedia.org/wiki/Jaiku
Edmodo	A social learning platform used primarily in schools to respond to student work; blog with students, teachers, parents, etc.	http://en.wikipedia.org/wiki/Edmodo
Facebook	Individuals or groups join to interact with others; exchange information, posts, photos, videos, etc.	http://en.wikipedia.org/wiki/Facebook
MySpace	Social media focusing on music and the arts.	http://en.wikipedia.org/wiki/Myspace
Pinterest	Massive storage area to "pin" articles, photos, lesson plans, videos, or any other items of interest. What is stored can be shared with others, re-posted on other social media sites such as Facebook.	http://en.wikipedia.org/wiki/Pinterest

Motivation and the Adult Learner

A culture of learning supports teachers in becoming more satisfied, gaining more self-confidence, and deriving value from their own work and from working with others. By working with others and engaging in deep conversations about teaching and learning, instructional practices, student work, and the impact of individual and collective efforts, we expose our vulnerabilities. Through our questioning and our pondering, we create imbalance. Personal and collective disequilibrium could possibly occur as our ideas are being challenged by colleagues or we are challenging ourselves, our colleagues, our practices, and perhaps digging deeper into challenging our own beliefs and assumptions.

Maslow's (1954) hierarchy of needs theory relates to adult learners. First, the theory sheds light on how and why people respond as they do. Second, Maslow's theory clarifies the meaning and significance that people place on work. Maslow believes that human needs extend from the physiological (lowest) to self-actualization (highest). Figure 2.2 illustrates the range of human needs according to Maslow.

From Maslow's hierarchy of needs, we know that adults want to feel psychologically safe, secure, have a sense of belonging with others, be productive, and to feel useful. Adults often seek new knowledge in response to a need. Cross (1992) indicates that adults are motivated by the need to:

◆ achieve practical goals;

◆ achieve personal satisfaction and other inner-directed goals;

◆ gain new knowledge; and,

◆ socialize with others.

Adults also want to have a strong sense of affiliation (McClelland, 1987). Affiliation is important because people who are motivated by collaborative needs value

Figure 2.2. **Maslow's Hierarchy of Needs**

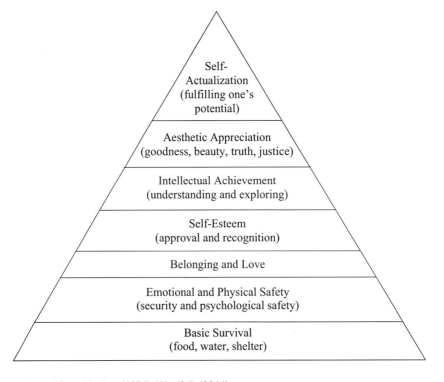

Source: Adapted from Maslow (1954); Woolfolk (2014).

human relations, open communication, and lasting relationships with others. In a community of learning, teachers form a safety net, giving and receiving support during challenging times (Zepeda, 2012a).

Through problem-posing, problem-solving, analyzing, and active inquiry, teachers can continue to build and construct, and then reconstruct what they are learning as they apply this new knowledge or strategy into practice.

Constructivism and Adult Learning

Dewey (1938) advocated learning from experience, and according to Seimears, Graves, Schroyer, & Staver (2012), the constructivist model "contends that learners actively construct knowledge" (p. 266), and that "the construction of knowledge is a lifelong process and at any time, the body of knowledge individuals have constructed makes sense to them and helps them interpret or predict events in their experiential worlds" (p. 266).

As active learners, teachers need to construct their own meanings based on what they do and experience. For the purposes of professional development and adult learning, the focus on constructivism really centers on three main ideas: 1) learners are active in the process of learning, 2) social interactions are important in the process of learning, and 3) the zone of proximal development is important as colleagues support one another in their growth and as individuals recognize where they need support. The zone of proximal development (Vygotsky, 1978) is examined more fully during peer observations (Chapter 4) and during coaching conversations (Chapter 5).

A major stream in adult learning is self-directed learning. Many school systems are turning to self-directed learning and subsequent plans as either a complement to larger initiatives such as the teacher evaluation system or as a way to ensure that 1) teachers are moving forward in a systematic way with their professional learning and 2) learning within the school and system can achieve greater coherence with knowing the patterns of what professional development and learning needs exist and hence what resources are required to meet these needs.

Self-Directed Learning

In the field of supervision, self-direction, developmental, and differentiated forms of support are considered best practice (Zepeda, 2012b, 2013). Nolan and Hoover (2011) champion that differentiated and developmental approaches assist teachers in the refinement of current practices by allowing them to focus on specific areas in which they want to grow, to improve on, or to refine, and that, moreover, efforts are directed and differentiated according to the needs of teachers. The individually guided nature of professional learning centers on professional goals and the active role adults play in the process, elaborated by Tkatchov and Pollnow (2011, based on Guskey's 2000 work) as follows:

Professional Goal—First, it is important to have a clear professional goal in mind for yourself and determine what outcomes you will expect as a result of the professional development.

Meaningful—Second, the goal should be meaningful to you and your practice.

How do you know?—Finally, decide how you will know you have reached your goal and set benchmarks to gauge your progress along the way. What results do you expect for you and your student? (p. 128).

Self-directed learning allows learners to "augment . . . professional expertise" (Bhatta, 2011, 1.3), to engage in formal and informal learning experiences (Tkatchov & Pollnow, 2011), to capitalize on incidental and informal learning (Marsick, Watkins, & Lovin, 2012), and to assume responsibility for their own learning and development (Brookfield, 1995).

Self-directed learning needs to go beyond a piecemeal approach, to one focused on teacher and student learning. Self-directed learning that becomes a part of a teacher's career path increases the likelihood that learning will sustain over time. Self-directed learning takes into account perceived needs or gaps as well as past experiences with students, instructional strategies, assessment practices, and other experiences with professional learning, degree attainment, etc. A framework for building an Individual Professional Development Plan (IPDP) is presented next.

Framework: Individual Professional Development Plan (IPDP)

The objective of learning is to provide teachers with windows of opportunities for growth and development, and to provide opportunities to work solo or in the company of others, all while moving toward deeper understandings about their work with students and with their peers. The following framework, the Individual Professional Development Plan (IPDP), can support individuals or even teams of teachers in reflecting about professional learning needs and opportunities. As with all plans, they should be differentiated and developmental and situated within the context of the school, the classroom, the grade level, etc. The Individual Professional Development Plan (IPDP) Framework gets to the point by helping teachers or teams to develop goals that focus their individual or group efforts on learning from their work.

The three parts of the Individual Professional Development Plan (IPDP) include identifying through a self-assessment: 1) strengths, and identifying 2) two self-perceived needs based on evidence of practice, and then, 3) framing goals, self-monitoring strategies, and reflective blogging.

Individual Professional Development Plan

Part I: Self-Assessment: Acknowledging Strengths—Where am I Now?

   a. Look at the Following Areas and pick two that you believe you excel in in your classroom practices and would be willing, if asked and time permitting, to coach or mentor other teachers in to help them gain more expertise in the areas you identified.

☐ Assessment (formative/summative)
☐ Instructional Planning
☐ Pacing
☐ Differentiated Instruction
☐ Formative Assessment
☐ Classroom Openings
☐ Essential Questions
☐ Sequencing Lesson and Content
☐ Setting Realistic Student Behavior Expectations
☐ Rigor
☐ Student Engagement
☐ Classroom Rituals and Routines
☐ Building Relationships with Students and Families
☐ Transition Strategies
☐ Questioning Skills and Strategies
☐ Higher-Order Thinking
☐ Use of Digital Learning Tools
☐ Feedback

Other Areas: _____

_____

_____

b. What is it about these areas that you could share with your colleagues?

_____

_____

_____

Part II: Identifying Self-Perceived Needs—Digging into the Weeds

a.   Identify two self-perceived needs you believe you have. Needs could be related to instruction, assessment, a grade-level initiative, a content area specialization, a related collaborative project, for example, or studying student work, etc.

Need Area 1 _____

Self-Perceived Need:

Evidence of Need: What makes you believe "this" is a need?

Digging into the Weeds: What gets you pondering?

Need Area 2 _____

> Self-Perceived Need:
>
> Evidence of Need: What makes you believe "this" is a need?
>
> Digging into the Weeds: What gets you pondering?

Part III: Framing Goals—To Self-Direct Learning

    a. Self-Directed Learning Goals: Develop two self-directed goals using the following as your guide. Note there is a private blog space for reflections.

> Self-Directed Learning Goal 1 to Correlate with Identified Need Area I
>
> **Learning Goal I**
>
> a. Identified Need Area I
> b. Broad Area of Focus based on i) evidence and ii) what gets you pondering
> c. The Specific Goal for this year and perhaps to build upon for next year
> d. Resources that I need: _____ Peer Support
>   _____ Administrative Support
>   _____ District Staff Support
>   _____ Content Materials
>   _____ Digital Learning Environment Support
>   _____ Coach/Mentor
>   _____ Professional Development (off-site)
>   _____Other
> e. Resources I have
> f. Self-Monitoring Strategies
> g. Artifacts and Evidence/Markers of Success
> h. Reflections on Progress (ongoing/private blog)
> i. Moving into Next Year . . . Future Plans . . .

> Self-Directed Learning Goal 2 to Correlate with Identified Need Area II
>
> **Learning Goal II**
>
> a. Identified Need Area II
> b. Broad Area of Focus based on i) evidence and ii) what gets you pondering
> c. The Specific Goal for this year and perhaps to build upon for next year
> d. Resources that I need: _____ Peer Support
>   _____ Administrative Support

_____ District Staff Support
_____ Content Materials
_____ Digital Learning Environment Support
_____ Coach/Mentor
_____ Professional Development (off-site)
_____ Other
  e. Resources I have
  f. Self-Monitoring Strategies
  g. Artifacts and Evidence/Markers of Success
  h. Reflections on Progress (ongoing/private blog)
  i. Moving into Next Year . . . Future Plans . . .

We shift to the Case from the Field that details a highly personalized form of self-directed learning using online platforms to extend learning at the local level.

A Case from the Field

Self-Directed Online Learning Opportunities—Increasing Personalized Learning

Mr. Nicholas Hussain, 7th Grade Mathematics and Social Studies Teacher, Hilsman Middle School; Dr. Selena Blankenship, Principal, Clarke County School District, GA

Case Organizer

The digital learning environment has changed the ways in which many people learn across the career continuum. Teachers use digital resources to become more self-directed and to embed further the lessons, the practical wisdom, and craft knowledge they learn daily from their practices. Nicholas Hussain, a 7th Grade Mathematics and Social Studies teacher, is a lifelong learner who embraces technology and digital tools, platforms, and professional learning networks as well as more traditional learning formats—books and workshops—to build capacity—his own and his colleagues'—at Hilsman Middle School in Athens, GA.

Because time is always scarce for teachers during the school day, using digital environments for professional development opportunities can serve as both a time-saving and cost-efficient strategy for teachers and schools. An additional benefit of digital professional development is that it allows learning to occur at the teacher's convenience; online resources are always available. Mr. Hussain praises digital learning opportunities that foster "asynchronous communication" or communication that takes place outside of a particular time and place.

The Context of Hilsman Middle School

See Case from the Field in Chapter 1

Using Digital Learning Environments to Increase Personalized Learning

Although Mr. Hussain sees much value in the face-to-face professional development that occurs in his school and through the education books he reads to help improve his teaching practice, he notes that there is one limitation to these umbrella approaches to learning: the lack of opportunity to personalize the material to suit the unique needs of his teaching practice, his students, classroom, and content. Mr. Hussain believes that digital learning environments may serve as a supplement to face-to-face professional development that can increase personalized learning for every teacher and their unique classroom situation.

Mr. Hussain sees that the same social media and digital environments that teachers use in their personal lives have begun to spill over into their professional lives. In his experience, some of the digital learning environments that teachers are most excited about are Pinterest, Facebook, Twitter, Google+, the Teaching Channel and TED-Ed. These and many other digital resources offer access to different types of educational ideas that teachers can sift through to choose the material that will be most useful to their particular teaching practice.

One Digital Site Leads to Another

Stumbling on a TEDx talk on math education by Dan Meyer, a former math teacher in California, Mr. Hussain connected with the speaker's insights and decided to follow a link in Dan Meyer's biography to his personal website, dy/dan (http://blog.mrmeyer.com/). There he found reflections and brainstorming, as well as shared frustrations, all of which resonated deeply with Mr. Hussain.

Dan Meyer's site has a blogroll, or list of other educators and links to their blogs, whom Mr. Meyer regularly follows and reads. Mr. Hussain began to follow this trail of educators and this cascaded to additional blogrolls. He found link after link that connected him to a broad array of educators and their websites and blogs. By engaging in this process, Mr. Hussain is regularly introduced to new educators through the writings and Tweets in his circle of educators.

Mr. Hussain follows around 100 education blogs and about 60 educators via Twitter. These people write about their experiences in a relatable way and share innovative and creative lesson plans that Mr. Hussain incorporates into his own teaching practice. Mr. Hussain shared, "Every post or tweet is not revolutionary for my practice, but the proportion of great nuggets versus non-relevant learning is much higher using these digital environments." As Mr. Hussain incorporated what he learned from these digital learning environments, substantial results began to show in his practice.

Tangible Rewards in the Digital Era of Professional Learning Networks

Mr. Hussain's online professional learning network provides him with lesson ideas, classroom management techniques, exposure to research and best practices, access to a community of people striving for success in the classroom, and colleagues with varying degrees of experience and expertise. He expressed that being connected to a digital professional learning network "is like having a large department filled with intensely passionate, intelligent, helpful colleagues whom you get to choose. They certainly make my teaching life richer and easier."

Mr. Hussain's colleagues at Hilsman consistently share what they have learned in workshops or conferences with teachers who were not able to attend. Digital professional learning allows this to happen regardless of time or place and allows learning to spread across grade levels and content areas. Mr. Hussain frequently emails his colleagues when coming across a resource that he thinks is relevant to their practice: "By now, I'm sure that some of my colleagues grin to themselves when I pass them in the hall and say that I'm going to send them something that made me think of them." The practice of sharing digital resources has made his school a better place, and Mr. Hussain explains:

> As states across the country are implementing Common Core Standards in mathematics and language arts, many educators are sharing their ideas and resources online. One of the best features of digital professional learning is access to rich and creative ideas for lessons. With so many people teaching the same standards, it is significantly easier to find those great resources. A small department can gain access to a world of ideas and resources that was not as easily available before.

How Do I Start?—How You Can Use Digital Environments for Professional Learning

There are countless communities for education that exist online, with new sites and communities emerging frequently. Some communities focus on a specific topic such as leadership, technology, math, or science and exist across Twitter, Facebook, Pinterest, and many other websites. One of the best ways to connect to a particular community is to look for its Twitter hashtag (#), which functions as a tag or category aggregator. A comprehensive list of Twitter hashtags can be found using the Google search "twitter hashtags for education." Search Twitter (http://twitter.com/) for the hashtag (e.g., search #scichat to find science education tweets), then follow some of the links that people include in their tweets. Educators can easily bookmark their favorite resources using this site.

Other digital professional learning communities center on a specific person and their website. Mr. Hussain recommends sites like Angela Watson's website, The Cornerstone for Teachers (http://thecornerstoneforteachers.com/), or Grant Wiggins' blog, Granted (http://grantwiggins.wordpress.com/). Websites and blogs such as these allow for comments after each post where readers can share their thinking or related ideas, and these comments form a conversation about the topic of the post. Comment threads are a valuable resource on websites and blogs because they allow for conversation to continue without being constrained by time and location. "The opportunity that educators have in a digital-rich era is immense," Mr. Hussain explained. He further elaborated, "They can collaborate with almost anyone at almost any time of day. It's not uncommon to see a call for help on Twitter at 10:00 p.m. with a half-dozen replies by 7:00 a.m."

While there is an online community for practically every topic, Mr. Hussain has ventured mainly into the online world of math educators. He explains that many

Table 2.4. Digital Learning Environments for Teachers of Mathematics

Website	Description	What Does it Mean?
www.twittermathcamp.com/	Twitter Math Camp	TMC is an in-person professional development workshop that takes place during the summer. It is organized and hosted by members of the MTBoS.
http://mathtwitterblogosphere.weebly.com/	A "MTBoS"-themed blog	This is a welcome site for educators looking for an introduction to the online math community. It includes an extensive list of math educators who actively contribute resources developed by members of the community.

math educators who blog and Tweet have collectively begun calling their community the MathTwitterBlogosphere, or MTBoS (pronounced "mitt-boss"). Table 2.4 shows multiple websites that can help anyone interested in joining the MTBoS community get started.

In addition to content-specific resources, Mr. Hussain shared a few ideas gleaned from his online professional learning communities:

♦ At the beginning of the school year, use a fill-in-the-blank syllabus with middle school students.

♦ Engage in team-building activities such as the Marshmallow Tower activity with other teachers on your team.

♦ When students write stories, showcase their work on a bulletin board by placing a QR code next to their writing; the QR code can link to a video of the student reading his or her writing.

♦ On day 100 of the school year, have students walk into class under a banner that reads "You are 100 days smarter!"

♦ Place extra handouts in a file drawer with 31 folders, one for each day of the month. This makes it easy to find an extra handout when needed, and files are only emptied monthly.

♦ When there are a few minutes of unplanned time, teach students how to play Ultimate Tic-Tac-Toe or about the Seven Bridges of Konigsberg.

♦ When students need a visual reminder to work quietly, use the webpage Bouncy Balls (http://neave.com/bouncy-balls) in conjunction with a projector and microphone.

Case Summary

This case illustrates how engaging in digital learning opportunities can help supplement and extend job-embedded learning, face-to-face professional development, and other activities regardless of time or location. The opportunity to connect with online professional learning communities means that teachers can easily pose a question on a blog or message board, receive multiple responses with as many perspectives, and reflect on what makes sense. Online professional learning offers valuable opportunities for teachers to personalize professional learning, to be more self-directed in what they pursue to learn, and to embed through extended online discussion and reflection what they are learning during the day from teaching students and working with peers.

Chapter Summary

Adults learn in ways that can be supported through collaboration with peers, clear goals that are self-directed, and by focusing on learning skills that have immediate applicability in their classrooms. In standards-based classrooms, teachers engage in complex tasks in which their own learning at the site can be extended through reflection that occurs solo, with team members at the site, or with colleagues who connect through membership in professional learning networks and other social platforms. Job-embedded learning is examined in Chapter 3.

Suggested Readings

Drago-Severson, E. (2009). *Leading adult learning: Supporting adult development in our schools*. Thousand Oaks, CA: Corwin Press.

Keay, J. K., & Lloyd, C. M. (2011). *Linking children's learning with professional learning: Impact, evidence and inclusive practices*. Netherlands. Sense Publishers.

Swanson, K. (2013). *Professional learning in the digital age: The educator's guide to user-generated learning*. New York, NY: Routledge.

Thompson, R., Kitchie, L., & Gagnon, R. (2011). *Constructing an online professional learning network for school unity and student achievement*. Thousand Oaks, CA: Corwin Press.

Job-Embedded Professional Development in Action

3

In This Chapter . . .

♦ What Is Job-Embedded Learning?

♦ Job-Embedded Learning—No Time Like the Present

♦ Trust, Teamwork, and Job-Embedded Learning

♦ The Markers of Job-Embedded Learning

♦ Case from the Field

♦ Chapter Summary

♦ Suggested Readings

We know that teachers value working collaboratively with one another, and that "professional development should be intensive, ongoing, and connected to practice" (Darling-Hammond *et al.*, 2009, p. 9). Job-embedded learning occurs when teachers engage actively in the work of growing as professionals, and Mizell (2008) emphatically reminds us that "educators must experience learning as integral to their normal work week and it must be as easily accessible in their schools as walking to a room down the hall" (p. 5).

With the opportunities technology offers and the push toward increasingly sophisticated and digitally rich learning environments, teachers can meet with colleagues within their system, across the state, or even meet new ones who share similar learning interest from around the world. Professional learning networks (PLNs) are akin to professional learning communities but reside "out there" in addition to including perhaps members from within the buildings in which teachers work. Applications such as blogging and Tweeting and social media platforms such as Facebook and Pinterest encourage a different type of learning that also supports job-embedded learning but may be pushing by degrees of time, space, and speed the limits of our definition of job-embedded learning. Regardless of definition, digital tools and platforms have the ability to support and enhance job-embedded learning at the site and to extend learning beyond "the moment" as teachers engage on their own time ideas through reflection, reading a book, Tweeting with an expert, following a blog, etc.

What is Job-Embedded Learning?

Job-embedded learning is what occurs during a teacher's "daily work activities" (Wood & Killian, 1998, p. 52) that signals collaboration, joint problem-posing, problem-solving, and a sincere desire to improve practice from the lessons learned on the job from teaching and interacting with peers (Zepeda, 2012a). Parise and Spillane (2010) offer that on-the-job learning opportunities include "interactions with colleagues around teaching and learning, including conversations about instruction, peer observations, feedback, and advice-seeking about instruction" (p. 324).

Job-embedded learning can be both formal and informal. Teachers learn from teaching their students, while studying student work, while engaging in conversations with their colleagues, analyzing student data during grade-level data team meetings, and during other such opportune times. Teachers learn during conversations. Teachers learn from reflecting on their own and from reflecting after a conversation with a colleague. Teachers learn while they are blogging, Tweeting, or constructing an electronic portfolio. Teachers learn from listening to students respond to questions.

Every one of these examples situates the teacher as actively engaged in learning from the work associated with teaching and the work needed to support student learning. Job-embedded professional development

- ♦ holds relevance for the adult learner;

- ♦ includes feedback as part of the process;

- ♦ supports inquiry and reflection;

- ♦ facilitates the transfer of new skills into practice; and

- ♦ promotes collaboration. (Zepeda, 2012a)

Holds Relevance for the Adult Learner. Adults want to be successful and derive value from their learning. Job-embedded learning is highly individualized; it can be chronicled through electronic portfolios, public and reflective blog postings, and the use of an Individual Professional Development Plan (IPDP) as described in Chapter 2.

Includes Feedback as Part of the Process. Job-embedded learning includes feedback and collaborative supports as built-in processes. Processes that can generate feedback include mentoring, peer coaching, reflection and dialogue, study groups, videotape analysis of teaching and discussion about the events on tape, and journaling. Teachers can use these tools to chronicle implementation of new instructional skills, to provide artifacts for assessing transition from one learning activity to the next, or to use as material to frame future initiatives.

Supports Inquiry and Reflection. Job-embedded professional development supports inquiry that over time promotes thinking more critically and reflectively about practice (Bold, 2011). Inquiry and reflection can certainly occur at the individual level; however, there is value and benefit when peers inquire and reflect collaboratively in pairs and in teams. Although reflection is examined in Chapter 2, Pappas (2010a) offers a fresh perspective of reflection creating an application for using Bloom's Taxonomy. First as overview, Bloom (1956) and his colleagues developed a continuum for categorizing questions and responses from a hierarchy that ranged from lowest to highest levels of thinking in a taxonomy:

◆ Evaluation: making value decisions about issues   HIGHEST LEVEL

◆ Synthesis: creating a unique, original product

◆ Analysis: subdividing something to show how it is put together

◆ Application: applying information to produce some result

◆ Comprehension: describing in one's own words

◆ Knowledge: recalling specific facts.   LOWEST LEVEL

Figure 3.1 offers Pappas' Taxonomy of Reflection (2010a), where a teacher would move from a lower level of thinking and reflecting on the continuum of recall through higher levels getting to reflecting and thinking about the creation of new plans.

Pappas (2010b) provides a series of questions along his continuum that could be used to prompt reflective discussions and thinking. To better our understanding, these reflective questions developed by Pappas (2010b) are offered in Table 3.1.

Figure 3.1. Pappas' Taxonomy of Reflection

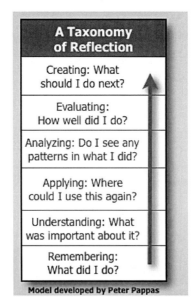

Source: © Pappas, P. (2010a, January, 4). A taxonomy of reflection: Critical thinking for students, teachers, and principals (Part 1). [Web Log Post] Retrieved from Copy/Paste http://www.peterpappas.com/2010/01/taxonomy-reflection-critical-thinking-students-teachers-principals.html. Used with Permission. peterpappas.com

Table 3.1. Pappas' Reflective Taxonomy—Reflective Questions along Bloom's Continuum

Bloom's Remembering: What did I do?

Teacher Reflection: What was the lesson? Did it address all the content? Was it completed on time? How did students "score" on the assessment?

Bloom's Understanding: What was important about what I did? Did I meet my goals?

Teacher Reflection: Can I explain the major components of the lesson? Do I understand how they connect with the previous/next unit of study? Where does this unit fit into the curriculum? What instructional strategies were used? Did I follow best practices and address the standards?

Bloom's Application: When did I do this before? Where could I use this again?

Teacher Reflection: Did I build on content, product, or process from previous lessons? How does this lesson scaffold the learning for the next lesson? How could I adapt the instructional approach to another lesson? How could this lesson be modified for different learners?

Bloom's Analysis: Do I see any patterns or relationships in what I did?

Teacher Reflection: What background knowledge and skills did I assume students were bringing to the lesson? Were the instructional strategies I used the right ones for this assignment? Do I see any patterns in how I approached the lesson—such as pacing, grouping? Do I see patterns in my teaching style—for example do I comment after every student reply? What were the results of the approach I used—was it effective, or could I have eliminated or reorganized steps?

Bloom's Evaluation: How well did I do? What worked? What do I need to improve?

Teacher Reflection: What are we learning and is it important? Were my assumptions about student background knowledge and skills accurate? Were any elements of the lesson more effective than other elements? Did some aspects need improvement? Were the needs of all learners met? What levels of mastery did students reach? What have I learned about my strengths and my areas in need of improvement? How am I progressing as a teacher?

Bloom's Creation: What should I do next? What's my plan/design?

Teacher Reflection: How would I incorporate the best aspects of this lesson in the future? What changes would I make to correct areas in need of improvement? How can I best use my strengths to improve? What steps should I take or resources should I use to meet my challenges? Is there training or networking that would help me to meet my professional goals? What suggestions do I have for our leadership or my peers to improve our learning environment?

Source: © Pappas, P. (2010b, January, 6). The reflective teacher: A taxonomy of reflection (Part 3). [Web Log Post] Retrieved from Copy/Paste http://www.peterpappas.com/2010/01/reflective-teacher-taxonomy-reflection.html. Used with Permission. peterpappas.com

Facilitates the Transfer of New Skills into Practice. Job-embedded professional development facilitates the transfer of new skills into practice. When ongoing support is linked to professional learning, transfer of skills into practice occurs. Various studies indicate that more active engagement and focus on content and its application to classroom practice coupled with practice yield higher transfer rates—up to 90–95 percent (Joyce & Showers, 2002).

Promotes Collaboration. Collaboration *is* a form of job-embedded learning (Darling-Hammond & Richardson, 2009). It is through collaboration that teachers share with one another, support one another, engage in discussions, and reflect about their experiences.

Job-Embedded Learning—No Time Like the Present

Given the structures in which teachers work, there is no time like the present to look at job-embedded learning as the ticket to enhancing teacher learning. Let's just brainstorm the ways in which teachers are "scheduled" and the configurations that the work of "education" unfolds outside of the classroom.

Teachers regularly meet in teams during the school day in these types of configurations:

♦ Team meetings

♦ Grade-level meetings

♦ Data team meetings

♦ School improvement teams

♦ Vertical team meetings (content, grade level)

♦ Horizontal team meetings (content)

♦ Department meetings (content)

♦ IEP meetings.

This list could probably continue in accordance with the context of the school and its configuration (e.g., elementary, middle, high school). The possibilities are endless. The work is to build a collaborative culture that supports professional learning that is "situated in practice [and] focused on student learning" (Whitcomb, Borko, & Liston, 2009, p. 208). Our list of configurations situates teachers as members of teams.

Needed—Teachers Who Can Work and Learn in Teams

Isolation from peers defies every principle of job-embedded professional development. Teams thrive in a collaborative culture in which peers can learn from each other. Everyone brings something to the table. Awareness of group development within teams can be helpful and reassuring. There are many theories of how groups develop that have evolved over time, including stage theory (Tuckman, 1965; Tuckman & Jensen, 1977). For example, Tuckman's (1965) Team Group Development Model (Table 3.2) originally included four stages (forming, storming, norming, and performing) and later Tuckman and Jensen (1977) added the fifth step, adjourning, to the model. One caveat is offered as you review these stages—team development entails learning, and learning is not linear. Learning is cyclical, recursive, and messy, as is team development.

Although members of a team or learning community change, the work and mission must stay focused on student achievement and the work teachers do to learn from their efforts.

Table 3.2. **Tuckman's Team Group Development Model**

Stage 1: Forming: The forming stage includes orientation to the work, tasks, and goals of the team. Members seek leadership, look for safety, are polite, but controversy is avoided and conversations are guarded. Initial concerns emerge. To get to the next stage, team members begin to take risks and offer differing points of view that lead to storming.

Stage 2: Storming: The storming stage is marked by testing the waters and conflict. Without storming and possibly agreeing to disagree, team members have difficulty moving toward interdependence (see norming stage). Conflict escalates when members move from an individual orientation to a team orientation to organize for teamwork and learn they have to make concessions about their own beliefs to achieve the work of the team. Interdependence between team members will not occur until the team has unearthed distrust and conflict. When conflict subsides, the team is ready to transition to the next stage, norming.

Stage 3: Norming: Team members adapt common work, reconcile their own opinions with the greater needs of the team, and members cooperate so they can begin performing.

Stage 4: Performing: The emphasis is on reaching the team goals, rather than working on team processes, establishing norms, and building trust. Members are loyal to the work of the group and its members. The team manages more complex tasks and copes with greater change.

Stage 5: Adjourning: The work of the team is complete, and the end-result has been reached.

Source: Adapted from Tuckman (1965) and Tuckman and Jensen (1977).

Trust, Teamwork, and Job-Embedded Learning

Without trust, little can be accomplished, and trust "can [only] occur when people have trust [in] each other" (Javadi, Zadeh, Zandi, & Yavarian, 2012, P. 213). Miranda (2012) reminds us that "critical reflection, validation, and development of trust with colleagues" occur in an environment in which people are embraced for the individual and collective gifts and values they bring to the community (p. 77). Moreover, in communities where trust is the norm, "teachers and leaders respond favorably to invitational, planned, safe places for professional development" (Miranda, 2012, p. 77). Learning communities are dependent on relational trust that serves as the glue (Cranston, 2011). In the final analysis, Miranda (2012) concludes: "Everything that must happen for a learning community to grow, develop, and transform rests on how much its members learn to trust each other" (p. 83).

Teamwork Needed to Engage in Collaborative Job-Embedded Learning Opportunities

A sense of teamwork is needed for teachers to engage in the work of job-embedded learning (Wynne, 2010). Darling-Hammond and McLaughlin (2011) remind us that teachers need to have opportunities to collaborate in ways to be "grounded in inquiry, reflection, and experimentation" as they "engage in concrete tasks of teaching, assessment, observation, and reflection that illuminate the processes of learning and development" (p. 82).

There are key markers of best practices related to job-embedded learning found in the literature and research.

The Markers of Job-Embedded Learning

The research and literature on best practices about job-embedded learning and teacher professional development have evolved since the early works of such pioneers including, for example, Joyce and Showers (1981, 1982), Wood and McQuarrie (1999), and Wood and Killian (1998). We have learned more about the differentiated and developmental ways in which adults learn (Drago-Severson, 2009), new technologies and the digital learning environment have pushed the envelope, and new forms of collaborative professional learning continue to evolve (e.g., instructional rounds). The markers of job-embedded learning remain constant and are examined.

Job-Embedded Learning Occurs in the Context of the Work Day. Given the complexities of schools, professional learning must be efficient, swift, and relevant in helping teachers to develop as professionals. There has been a steady resurgence of interest in team learning. *Job-embedded learning honors the principles of adult learning.* Recognizing how adults learn and what motivates teachers to learn justifies the shift away from "sit-and-get" professional development sessions to learning opportunities that are ongoing and continuous.

Job-Embedded Learning is Coherent. The content, pace, and processes of learning must be coherent, and *job-embedded learning promotes reflection* so teachers can think through what they are learning from their practices and from their interactions with students and their peers. *Job-embedded learning promotes collaboration and fosters collegial relationships* built around the work of teaching. In a school that promotes job-embedded learning, there would be lively discussions centered on practice.

Throughout these discussions, teachers would be actively digging deeper about what they are learning and how they are going to apply these lessons in their daily practices—tomorrow. To this end, *job-embedded learning supports the transfer of practice with the adoption and application of new skills.*

Job-embedded learning would not be complete without feedback and opportunities to debrief with peers. When teachers analyze their own work and share critical feedback in a collaborative exchange with peers, powerful learning occurs.

Case from the Field

Before Getting to Co-Teaching: The Nuts and Bolts of Establishing Collaborative Norms

Mr. David Forker, K–12 ESOL Specialist, Division of Instructional Services and School Performance, Clarke County School District, GA; Mr. Dwight Manzy, Principal, W. R. Coile Middle School, GA

Case Organizer

Learning from the work of teaching occurs through all interactions including those with children, teachers, administrators, parents, and anyone else who comes in contact with the schoolhouse. Working in a team requires learning how to collaborate and to set norms, for example.

Mr. David Forker shares how he learned to work collaboratively after entering teaching through a non-traditional preparation program and being asked to co-teach at the beginning of his second year of teaching.

The Context of W. R. Coile Middle School

W. R. Coile Middle School is on the outskirts of Athens, GA in Athens-Clarke County. It is situated in northeast Georgia within a rural setting fed by an urban population. Coile serves a population of about 698 students in Grades 6–8. Of the total population of Coile, about 51 percent are Black, 36 percent are Hispanic, 7 percent are White, and 6 percent are of other cultural backgrounds. About 7 percent of the students have been identified as English Language Learners (ELLs), and 94 percent are enrolled in the free and reduced lunch program.

David Forker Shares His Story About Entering Teaching

This approach to establishing collaborative norms was developed in response to the uncertainties I experienced when assigned to work as a collaborating co-teacher for the first time.

As context, I am a non-traditional teacher. After trying a few different careers, I earned a non-renewable teaching certificate, was hired as a teacher of English to Speakers of Other Languages (ESOL), and found teaching to be an excellent fit. My first year of teaching was similar to any other teacher working with a non-renewable certificate. I taught every day and was enrolled in coursework for a clear and renewable certificate at night. My time not at work was spent planning, grading papers, going to class, and doing my own coursework.

First-Year—Isolation Served

During the first year, I was fairly isolated from other teachers. I taught in an instructional model that is known as a scheduled ESOL environment. This meant that the classes I facilitated were clustered by grade level and consisted only of students identified as English Language Learners (ELLs). There was no particular content focus as these classes were intended to provide support with English-language acquisition in a very general sense. I was the only adult in the classroom and I was not part of any particular grade level or content team. Based on the way my class schedule was configured, I shared planning time with the connections/specials (Band, Art, PE, Consumer Science, etc.) team. Consequently, there was minimal interaction with the content/disciplinary grade-level teachers.

Second Year—Second Chance for Collaboration

Approaching the second year of teaching, I was assigned to work in a "collaborative" environment as a co-teacher in content grade-level classes. This meant that, by grade level, the English Language Learners were going to be clustered into particular content classes, and I was going to be assigned to their classes. For example, I was assigned to an 8th Grade math class, a 7th Grade English-language arts class, and a 6th Grade science class. The classes were no bigger than 28 students, and the English Learner clusters could be no larger than 14 students. Within these classes, there were two teachers. It was my understanding that the content teacher was going to be responsible for providing access to the subject matter, while I was going to be responsible for supporting English acquisition. We were expected to do this together as a team.

The Journey from Isolation to Collaboration— Learning How to Collaborate

Although typically very supportive, my administration did not have any resources or professional learning sessions prepared to help me develop an under-standing of what to expect in or to prepare for co-teaching/collaborative environ-ments. I was able to figure out that if I was going to be spending a considerable amount of time working in an often-challenging environment with someone I did not know, the most logical thing for me to do was to find out as much information about working in collaborative and co-teaching situations as I could. Fortunately, I was able to initiate conversations with some experienced veteran teachers and my college professors and classmates. I also used a vast amount of free resources on the internet.

Additionally, a considerable amount of mental energy thinking about possibili-ties and the approaches that could be undertaken to co-teach and to learn how to collaborate were reflected upon. My thinking centered on the lessons learned about the positive and negative experiences working with people in the past as I tried to visualize how my new working arrangements could develop.

Co-Teaching and Team Dynamics

Based on my experiences working with different teachers on different grade levels and in different content areas, there is no "one-size-fits-all" approach to work-ing in a collaborative/co-teaching environment. Each teacher team has been unique in its own ways. Individuals bring their own sets of strengths, challenges, expecta-tions, and beliefs. The ways in which people interact with each other and students vary. However, the constant is that teacher teams will take on some sort of dynamic. Whether it occurs organically or it is addressed in a deliberate and intentional man-ner, some sort of dynamic will develop.

How Will We Work Together?

There is an amazing amount of potential embedded in the notion that *a team dynamic will develop*. Considering how wide ranging the possibilities can be, it is advantageous for all parties involved (teammates, students, parents, administrators, etc.) if the members of the collaborative team dedicate time to establishing norms for their working relationship.

So what does this mean? In its most basic form, it means that collaborating teammates should talk about what their working lives together are going to look like before they dive in and get started. There is uncertainty in assuming every-thing is going to work itself out and all teammates are going to be able to contribute to their maximum potential without thinking through norms of how people will work together. To lay the groundwork, some conversation about each participant's visions, approaches, and expectations should occur to help create space for each participant's voice.

After a short preliminary analysis, I realized that I was about to spend a significant amount of time working with some new collaborating teammates that I knew virtually nothing about. This led me to the conclusion that, before we started planning and teaching our students, we needed to figure out a way that we could establish an environment in which we would be able to communicate openly.

Although this notion is not particularly profound or time consuming, I have seen many teacher teams neglect to take the time prior to starting their work together to establish collaborative environments. In many instances, this has led to poor communication, misunderstandings, lack of resolution, and in some cases resentment. Consequently, instructional shortcomings take place as a result of a break down in the learning environment. Even worse, this could result in a poorly developed learning environment that has the potential to discourage students from developing a passion for a particular content or disciplinary area, subsequently missing opportunities to realize their potential.

There is meta-cognitive component at work here that should be considered. On the one hand, there is the option of spending time with your teammates to think and talk about the work you are going to be doing before you begin. Conversations could lead teammates to learn about each other and their respective visions for the work they are going to be doing together. On the other hand, there is the option of diving right into the work. In this case, there would no mutual thinking about how the working relationship and environment will develop or how tasks are going to be approached.

Establishing Collaborative Norms—The Nuts and Bolts

Establishing collaborative norms with your co-teacher(s) comes down to taking the time to talk about how you each would like your work together to go. Teachers who are going to be working with each other in any capacity will benefit if they take the time develop a collaborative perspective of what their work together will look and sound like.

Ideally, before working together, teacher teams should take time to get to know each other, and to discuss some of their expectations and visions for the work they are going to do together. Here are some ideas that team members might want to think about as they begin the process of establishing collaborative norms.

The initial consideration of time: It is most unlikely that every school is going to be able to build in designated time for teacher teams to get together and establish collaborative norms, so, in many cases, teammates will need to make time on their own. This could be during preplanning, collaborative planning time, at lunch, after school, via Skype, or even at a coffee shop on the weekend. Regardless of when and where, teammates should find and protect time to establish collaborative norms for the work they are going to be doing together.

What do we talk about? The human component is the most important element of the initial meetings designated to establish collaborative norms. Rather than diving right into planning for instruction, this is well spent if teammates discuss to establish collaborative norms. There are some topics that particularly address collaboration through discussion based on teacher personality, style, and expectations (see Figure 3.2).

Figure 3.2. **Conversation That Facilitates Collaboration**

◆ Tell me about your experience as an educator (positions, contents, grades, etc . . .).

◆ What is your teaching philosophy?

◆ Do you have a particular teaching style?

◆ What are some negative and/or positive collaborative teaching experiences you have had?

◆ What do you envision as your role in the classroom?

◆ What do you envision as my role in the classroom?

◆ How can we present constructive criticism to each other?

The communication checklist (see Figure 3.3) provides a list of possible topics for discussion during the first meeting with teammates. These topics provide perspective into teammates' schedules and responsibilities. The amount of time spent on any of the topics remains at the discretion of the teammates.

Figure 3.3. **Communication Checklist**

◆ Class Schedule

◆ Teacher Personality

◆ Classroom Routine and Management

◆ Instructional Responsibilities

◆ Assessment, Homework, and Grading

◆ Collaborative Planning Time

◆ Other Issues to Address

Attention now goes to how the collaborative environment should be maintained. In particular, teammates should take time to give perspective regarding how they would like both glowing and growing input from each other. Often overlooked, this element provides insight into how each of the participants gives and receives input. Respectful dialogue over differing perspectives can be very healthy and productive. At the same time, if teammates have not discussed how to approach each other regarding such issues, they have created the potential for disaster. Conversation could easily lead to arguments.

Mutual Benefits

Learning about each other's strengths and weaknesses can increase your efficiency as an instructional team. When it is time to plan, facilitate instruction, correspond with parents, address discipline issues, or handle any other duties as assigned, insight into you and your teammates' strengths and weaknesses can be very useful. One member may have more experience with a particular type of teaching model. One member may be more comfortable having tough conversations with students, parents, or administrators. You both may have a common interest in a specific author or genre. You have no idea what you may learn about each other, but the power resides in the notion that learning about your teammate provides you with perspective that you can use to complement your teammate and position yourself to be complemented.

Student Benefits

The most important result of working to establish collaborative norms in this capacity is it supports teachers in their work together in a communicative environment that can be responsive and adaptive to the needs of the teammates and most importantly their students. As anyone who has worked around children and young people is fully aware, students have an intuitive sense of emotions and dynamics. If teachers are able to work with each other efficiently, students should experience a learning environment that is responsive and adaptive to their needs.

Lessons Learned and Future Directions

I hope not to present the illusion that establishing collaborative norms creates an environment in which no disagreements occur. There will be moments that shine and moments that do not; good days and bad; successes and failures. With that understanding, working to establish collaborative norms in some capacity allows teammates to communicate and to overcome the challenges that inevitably emerge.

As a final thought, teachers have a lot to learn from each other. We all bring experiences and knowledge that are valuable in a wide range of capacities. Some of my most insightful "professional learning" came from dialogue with co-teachers. Whether conversation was related to content, student achievement, behavior, or life in general, my collaborators and I came to know each other in a capacity that allowed us to provide each other with support, or space when we needed it most. Unquestionably, our students were able to reap the benefits.

Case Summary

Mr. Forker's story is an interesting one that shines a light on how teachers learn to work together in a collaborative teaching arrangement. The highlights of this narrative align with the major ideas presented in this chapter related to trust, teamwork, and job-embedded learning focusing especially on how and why it's important to establish norms and other "rules of engagement" so that team members can focus attention on learning.

Chapter Summary

Job-embedded learning supports teachers from the very work they do every day as they teach and work with peers. The work of teaching has become much more complex and multifaceted. Inquiry, reflection, and collaboration are necessary, as well as the ability to work in teams. There are several ways in which peers work to support learning. One such way is to engage in peer observations, examined in the next chapter.

Suggested Readings

Troen, V., & Boles, K. C. (2012). *The power of teacher teams: With cases, analyses, and strategies for success*. Thousand Oaks, CA: Corwin Press.

Venables, D. R. (2011). *The practice of authentic PLCs: A guide to effective teacher teams*.Thousand Oaks, CA: Corwin Press.

Villa, R. A., Thousand, J. S., & Nevin, A. I. (2013). *A guide to co-teaching: New lessons and strategies to facilitate student learning* (3rd ed.). Thousand Oaks, CA: Corwin Press.

Zepeda, S. J. (2012). *Professional development: What works* (2nd ed.). New York, NY: Routledge.

4 The Power of Peer Observations

Many schools have peer coaching and mentoring programs that include opportunities for peers to observe each other teach and then to engage in conversations. A teacher does not have to be a peer coach to engage in peer observations. All one needs is a colleague, a member of a grade-level team, a mentor, or a peer willing to spend some time before a classroom observation and then after a classroom observation engaging in conversation. Peer observations play an integral part in numerous professional development models including, for example, lesson study, peer coaching, cognitive coaching, critical friends groups, and other system improvement strategies such as learning walks, instructional rounds, and walk-throughs.

Technological advances have made some inroads in making peer coaching go "virtual" in some contexts. In a digital environment, teachers can view another colleague teaching in the same building or school system or as far away as the other end of the state or in a different continent, then meet, Skype, or blog with the observed teacher. As the digital environment advances, so too will opportunities to discover how professional learning can be enhanced through various applications that could influence peer observations and other forms of coaching.

The objective of this chapter is to examine the POP Cycle as a viable way for conducting peer observations. The POP Cycle is derived primarily from the field of instructional supervision that has evolved from a nine-phase process (Cogan, 1973; Goldhammer, 1969) to a more streamlined three-part cycle (Acheson & Gall, 2011; Sullivan & Glanz, 2013; Zepeda, 2012b, 2012c, 2013).

There is a proliferation of classroom observation models that includes a variety of methods, protocols, and tools. Some classroom observations conducted by peers are done in groups (e.g., instructional rounds, walk-throughs) and others are done "one-on-one," as in teacher-to-teacher. Some schools have instructional coaches that are specialists in a content area (e.g., mathematics, science, literacy), and these coaches are also engaged in observing peers teach. The type of peer-to-peer observation examined in this chapter is not tied to teacher evaluation.

Peer Observation

Engaging in peer observation signals two-way, reciprocal learning for teachers. Peer observation gets teachers into the classrooms of their peers. Peer observations allow teachers to go deeper into their work by supporting conversations about teaching among teachers. Regardless of type, who, or how many peers are involved, peer observation is a collaborative form of professional development situated in the context of the teacher's classroom and is therefore a job-embedded professional learning strategy. Peer observations situate teachers as active learners engaged in a variety of practices such as examining assessment strategies, student responses, and work artifacts from a lesson, and then perhaps planning for making mid-course changes in practices based on discussion points during conversations.

It is through conversation and reflection that teachers make more sense of their practices, see the possibilities, and make decisions. With a "second point of view" or an idea sparked during a conversation with a peer, teachers can focus with more precision on specific teaching practices. Collecting objective data during an observation provides evidence that a teacher can use while considering options about practice. Reflection can be pointed toward results—Are the kids getting it? Does "this" make sense? Actions such as tweaking a strategy or making a mid-course change in plans can be made with more confidence.

Fullan (2008b) believes that learning opportunities can be unified as a change strategy if we "connect peers to purpose," and if we embrace the notions that "learning is the work" and that "capacity building prevails." These notions are important because peer observations hold potential to connect peers to the purpose of learning more about their practices, to build system and student capacity while simultaneously supporting the needs of teachers who consistently focus their attention, best interests, and hearts on students and their learning needs.

Peer Observation Supports Job-Embedded Learning. People learn by the action of doing, reflecting, and making modifications to their practices (Darling-Hammond & Richardson, 2009). It is clear that everyday practice is the foundation of peer observation.

Collaboration Is a Requisite for Peer Observations. According to Waldron and McLeskey (2010), "collaborative activities result in added value by generating multiple solutions to complex problems and by providing opportunities to learn from others as school professionals express and share expertise" (p. 59).

Social Support Can Be Built Through Peer Observations. Peer observations provide social and emotional support. Learning is messy and recursive especially as people develop and transfer new skills into practice. There is a certain disequilibrium that occurs. As task complexity increases, teachers might want and need more or different types of support—specifically, social support that can come from trusted colleagues.

Malecki and Demaray (2003) define social support as an "individual's general support or specific support behaviors (available or enacted upon) from people in the social network, which enhances their functioning and/or may buffer them from adverse outcomes" (p. 232). Although Mercer, Nellis, Martinez, and Kirk's (2011) summary of these categories dealt with children, there is applicability to the adult learner's need for social support:

> *Emotional support* includes feelings of empathy, concern, and trust. *Instrumental support* consists of direct intervention by spending time with someone and providing assistance, materials, and help. *Informational support* is providing someone with verbal directions, advice, or suggestions. *Appraisal support* consists of providing someone with affirmation and evaluative feedback. (p. 324, emphasis added)

Conversation Skills. It is during the conversations before and after the peer observation that teachers engage in the real work—digging deeper into teaching practices based on the classroom observation and the sense that is made of the observation within the overall context of what's happening—is the team in the middle of a lesson study; is the teacher collecting data for an action research project; is the teacher being observed a first-year teacher who is being mentored? Context is everything and guides the conversation and the sense that is made during and after it.

Norms that Drive Peer Observations. In schools that engage in peer observations, teachers develop norms that guide this work. Norms are rules and beliefs about how people should operate under certain conditions. Norms do not have to be elaborate; they just have to fit the context of the school, and members need to commit to them. In Figure 4.1 there is an example of norms expressed as "rules" that were developed by a large urban high school in which the teachers involved in the peer observation program wanted "their" program to be a strengths-based one.

Although there are many variations, the peer observation process examined in this chapter is the POP Cycle (Zepeda, 2013, 2012c).

Figure 4.1. **Rules for Observing Peers' Strengths**

- ◆ Talk to each other ahead of time to gain awareness of the lesson, the students, and how an instructional strategy will be used.
- ◆ Comment only on the strategy you are observing. Staying within this parameter allows the host teacher to trust that you will not tread where you have not been invited to do so.
- ◆ Observations and conversations before and after are confidential.
- ◆ The purposes of peer observations are to improve student learning and to support teacher development.

Source: Arnau (2013).

POP Cycle

From the field of instructional supervision (Nolan & Hoover, 2011; Sullivan & Glanz, 2013; Zepeda, 2012b, 2012c, 2013), the basic phases of the clinical supervisory model have been morphed into the peer observation POP Cycle (Zepeda, 2012b, 2013). Peer observation using the POP Cycle involves three phases including: the *Pre-observation conversation*, the *Observation*, and the *Post-observation conversation* as depicted in Figure 4.2.

Figure 4.2. **POP Cycle**

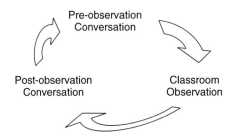

Pre-Observation Conversations

The pre-observation conversation opens the door to the teacher's world (Zepeda, 2013) so that a peer can get ready to observe in another peer's classroom. Here are some ideas to help frame this conversation. The conversation should:

♦ take place in the classroom where the observation will occur;

♦ define a clear focus for the observation, with the teacher whose class is being observed taking the lead; and,

♦ give the teacher the opportunity to "talk through" teaching—paint the context of the classroom and provide a snapshot of the characteristics of the students. (adapted, Zepeda, 2013)

This conversation sets the stage for all that follows in the classroom observation and during the next conversation.

Keep It Simple—Keep It Real

Conversations before the observation help create understanding of what will be observed, and help teachers "talk through" the lesson, and help peer observers understand the context of what is going to be taught. Moreover, the observer needs to be able to focus attention on "something" during the observation. Generally, what would teachers want a peer observer to focus on during a classroom observation? "It depends" is the first response because of the context-specific nature of the world of teaching and the experience, background, etc. of the teacher. Generally, a focus area would land on an area surrounding:

♦ a perceived need to improve in a specific area;

♦ a follow-up on professional development; and/or,

♦ areas under construction (e.g., trying a new technique). (Zepeda, 2013, p. 92)

Two conversation forms are provided in Figures 4.3 and 4.4 as examples to be adapted to fit the context of your needs.

Conversations Are About Looking at Practices

Looking at Figure 4.3, there is a conversation opener, "Tell me about your proudest moment in this classroom with these students," to help ease into the discussion about the upcoming classroom observation. The focus is important because it helps to determine what types of teacher or student (or both) behavior, artifacts, or evidence should be examined when in the classroom. The teacher being observed ideally determines the focus. The peer observer helps the teacher look at why the focus is important and what types of information about his/her practice would help bring into "focus" the area being analyzed. The focus will frame the classroom observation and then the conversation between the peer observer and the teacher after the observation.

Figure 4.4 gets right to the focus for the peer observation and asks for very specific information related to logistics (e.g., how long should the peer observer stay, where to sit, and then when to meet for the follow-up conversation).

Figure 4.3. **Sample Pre-Observation Conversation Form # 1**

Pre-Observation Conversation Form # 1

Teacher _____ Date of Pre-conversation _____

Peer _____ Date for Post-conversation _____

Observation Date _____ Time _____ to _____ Room Number _____

1. Tell me about your proudest moment in this classroom with these students.

2. What area [instruction, assessment, classroom management, etc.] would you like feedback on for further analysis?

3. What data led you to this focus?

4. What kinds of observation notes (information) would help you look deeper at your practices?

To recap, the purpose of the pre-observation conversation is to:

1. Open lines of communication before the classroom observation and to develop further collaborative relationships with peers.

2. Land on a focus for the observation so that the peer observer can take more useful notes related to that focus (teacher action or words, student action or words, etc.).

3. Get a feel for the context of the lesson (content, instructional methods, etc.) and the characteristics of students.

4. Negotiate follow-up meeting date, time, and location for the follow-up conversation after the classroom observation (adapted, Zepeda, 2013).

Figure 4.4. **Sample Pre-Observation Conversation Form # 2**

Pre-Observation Conversation Form # 2

1. What would you like for me to focus on intently?

2. Is there anything you want me to know about before I visit?

3. Are there any students that you would like for me to focus on during the visit?

4. How long should I stay in your room and where would you like me to sit?

5. When and where can we meet to have a conversation about our experience?

Timing is everything. It is advisable to conduct an observation within a day or two after a pre-observation conversation.

Classroom Observations

There are many approaches to collecting data, and there are a variety of tools that have been developed to assist peer observers, peer coaches, literacy coaches, school leaders, and any other school personnel who conduct classroom observations. In addition to these approaches and tools, many hybrid tools are developed "on the fly" based on the focus of the classroom observation.

A few examples of peer observation tools are offered. Technology can assist with the development of classroom observation tools that can be stored on Google Docs and then be easily shared.

Again, these tools are offered as an illustrative sampling of tools that are available to support the work of conducting peer observations. The main point to remember is that the tool has to be able to help the peer coach collect usable data that matches the focus—the area in which the teacher wants data collected during the observation.

TOOL 1

Tool 1	Anecdotal Scripted Notes Using Time

Directions: Simply use a sheet of paper and take notes chronicling in 5-minute increments around the focus identified by the teacher.

Time	Notes

TOOL 2

Tool 2	Bloom's Taxonomy: Levels of Questions

Directions: Chronicle the time of the question, the question, and examine at what level of the taxonomy the question falls.

Time	Question(s)	Levels of Questions Thinking					
		Knowledge	Comprehension	Application	Analysis	Synthesis	Evaluation

Source: Zepeda, S. J. (2012c).

TOOL 3

Tool 3	T-Chart of Teacher Stimulus and Student(s) Responses

Directions: Make a T-chart and record teacher actions, directions, physical proximity, etc., and specific student responses, include time to chronicle this information.

Time	Teacher Actions/Directions	Student Responses

Source: Zepeda, S. J. (2012c).

TOOL 4

Tool 4	Sequencing the Lesson

Directions: Check and comment on all that apply about the sequencing of instruction, activities, closure, etc.

		Comments/Notes:
☐	Essential Question runs through entire lesson/is referred to throughout the lesson	
☐	The lesson follows the lesson plan	
☐	Introduction	
☐	Previews	
☐	Purpose	
☐	Standards are identified and addressed	
☐	Outlines learning objectives	
☐	Develops introduction	
☐	Activating prior knowledge/anticipatory set	
☐	Specific learning activities	
☐	Checking for understanding	
☐	Clear assessment criteria	
☐	Conclusion	

Now that the observation has concluded, it's time to head into the third phase of the POP Cycle—the Post-observation Conversation.

Approaches to the Post-Observation Conversation

The purpose of the post-observation conversation is to debrief about the focus established before the classroom observation and what was observed in the classroom. Through discussion, probing questions, and a sincere desire to support a peer, the objective is to reconstruct the events of the classroom so that deeper meanings and insights can be gleaned from the observation. At the end of the conversation, it would be a reasonable expectation that a teacher would:

1. have a new insight about some aspect of teaching (the area of focus);

2. have ideas to reflect about and perhaps seek a follow-up discussion (a good sign!);

3. have some unanswered questions that spark more probing discussions with team members;

4. want to continue with ongoing peer observations or engage in other forms of collaborative learning (e.g., action research, portfolio development, join a professional learning network, read a book, blog with an expert); and so on.

The timing of the conversation after the observation is important because teachers want feedback quickly and there is a tendency to be "wound tight" when we are being observed.

Let's Get the Conversation Started. Engaging in a professional conversation after a peer observation serves to break the isolation experienced by many and helps to make instructional practice more public. Here are a few ideas to get the conversation started.

Frame an Opening to Get the Teacher Thinking About the Lesson that Was Just Observed. Effective openings are open-ended and serve a purpose—to put the other person at ease and to act as a jumping point to get to the focus—what the teacher wanted to focus his/her attention on.

Figure 4.5 presents some sample conversation openers.

Figure 4.5. Conversation Openers

Conversation Openers. . .
♦ Tell me how you thought the lesson went related to your focus. ♦ What was a high-beam teachable moment for you? ♦ Did things go as you had planned? Explain . . .

Embrace the Spontaneity of the Discussion. Although a focus was developed, spontaneous interactions surrounding the events of the classroom can help the teacher talk through ideas, see how one area might affect another area, etc.

Use Notes, Artifacts, and Other Items from the Classroom Visit. Let the data and other types of evidence help inform the teacher's sense-making about practice. A few detailed examples that can illustrate a point related to the focus can help more than incomplete examples. As a peer observer, the work is to help keep the conversation moving by asking questions, probing the teacher to think and reflect on practice, and to serve as a confidant as discussion points, questions, or other thorny issues of practice surface during the conversation.

Extending Conversations Through Questions

"Listen more, speak less," should be the maxim for peer observers because it is the teacher who was observed who needs to talk about teaching and the meaning of the data. Through the discussion will come the reflection and the impetus for further inquiry. The way questions are framed and the types of questions that are asked influence the quality of the conversation and the depth of the reflection.

The four types of questions examined include:

◆ probing questions (more Socratic in nature, use higher-order type questions and probes to support new ways of thinking and reflection);

◆ open questions (designed to get people to open up more to share more information);

◆ closed questions (designed to limit responses); and

◆ extended recall questions (designed to get people to elaborate in depth about a specific incident that occurred in the classroom).

Types of Questions

Probing questions do not necessarily introduce a new topic but allow a peer to probe further so the person responding can go deeper into thought. According to the National School Reform Faculty at the Harmony Education Center and the Southern Maine Partnership (n.d.), good probing questions have several qualities to support conversations as explicated in Figure 4.6.

Examples of probing questions include:

◆ Could you tell me more?

◆ Could you give me an example?

◆ Why was that?

◆ Could you expand?

Open questions attempt to get teachers to go beyond short one- or two-worded responses to talk more, to relate more details about specific practices, or to help fill in the blanks with information that might not be readily known by the observer.

Figure 4.6. **Good Probing Questions**

Good probing questions . . .

♦ are for the benefit of the receiver and the colleagues and students he/she impacts;

♦ deepen and expand thinking and conversation;

♦ sustain thinking beyond the moment;

♦ are relevant and important to the receiver;

♦ keep learning at the center;

♦ help foster a sense that participants are a community of learners;

♦ are concise;

♦ elicit a slow, reflective response;

♦ are exploratory—they do not contain explicit recommendations or directives;

♦ are non-judgmental—neutral rather than positive or negative. (p. 1)

Closed questions fall in the lower levels of Bloom's Taxonomy and these types of questions really elicit simple "yes," or "no," or other one- or two-worded responses. In many ways, closed questions place the control of the conversation with the person asking the questions and, moreover, closed questions do not promote two-way, interactive conversations.

Extended recall questions are designed to get teachers to go into great detail about a specific incident that occurred in the classroom. However, the objective is to start thinking more critically about the totality of the incident, to recall more details of the incident, and to start attaching more meanings through reflection and questioning. Extended recall is about meaning through the reflection. Figure 4.7 offers some examples of extended recall questions.

Figure 4.7. **Extended Recall Question Examples**

Think back [to some aspect of the lesson or the class] and tell me about it.
The approach you chose to break students into small groups helped students learn how to cooperate. Tell me how you were able to get students to this level of cooperation.
Tell me more about [some aspect of the class, student response, an instructional method, predictions about how students will perform on an assessment].
When you looked at Johnny, he knew immediately to stop talking.
How did you know that the student would try to . . .
After the small group activity began, you used the down time to help students who had been absent the day before.

The Nature of Post-Observation Conversations

Conversations support inquiry and reflection. For a culture of learning that supports inquiry on practice to emerge, Cunningham (2011) reminds us that certain "non-negotiables" must be present to support this type of work. The non-negotiables for "collegial inquiry" must:

◆ work for deep understanding;

◆ develop intellectual perseverance;

◆ commit to reflective practice;

◆ build a commitment to collaborative and collegial work;

◆ recognize and honor each other's expertise; and

◆ be courageous. (p. 5)

Conversations in such a culture would hold true to these same commitments that peers make to one another and to their students. Through purposeful conversations, teachers come to deeper understandings about their practices. Conversations situate teachers as architects continually constructing and reconstructing knowledge about practice.

Conversations Embrace Constructing Knowledge about Practice. Constructivist-based learning activities for adults lead to learning about practices and the impact on student learning where "the focus is puzzling," and therefore should require active "inquiring and problem solving" (Sergiovanni & Starratt, 2009, pp. 266–267). By actively pushing our limits seeking to better understand our practices and student learning, we do at least two things right. First, we get away from blaming students for not learning. Second, we channel energy "actively constructing knowledge" (O'Neil, 1998, p. 51), about our instructional practices.

With a laser-focus on students embedded in practices that engage peers in learning activities, teachers are in a position to learn through conversations. Closely associated with constructivism is the zone of proximal development, important to consider while thinking about conversations.

Conversations Allow Peers to Enter the Zone of Proximal Development. In the zone of proximal development, Vygotsky (1978) asserts that the learner individually constructs knowledge with the assistance of another person who can help the learner rise to higher levels of knowledge or practice. Working in the zone of proximal development, learners keep stretching to construct new knowledge slightly above their current level of knowledge or perhaps performance. Figure 4.8 depicts the zone of proximal development as described by Vygotsky (1978). Conversations nudge peers through the zone.

Conversations Lead to Further Reflection and Inquiry About Practice. Originally published in 2004, Tice (2011) wrote about a self-reflective action model where teachers would start inquiring about and reflecting on their practices with or without the assistance of a peer. After viewing Tice's article, the components are examined in the context of what can occur after a POP Cycle. Consider the distillation of Tice's work as envisioned in the rendition presented in Figure 4.9.

After a POP Cycle, job-embedded learning does not stop. There are several windows of opportunity for teachers to engage in learning (e.g., action research,

Figure 4.8. **The Zone of Proximal Development**

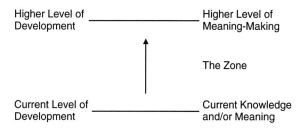

Higher Level of Development _____ Higher Level of Meaning-Making

The Zone

Current Level of Development _____ Current Knowledge and/or Meaning

Figure 4.9. **Self-Reflective Action Model**

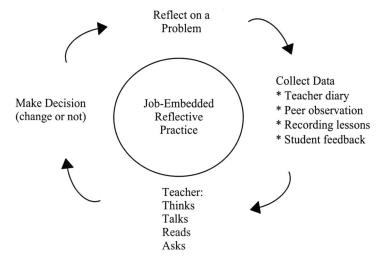

Reflect on a Problem

Collect Data
* Teacher diary
* Peer observation
* Recording lessons
* Student feedback

Job-Embedded Reflective Practice

Make Decision (change or not)

Teacher:
Thinks
Talks
Reads
Asks

Source: Based on the work of Tice (2011).

examining student work). In the following Case from the Field, coaching as a form of job-embedded learning is offered where teams are being coached and the members within the teams are engaging in variations of the POP Cycle.

Case from the Field

Job-Embedded Professional Learning to Enhance Collaborative Co-Planning

Ms. Marie Yuran, Special Education Team Leader; Dr. Linda Boza, Instructional Coach; Ms. Mary Thielman, Associate Principal; Dr. Robbie Hooker, Principal, Clarke Central High School, GA

Case Organizer

This case examines how a group formed as a job-embedded learning team to support the multiple co-planning and teaching teams. Coaching included walk-through classroom observations and more focused classroom observations that followed the POP Cycle. Coaching included targeted conversations, provision of resources, and other supports.

The Context of Clarke Central High School

Clarke Central High School (CCHS) is an urban school with nearly 1,450 students. The school serves a predominately minority population, which represents 79 percent of the total student body. The breakdown is as follows: 53 percent African-American, 21 percent Hispanic, 21 percent White, 3 percent Multiracial, and 2 percent Asian. Seventy-four percent of the teachers have advanced degrees. The graduation rate at CCHS has grown in a four-year period from 68.7 to 76.7 percent in the 2011/12 academic year. Students with disabilities have a graduation rate of 37 percent. Eighteen percent of the students receive gifted services, 13 percent receive special education services, and 3 percent are English Language Learners.

Collaborative Teaching

Under the state of Georgia's new College and Career Readiness Performance Index (CCRPI), Clarke Central High School was designated as a Focus School by the Georgia State Department of Education because of the gap in graduation rate between White students and students with disabilities. Being a large high school with many collaborative classes, CCHS needed to focus on stronger collaboration between special education and general education teachers. In 2003, CCHS had approximately 10 sections of collaborative classes; today, CCHS has 83 sections.

Collaborative classes are classes taught with two educators, one who has content certification and the other of whom has a special education certification. Often, the special education teacher also has content certification. These classes have two rosters, one comprised of general education students and one comprised of students with disabilities served through an Individualized Education Plan (IEP). The IEP is a legal document detailing the disabilities services to be provided, accommodations that are required for the student to experience success in the classroom, and other information as necessary.

Job-Embedded Professional Learning Team—Forging Partnerships

To keep up with the number of teams and to support the collaborative effort of our teachers, a job-embedded professional learning team was formed. For the 2012/13 school year, the team consisted of Marie Yuran (Special Education Team Leader), Dr. Linda Boza (Instructional Coach), Sue Rickman (Clarke County School District Special Education Coordinator); Allison Nealy (Professor-in-Residence, University of Georgia), and Chuck Bell (School Improvement Specialist, Northeast

Georgia Regional Educational Service Agency). In 2014, Jennifer Leahy (Collaboration Coach Northeast Georgia Regional Educational Service Agency) joined the team.

Assessing Collaborative Team Needs—Instruction

Initially, the team conducted walk-through observations to gather team data (Table 4.1 portrays the types of data collected during walk-through observations). This data provided the team with information regarding areas where efforts needed to focus. Next, the job-embedded professional learning team divided the collaborative teams, based on content, needs, and personality. Throughout the year, collaborative team members discussed goals, individual learning needs of students, suggested strategies to implement, observed teams, and gave feedback during debriefing sessions following the cycle presented in Figure 4.10.

Table 4.1. **Comparative Collaborative Data Points from Walk-Throughs**

	August 2012	November 2012	January 2013
Standard Posted	87%	87%	85%
Essential Question Posted	87%	83%	85%
Instruction Is Aligned to Standard	87%	80%	35%
Flexible Groups/Type of Model			
Team Teaching	33%	21%	33%
Parallel Teaching	10%	4%	7%
One Teach/One Assist	50%	33%	4%
One Teach/One Observe	7%	8%	15%
Alternative Teaching	0%	4%	0%
Station Teaching	7%	17%	0%
Co-Assisting	23%	21%	19%
Type of Differentiation/Specialized Instruction			
Content	n/a	16%	5%
Process	n/a	40%	67%
Product	n/a	8%	14%
Learning Environment	n/a	16%	10%
None	n/a	20%	14%
Most Students Are Actively Engaged	70%	90%	96%
Student Learning Is Monitored and Assessed Throughout Instruction	76%	71%	93%

(Continued)

Table 4.1. (Continued)

	August 2012	November 2012	January 2013
Evidence of Specialized Instruction/ Differentiation			
Individualized Learning Issues/Needs	0%	38%	33%
Assessment/Data Collection	0%	4%	4%
Effective Strategies for All	13%	33%	41%
Scaffolding	27%	29%	20%
Universal Design	0%	8%	8%
Previewing/Acceleration	0%	0%	4%
None Observed	53%	25%	24%
Other	0%	4%	0%
Bloom's Taxonomy			
Lower Level	57%	51%	37%
Middle Level	30%	44%	46%
Higher Level	13%	5%	17%

Co-Planning Using Data Points from Walk-Throughs

Teams met together to plan lessons using data from the walk-throughs (see Table 4.1). Department chairs served as instructional leaders. This collaborative planning time lent itself to natural meetings with teams that did not go beyond the school day.

Data Points Lead Efforts

At the end of the year, End of Course Test data were analyzed for students with disabilities. There was no change for math or science courses and a decrease for economics. However, there was an increase in proficiency scores for language arts courses (46% for 9th Grade literature up from 31%; 46% for 11th Grade literature up from 33%). Further data were pulled for 9th Grade literature to compare the district benchmark data to course pass rates. Students with disabilities passed the benchmark tests in the 40th percentile, and they passed the actual course (teacher grades) in the 80th percentile. These data were presented to the teachers to help support the case for increasing rigor and implementing higher-order thinking with continued differentiation.

Helping To Organize Co-Teaching Support Team Meetings

Minutes of the meetings were taken and recorded on the Co-Teaching Support Team Meeting Form (see Table 4.2). These notes are used to discuss progress and to solicit ideas for further action and support.

Table 4.2. Co-Teaching Support Team Meeting Form

Co-Teaching Team:

Content Area:

Block/Room:

Meeting Date:

Members of Team Present:

Minutes of Discussion:

Meeting Outcomes:

Identified Needs:

Identified Supports with Timelines (short and
    long term):

Personnel Responsible for Supports (to
    include with whom and by when):

Next Meeting:

Coaching Cycle

The job-embedded professional learning team used the Coaching Cycle to support professional learning with their teams (see Figure 4.10). Using this formative cycle, teachers could get feedback that was relevant to their practices, timely, and focused on what they could possibly explore to support their instructional efforts. Classroom observations are taking place with the use of tools from the book *Informal classroom observations on the go: Feedback, discussion, and reflection* (Zepeda, 2012c). It is important to note that classroom observation tools are being modified to meet the needs of team members.

Figure 4.10. Coaching Cycle

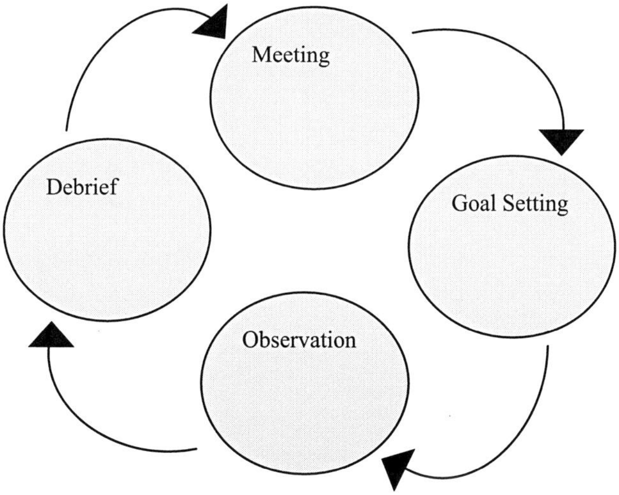

Meeting

Goal Setting

Observation

Debrief

Electronic Curating of Team Materials and Resources

Teachers wanted a physical "tool box" to aid in their development of co-planning materials and supports. At first, a giant notebook of resources and tools was envisioned. The solution was a Google site with organized folders. Forms for teachers to help them document their meetings were uploaded as well.

Case Summary

The collaborative approach allowed this job-embedded professional learning team to support teachers as they readied to co-plan and then co-teach. External personnel from the district office, a local university, and an educational service agency rounded the team as well as the support and encouragement of the administration. Tools were electronically curated, and team walk-throughs and individual classroom observations were part of the support structures.

Chapter Summary

Regardless of form, peer observations are a "teacher-to-teacher" type of support that includes a classroom observation sandwiched in between a conversation before and after it. Conversations matter. It is through conversations with peers that the thorny issues of practice can be examined and solutions bantered in a space where teachers can actively reflect about the impact their instruction is having on student learning. There are many types of tools to help frame the pre-observation conference, the data collection that occurs during the classroom observation, and the conversations in the post-observation conference. The next chapter examines peer coaching and coaching.

Suggested Readings

Patterson, K., Grenny, J., McMillan, R., & Switzler, A. (2012). *Crucial conversations: Tools for talking when stakes are high* (2nd ed.). New York, NY: McGraw Hill.

Roberts, S. M., & Pruitt, E. Z. (2009). *Schools as professional learning communities: Collaborative activities and strategies for professional development* (2nd ed.). Thousand Oaks, CA: Corwin Press.

Sullivan, S., & Glanz, J. (2013). *Supervision that improves teaching: Strategies and techniques* (3rd ed.). Thousand Oaks, CA: Corwin Press.

Zepeda, S. J. (2012b). *Instructional supervision: Applying tools and concepts* (3rd ed.). New York, NY: Routledge.

Zepeda, S. J. (2012c). *Informal classroom observations on the go: Feedback, discussion, and reflection.* New York, NY: Routledge.

5 | Best Practices in Peer Coaching

Peer coaching is its own model of professional development. However, certain components of the model have been adapted in practice and play an integral part in other models of professional development. Regardless of its form, all coaching models and configurations share at least one practice—a belief in conversations. In this chapter, a brief overview of the major models of coaching is presented and then the focus shifts to the peer coaching model as developed by Joyce and Showers (1981, 1982). This chapter is an important one because all models of professional development benefit from peer and other forms of coaching.

Coaching

Effective coaches know when and how to stretch, when and how to challenge, and when and how to guide those whom they are coaching. The foundational coaching skills include the ability to collaborate and to build trust with teachers. Coaching practices take into account the needs as well as the experience, maturity, and knowledge of the individual. Coaching must be developmental and differentiated, relying on the principles of how adults learn (see Chapter 2); coaching must be embedded in the work of teachers during the day while they are on the job (see Chapter 3); and coaching is also embedded in numerous professional development models and approaches (see Chapters 4, 6, 7, 8, and 9).

The Work of Coaching

The work of coaching includes such activities as modeling, demonstrating, providing professional development, sharing best translations of research, observing teachers, etc. Coaching, regardless of its form, is concerned with

♦ supporting teachers in the development of deeper understandings of content knowledge;

◆ extending thought processes needed to see different points of view about strategies;

◆ helping develop critical thinking skills through problem-posing and problem-solving to get at looking at the impact of instruction on student success;

◆ helping teachers boost student performance;

◆ providing translations of research and making connections to classroom practice; and

◆ giving feedback on performance to answer the question, "Are we getting closer to meeting the objectives?"(Zepeda, 2012a)

Figure 5.1. Cyclical and Collaborative Nature of Coaching

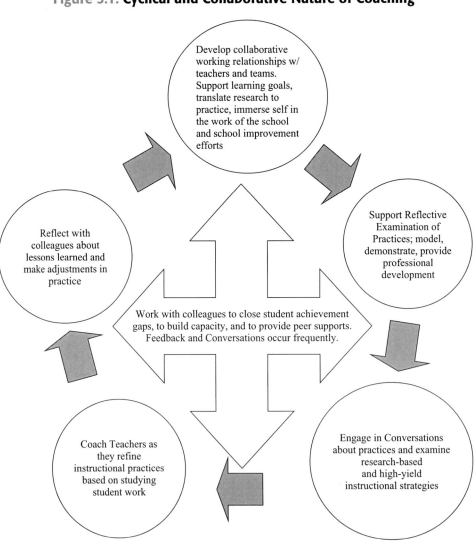

Based on the various models, constructs, and the literature on coaching, Figure 5.1 illustrates the cyclical and collaborative nature of the work that a coach engages in at the site level.

Virtual Coaching

Millennials in digital learning environments engage in coaching using varied platforms and applications such as "bug in the ear technologies" to give feedback during real-time instruction (Rock, Zigmond, Gregg, & Gable, 2011), and the use of video allows for teachers and coaches to review teaching episodes. As technology evolves, there will be increases in the uses of electronic tools and applications for coaching, and processes that will influence professional development.

Coaching Promotes Reflective Practice

In Chapter 2, reflection was examined in detail. Recall the work of Schön (1983, 1987), who examined reflection-in-action (in the moment) and reflection-on-action (looking back afterward), Killion and Todnem (1991), who brought forward the notion of reflection-for-action (acting on what was learned from reflection), and Bold (2011), who holds firm that critical reflection must lead to sense-making (see Figure 2.1 in Chapter 2). Coaching occurs in the moment, but typically the conversations occur after coaching; therefore, the conversations need to elicit reflective responses.

Overview of Select Models of Coaching

Because of their strengths, three models of coaching are briefly reviewed in this section: 1) cognitive coaching, 2) instructional coaching, and 3) literacy coaching.

Cognitive Coaching

Costa and Garmston (2002) developed the cognitive coaching model based on the idea that meta-cognition occurs when there is an awareness of one's own thinking processes and it is this awareness that fosters learning. Cognitive coaching builds flexible, confident problem-solving skills through self-appraisal and self-management of cognition with the assistance of a coach who promotes a focus on learner performance within a given focus (Costa & Garmston, 2002). The cognitive coaching cycle is cyclical, resembling the supervisory cycle of a pre-observation conference, a classroom observation, and then a post-observation conference (see Figure 4.2). Techniques that foster cognitive coaching include reflection, dialogue, problem-posing (identification), and problem-solving.

Cognitive coaching is based on the core beliefs that a) everyone is capable of changing, b) teaching performance is based on decision-making skills that motivate skill development and refinement, c) teachers are capable of enhancing each other's cognitive processes, decisions and teaching behaviors, and d) teachers and the coach examine and assess student learning through evidence to match the teacher's own goals (Garmston, 1987).

Instructional Coaching

Knight (2007) offers instructional coaching as an alternative to traditional professional development. Instructional coaches are defined by Knight as "individuals who are full-time professional developers, onsite in schools" (p. 12). Knight (2007) summarizes the range of work and the roles instructional coaches (ICs) assume:

◆ Coaching is about building relationships with teachers as much as it is about instruction. The heart of relationships is emotional connection.

◆ To get around barriers to change, coaches often start by working one-to-one with teachers.

◆ ICs adopt a partnership philosophy, which at its core means that they have an authentic respect for teachers' professionalism.

◆ The partnership philosophy is realized in collaborative work between the coach and the collaborative teacher. Together, coach and teacher discover answers to the challenges present in the classroom.

◆ ICs model in the classroom so that teachers can see what correct implementation of an intervention looks like.

◆ ICs model in the classroom so that teachers can see what research-based interventions look like when they reflect a teacher's personality.

◆ To be truly effective, coaches must work in partnership with their principals. (Knight, 2007, p. 33)

Literacy Coaching

In coaching, relationships matter. Dozier (2006) indicates that literacy coaching is based on the development of a "respectful, caring, instructional relationship" (p. 9), and Peterson, Taylor, Burnham, & Schlock (2009) add the "ultimate goal of working with a literacy coach is to deepen the teacher's understanding of how students learn by facilitating self-reflection to bring about change in classroom instruction, which has the potential to lead to increased student achievement" (p. 501).

Moving beyond the individual classroom level, the literacy coach often assumes many roles and responsibilities for an entire school. Walpole and McKenna (2012) describe the work of literacy coaches in terms of their efforts across school-wide reading programs and the support they provide in the development of reading assessments, intervention strategies, and professional support (book clubs, study groups, peer observation) in addition to disseminating and interpreting research about reading.

Peer Coaching

Peer coaching provides opportunities for teachers to support and to learn from each other while engaging in realistic discussions about teaching and learning. Peer coaching derives strength not only from the social nature of the model, but also from the constructivist nature in which meanings are developed with others from the processes (reflection, dialogue/conversation) of constructing meaning during conversations. Peer coaches also work with teachers as they engage in action research, book study, lesson study, and other collaborative forms of learning.

The Peer Coaching Model

Joyce and Showers (1981, 1982, 2002) provided the first documented model of peer coaching as a form of professional development. Peer coaching is a multifaceted model that can be implemented as an instructional strategy, a professional development strategy, and a complement to instructional supervision, peer observations, action research, and other forms of professional learning. The big question should be: How could one model be so many things to so many models? Amazing, isn't it! Originally conceived as a form of professional development, peer coaching consisted of a cycle that included the presentation of theory as well as a demonstration. Teachers were then led through practice, given feedback, and coached accordingly as depicted in Figure 5.2. The coaching aspects of the model mirror the clinical supervisory model by including extended "in-class training by a supportive partner who helps a teacher correctly apply skills learned in a workshop" (Joyce & Showers, 1982, p. 5).

As depicted in Figure 5.2, teachers are 1) presented with the theory, 2) watch a demonstration of the theory, 3) given the opportunity to practice the application, and 4) receive feedback on practice. However, the peer coaching model does not stop there, because coaching is an integral part of the model.

Figure 5.2. Peer Coaching Cycle

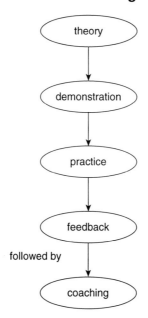

Coaching is the Bridge

Coaching occurs at two levels: in the classroom with a coach observing a teacher, and in the feedback conference. Because coaching occurs in the classroom, feedback is more realistic, steeped in the context where skills and techniques are applied. According to Joyce and Showers (1981), coaching involves a collegial approach to integrating mastered skills and strategies into:

♦ a curriculum;

♦ a set of instructional goals;

♦ a time span; and,

♦ a personal teaching style. (Joyce & Showers, 1981, p. 170)

Peer Coaching Includes Classroom Observations. Peer coaching includes classroom observations following the POP Cycle examined in chapter 4; however, the cycle is extended by including follow-up as part of the process (see Figure 5.3).

Peer Coaching Fosters Transfer of Knowledge into Practice. Peer coaching supports the transfer of newly learned skills from a learning opportunity into practice, the strength of peer coaching (Joyce & Showers, 2002). Transfer to practice is connected to four interrelated components of coaching linked to learning: a) learning the theory supporting the instructional strategy; b) watching a skillful demonstration of the instructional strategy; c) practicing the strategy; and d) engaging in peer coaching. Joyce and Showers report that if teachers only participate in the first three components of coaching, approximately "5% of the teachers transfer and master the strategy in their classrooms" (2002, p. 78). However, if these same teachers would

Figure 5.3. **Peer Coaching Classroom Observation Cycle**

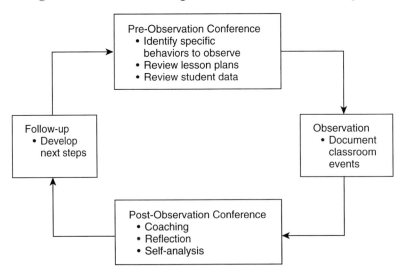

participate in all four components by adding coaching, "95%" of the teachers will transfer skills into practice (p. 78).

Coaching Conversations

A critical skill area for coaches is the conversation. Susan Scott's (2004) book, *Fierce conversations*, extols "the conversation IS the relationship," and relationships rest on a foundation of trust. Coaching conversations occur throughout the day, in the hallways, in the lunchroom, during team meetings, after school, or just about any place two or more teachers are present.

Coaches offer a different perspective. For example, if you were a coach, and conducting a classroom observation, you would act as another set of eyes (Acheson & Gall, 2011). You would see and hear things that the teacher would not necessarily be aware of and could offer insight through the feedback, reflective questions, or examples of what students or the teacher said or did during certain aspects of the class. If you were coaching a team of teachers as they were examining student work and they became stuck, you could lead the conversation to get the group's energy spinning out from the wheel ruts.

Coaching conversations are concerned about:

♦ building capacity of individuals;

♦ building relationships with people, one conversation at a time;

♦ bolstering individual and collective performance one person and team at a time; and

♦ focusing on student achievement, one student and one class and grade-level at a time.

It's important to examine conversations in the context of coaching. In teams or between two people "the pool of shared meaning is the birthplace of synergy," according to Patterson, Grenny, McMillan, & Switzler (2012, p. 25). Gross Cheliotes and Reilly (2012) outline that coaching conversations, "Stimulate thinking, growth, and change that lead to action" (p. 5); however, these aspirations can only be met if the characteristics of the conversations are:

1. intentional and often include pre-thought; and

2. focus[ed] on the other person, his strengths and challenges, and the attributes he brings to the conversation. (Gross Cheliotes & Reilly, 2012, p. 5)

Conversation Skills

Gross Cheliotes and Reilly (2012) identified four essential skills for holding conversations offered in Table 5.1.

Coaching conversations, whatever form they take, must be open invitations to continuing the talk about teaching throughout the year or even from one year to the next. Coaching conversations can be planned or spontaneous.

Table 5.1. **Four Essential Skills for Productive Conversations**

Skill	Explanation
Committed Listening	◆ connects you with others ◆ conveys value and a desire to engage in a dialogue ◆ helps build trust ◆ is foundational to all coaching conversations
Paraphrasing	◆ is a shorthand statement or summary ◆ helps the speaker clarify thinking ◆ aligns the thinking of the speaker and listener ◆ sends the message of attentive listening ◆ shows care for what is being shared
Presuming Positive Intent	◆ enters into a conversation with a positive mind-set about the other person ◆ understands language is critical
Reflective Feedback	◆ focuses on asking clarifying questions ◆ expresses the value or value potential of the idea or behavior ◆ poses reflective questions or possibilities; and ◆ is very specific

Source: Gross Cheliotes & Reilly (2012, pp. 6–12).

Zweibel's F.R.A.M.E. Coaching Conversation Model

Barry Zweibel, founder of LeadershipTraction® (2005/2014a), developed the Coaching F.R.A.M.E. of Reference Model (Figure 5.4) as a way to further empower coaching conversations. The F.R.A.M.E. Model has an embedded F.O.C.U.S. that supports coaching conversations that are non-judgmental, seek to extend conversations with open-ended questions, and to keep the momentum of the conversation on growth and development.

Zweibel (2005/2014b) further supports coaching conversations through the F.O.C.U.S. of each conversation (Figure 5.5). Zweibel asks, "So how does a coach help people focus?" His answer is to examine conversations from the perspective of the person being coached.

According to Zweibel (2005/2014c), there are two basic types of questions: questions that gather information, or look to blame, and questions that deepen the learning and increase the personal accountability of the person being asked. Zweibel elaborates:

> The latter category is far more powerful and thought provoking. Here's the test: if a client is telling you things s/he has already thought about or felt, or prolonged griping ensues, then you missed the mark. If, on the other hand, new thoughts, feelings, realizations, ideas, insights, and directions start to "pop," and the person is clearly starting to take full responsibility for his/her impact, then you're in the zone.

Figure 5.4. **The Coaching F.R.A.M.E. of Reference Model**

F—F.O.C.U.S. EACH INTERACTION—in increasingly relevant, and powerful, ways

R—RESPOND STRATEGICALLY—respectfully; collaboratively; engagingly; purposefully

A—ASK INTRIGUING QUESTIONS—to induce clarity, discernment, choice, and drive

M—MONITOR PROGRESS—acknowledging efforts made and outcomes enabled . . . or not

E—ENCOURAGE CONTINUED F.O.C.U.S.—inviting further exploration of one's goals, objectives, strengths, weaknesses, opportunities, challenges, self-limiting beliefs, and such

---

Source: © Zweibel, B. (2005/2014a). The Coaching F.R.A.M.E. of Reference Model. Used with permission of Barry Zweibel, LeadershipTraction®. Retrieved from www.ldrtr.com

Figure 5.5. **Coaching Helps People F.O.C.U.S.**

F—FACE IT—whatever "it" happens to be. Just getting people to talk about where they're stuck, or what they might be avoiding, is often enough to help them stare down their "scary monsters" and get back on track. So coaches have people talk about what's really important.

O—OUTSMART THE UEs ("the ewww-ies")—the Unhelpful Extremes. People often evaluate their next steps by looking at things in a binary fashion: all or none; black or white; what they'd do in a *perfect world scenario* or, because things *aren't* perfect, sustaining the *status quo.* By pointing out that the UEs are really end-points of a continuum, the coach can help the client brainstorm a number of concrete alternatives that are *in the middle.*

C—CHOOSE MORE INTENTIONALLY—more consciously, purposefully, and discerningly. William James said it best: "When you have to make a choice and don't make it, that is in itself a choice" (James, n.d.). Brainstorming possibilities is an important step, but the choosing of one's next steps is even more so. But make sure that you're not the one providing all the answers—that's not coaching, that's consulting. The more you can encourage your client to come up with seemingly absurd ideas, the better.

U—UNLOCK POTENTIAL—through specific actions and activities that create and sustain irrefutable growth, progress, and momentum. This is the "doing" part;

the action and accountability inherent in moving meaningfully forward, insuring proper follow-through, and honoring one's commitments to self and others. It's about actually implementing the specific assignments and plans that get things going.

S—SOLIDIFY THE LEARNING—by helping them better recognize their impact, take greater responsibility for it, and modify their thoughts, feelings, and behaviors, accordingly. Results are nice, but for learning to stick, it's essential to talk about the insights, discoveries, and lessons learned along the way. As Vernon Law said, "Experience is a hard teacher because she gives the test first, the lesson afterward" (Law, n.d.). A good coach makes sure the lessons are clearly understood.

Source: © Zweibel, B. (2005/ 2014b). Coaching Helps People F.O.C.U.S. Used with permission of Barry Zweibel, LeadershipTraction®. Retrieved from www.ldrtr.com

Consider the examples of questions that gather information versus deepen learning presented in Figure 5.6 offered by Zweibel (2005/2014c).

Figure 5.6. Questions That Gather Information Versus Deepen the Learning

Questions that Gather Information	Questions that Deepen the Learning
What have you tried so far?	What haven't you tried yet?
Why are you stuck?	How could you make that easier on yourself?
What do you mean?	What are you thinking but not saying?
What are you waiting for?	What are you now ready to do?
Why did you do it that way?	How is this challenge helping you grow?
Why is it their fault?	How is it your responsibility?

Source: © Zweibel, B. (2005/2014c). Questions that Gather Information versus Deepen the Learning. Used with permission of Barry Zweibel, LeadershipTraction®. Retrieved from www.ldrtr.com

Coaching situates teachers at the center of their own learning. The following Case from the Field illustrates how the coaching cycle supported the acquisition of new skills through a digital one-to-one rollout in one school.

Case from the Field

Mighty Morphin' Power Users: Mrs. Kiel and Mrs. Murrell become iDeb and FlubaSue

Mr. Ryan Berens, Director of Instructional Technology; Mrs. Deborah Kiel, 5th Grade Teacher; Mrs. Susan Murrell, 5th Grade Teacher; Mr. Gordon Walker, Headmaster, Southfield School, LA

Case Organizer

Coaching in the context of technology integration within a co-teaching model is described in Figure 5.7, the Technology Immersion Flow Chart. All the elements of coaching as envisioned by Joyce and Showers (1981, 1982, 2002) are present in this case—demonstration, practice, modeling, and feedback. iDeb and FlubaSue become Mighty Morphin' Power Users during a one-to-one rollout while being coached at Southfield School.

The Context of Southfield School

Situated in Shreveport, Louisiana, Southfield School is a pre-K2 through 8th Grade private institution that promotes a lifelong love of learning as its mission. Southfield serves 164 students in middle school, Grades 5–8, 182 students in the lower school Grades K–4, and 94 students in its pre-K programs. Southfield prides itself on finding and hiring highly qualified experienced teachers from around the United States.

The Southfield Technology Initiative launched with two of its most experienced teachers. Mrs. Susan Murrell (FlubaSue) is a 5th Grade Social Studies and Language Arts teacher who has been at Southfield for 28 years. While at Southfield she has also taught 4th Grade self-contained, 6th Grade geography, 7th Grade American history, and 8th Grade Louisiana history. Mrs. Deborah Kiel (iDeb), the 5th Grade Math and Science teacher, has taught at Southfield for 15 years. After leaving her career as a medical technologist, iDeb came to Southfield and taught 6th, 7th, and 8th grade math and science. Mr. Berens, the Director of Instructional Technology, chose FlubaSue and iDeb as the beta group for this project and soon discovered that they both disproved stereotypes that experienced teachers cannot "do" technology and that you have to master a device or program before you use it with students.

The Fast and the Furious

> If you would have told me a year ago that by the end of the first semester every student 5th through 8th Grade would have their tablet and be using it, I would have called you a liar . . . and meant it.
>
> Gordon Walker, Headmaster

In fall 2012, Southfield administrators broached the idea of increasing the use of technology in the classroom. Knowing that a major overhaul of the network was needed, the administration and Board of Trustees decided this was the time. In spring 2013, the administration brought the idea of using iPads in the classroom to the teachers, asking them to be prepared to begin the initial phases of rollout in the fall 2013. During summer of 2013, Southfield hired Mr. Berens as the Director of Instructional Technology to oversee the rollout of the technology initiative and to carry out professional development. The original rollout plan called for teachers to receive iPads for use during the summer months and for them to then receive a concentrated series of professional learning opportunities from August 2013 to November 2013. In November of 2013 a beta group (5th Grade) would begin the initial rollout of the iPad devices to students. The remaining grades would then see a graduated rollout commencing in the fall of 2014. While this plan was sound in theory and followed the generic protocol of how schools "do" professional learning and technology rollouts, it was not the most effective and efficient way to prepare teachers for what their new classrooms would look and sound like.

Taking Stock of Technology Rollouts

Through past experiences, Mr. Berens learned: 1) that technology rollout has less to do with the technology and more to do with shifting the culture of the school in a way that leads to changes in how teachers operated in their classrooms; 2) technology infusion is best done by providing intensive, hands-on, job-embedded, professional learning opportunities that put technology in the hands of teachers on day one; and 3) technology rollout has to move to an immersion program similar to foreign-language immersion programs. With these lessons learned, Mr. Berens worked with FlubaSue and iDeb, who were willing to delve into a situation where they had to "learn the language" to communicate with the "digital natives." With this idea in mind, the Southfield timeline was pushed forward allowing these teachers and their students to receive their iPads during the second week of school, followed by a graduated rollout that provided all students in Grades 5 through 8 with devices by the middle of November. Grades 3 and 4 received their devices in January and February of 2014.

Moving Past Industrial Revolution Era Professional Learning

Prior to the implementation of the Southfield Technology Initiative, two types of professional development existed in the school. The first type involved attending conferences, which exposed teachers to new and innovative ideas but often without examples of how to seamlessly integrate these skills into practice. With a lack of experts to coach teachers, this type of professional development impeded implementation. The second type of professional development involved bringing in a specialist or company representative to the school to share new and innovative ideas. Although the ideas were beneficial to the teachers, no one was able to come into the classrooms and demonstrate how to put theory into practice. Many of these whiteboard meetings often left teachers with more questions about how to incorporate what they learned into the reality of their own classroom.

Jump, I promise your Parachute Will Open—Learning by Doing

The technology plan was to train the beta teachers—iDeb and FlubaSue—through technology immersion that would include professional learning through experiences with observing, modeling, co-teaching, and coaching into a seamless job-embedded package. This model fully immersed the teachers and students in the technology. Luckily, iDeb and FlubaSue were more than willing to learn "on the go" and understood how this type of professional learning would prepare them to use the device while maintaining order and engagement in the classroom. FlubaSue explained:

> My first exposure to the iPad in an educational setting was only at faculty meetings. Administrators and teachers who had attended workshops gave presentations or demonstrations primarily centered around the use of Apps. A technology/iPad resource room was created to afford teachers the opportunity to become familiar with the iPad in a "hands-on" situation, which I preferred. So the technology immersion, while a little scary to begin with, it was the real hands-on experience that made me much more comfortable with the iPads in the classroom.

On the first day of the Southfield iPad launch, students went to "technology class" to receive their iPads and basic training on use of the iPad, email, and how to login to the Google Apps for Education. Afterward, FlubaSue, iDeb, and Mr. Berens planned out a few simple activities (using the Quizlet application in FlubaSue's classroom and completing a shared document in iDeb's classroom) that would allow all parties involved to take the first step toward technology integration. Both teachers attended these "technology classes" so they could observe what the students learned and how a Twenty-First Century Classroom could be managed.

To support FlubaSue and iDeb begin teaching with this new technology, Mr. Berens traveled to each of their classrooms. First, Mr. Berens went into FlubaSue's classroom and helped them log into Quizlet and showed them how to create notecard sets. FlubaSue then walked around the classroom making sure the students were on task and helped them with some of their questions. Next, Mr. Berens walked next door to help iDeb start her activity. Prior to class, she created a Google Doc that had leading and comprehension questions for a chapter they were working on in science. He helped the class login to their Google Accounts and then had them open the document that iDeb had shared with them. Students were then shown how to make their own copies of the document and answer the questions on their own.

Mr. Berens showed iDeb how to create a Google Form and how to have the students turn in their work on the form so that iDeb had a spreadsheet of all student submissions. Once that period was over, the students switched places and FlubaSue and iDeb began their transformation by teaching the lesson themselves while Mr. Berens was in the background for support.

Learning the Language is Easier Than it Looks

The technology immersion program continued with a new type of technology activity introduced about every three days. The teachers learned to give online quizzes through Google Forms and to have them automatically graded and those grades emailed instantly to their students; they learned to use Google Spreadsheets to help students create charts and find averages; and they learned that the students themselves were an excellent source of technical support. FlubaSue and iDeb continued to have the students use the iPads and began to build lessons that created differentiation in the classroom. Because their students had constant access to the devices, both teachers were able to avoid making technology use an event, and were able to incorporate technology as an integral part of their daily content and instructional activities. Following the technology immersion steps followed in Figure 5.7, Mr. Berens, FlubaSue, and iDeb were able to create learning environments that engaged students and allowed them to learn outside the classroom walls.

Figure 5.7. Technology Immersion Flow Chart Steps

Putting the Pieces of the Steps Together

Plan:

♦ Planning was not as daunting as the teachers originally thought.

♦ The key to this process is to start with activities that can replace what a teacher is currently doing and then to move to more advanced activities once they have mastered the basics.

   ♦ For instance, instead of having the students complete a reading comprehension activity on a worksheet, create a Google Doc and have them answer the questions on a virtual worksheet.

   ♦ This type of activity will help the teacher become fluent in "replacing" so they can advance toward recreating activities.

Observe:

♦ Mr. Berens modeled what the classroom would or should look like for the teachers, what the students should be doing, and how to manage any issues that come with using that tool.

   ♦ This was a great opportunity for the teachers to refresh their learning about the specific tool.

Co-Teach:

♦ Planning and observing was followed by a short period of Co-Teaching with Mr. Berens starting the lessons.

♦ Once started, iDeb or FlubaSue would take over and help students mold the technology they were using to the topic that needed to be covered in class.

♦ Co-teaching gave real-time experience to help the teachers understand how they could help solve issues that arose.

Coach:

♦ After co-teaching, iDeb and FlubaSue replicated that activity several times during the week.

♦ As they became more comfortable with the basic concepts of a tool, they would make the activities more and more advanced.

♦ When problems arose, Mr. Berens would go visit and help them through any issues.

♦ Mr. Berens shared that the most important part of coaching was to help teachers understand that it was OK to make mistakes, and that they didn't have to use a tool exactly the same way every time.

Collaborate/Re-Teach:

♦ Both teachers decided that each one would master a specific tool, and then they would teach each other.

♦ This helped to expedite the full integration of technology in the classroom.

To Infinity and Beyond—Life Lessons and Future Considerations

The technology initiative caused major changes in the educational experience of students at Southfield. Students showed a high level of engagement because the activities were presented at a digital level to which they were accustomed. Students collaborated across classes, pushing the classroom beyond the walls of the school. Southfield students learned many of the life skills that will be necessary for them to compete in the global workforce. Without realizing it, students learned to be responsible for the tools of their learning and how to troubleshoot their own problems.

Case Summary

This case illustrates how technology integration is achieved by promoting hands-on learning that allows teachers and students to "learn by doing" with the safety net of the coaching process including demonstration, practice, modeling, and feedback. This type of intensive coaching accelerated the ability of these two veteran teachers to move into the digital arena. FlubaSue and iDeb did, indeed, both disprove stereotypes that experienced teachers cannot "do" technology and that you have to master a device or program before you use it with students.

Chapter Summary

Peer coaching works regardless of the content, process, or environment. The applications and modifications that can be made to coaching models are limited only by imagination. The peer coaching model has endured the test of time as a viable model and, if enacted with fidelity, can support transfer of practice perhaps more or at least as much as any other form of professional learning. Coaching is complex because of the focus on conversations, a skill that needs constant practice and attention. Relationships and building trust are critical to the success of coaching, regardless of its form.

Suggested Readings

Gross Cheliotes L. M., & Reilly, M. A. (2010). *Coaching conversations: Transforming your school one conversation at a time*. Thousand Oaks, CA: Corwin Press.

Gross Cheliotes L. M., & Reilly, M. A. (2012). *Opening the door to coaching conversations*. Thousand Oaks, CA: Corwin Press.

Knight, J. (2007). *Instructional coaching: A partnership approach to improving instruction*. Thousand Oaks, CA: Corwin Press.

Marzano, R. J., Simms, J. A., Roy, T., Heflebower, T., & Warrick, P. (2013). *Coaching classroom instruction*. Bloomington, IN: Marzano Research Laboratory.

Patterson, K., Grenny, J., McMillan, R., & Switzler, A. (2012). *Crucial conversations: Tools for talking when stakes are high* (2nd ed.). New York, NY: McGraw Hill.

Walpole, S., & McKenna., M. C. (2012). *The literacy coach's handbook: A guide to research-based practice* (2nd ed.). New York, NY: Guilford.

Zepeda, S. J. (2012). *Professional development: What works* (2nd ed.). New York, NY: Routledge.

6

Learning from Collaborative and Reflective Professional Development

In This Chapter . . .

- ◆ Collaborative and Reflective Professional Development Models
- ◆ Case from the Field
- ◆ Chapter Summary
- ◆ Suggested Readings

Collaborative and reflective professional development finds a home—a learning community. Thus far, the foundation for collaborative job-embedded professional development has been established. One of the prevailing ideas in this book is that teachers work and plan differently, meeting daily or almost daily with peers to engage in professional work. This is the sweet spot of where learning on the job occurs—from the work itself and through collaboration with peers. Team structures then can form by smaller learning communities within the school at large. The ways in which teachers assemble to work are boundless, limited only by imagination. Digital tools have broadened learning opportunities.

The second prevailing idea is that the time is ripe for teachers and other school personnel to be opportunistic by making the work of teaching a collaborative job-embedded experience where we can learn from the very work we do. The third prevailing premise of this book is that there are numerous models and practices that can be differentiated to meet the needs of the adult learner.

This chapter offers a broad overview with brief descriptions of professional development models. Subsequent chapters continue to go into more detail on other professional development models and approaches.

Collaborative and Reflective Professional Development Models

The following collaborative and reflective professional development models and processes are illustrative of the many models that exist. There are other models and processes that are covered in greater detail in other chapters in this book.

Critical Friends Groups

The Northwest Regional Educational Laboratory (NWREL, 2005) report "critical friends groups (or CFGs for short) are cross-curricular groups of teachers that meet once a month, focusing laser-like on student achievement through [examining aspects of] teaching practice" (p. 8) and through the use of highly structured protocols (National School Reform Faculty, 2006). Critical Friends Groups (CFGs) improve teachers' collegial relationships, and increase teachers' awareness of research-based practices and reforms, their knowledge of their school, and their capacity to improve their instruction (Curry, 2008). Usually a CFG is made up of six to ten teachers who meet to address a focused topic (National School Reform Faculty, 2006).

Data—Learning from Benchmark Assessments

Teachers and schools work with data as a way to reach students and as a way for teachers to adjust the pace of a lesson, differentiate instruction, assessments, etc. Moreover, teachers learn a great deal about their own practices when they collaborate with colleagues to analyze data, especially formative data.

In learning communities, student learning is nurtured "by making teachers more effective in the work of teaching" (Venables, 2011, p. 10). Venables (2011) suggests bringing clarity to the uses of formative data by adding three *essential tasks*, which include:

1. Looking at student and teacher work
2. Designing quality common formative assessments (CFAs)
3. Reviewing and responding to data (p. 11).

Benchmark Assessments

Benchmark assessments are tests that monitor students' progress within specific subject areas over the course of the school year. Benchmark assessments are designed to measure achievement on standards within the curriculum; they are typically administered at prescribed intervals, and as a form of a common assessment, benchmark assessments measure proficiency on subsets of standards (Herman, Osmundson, & Dietel, 2010).

Based on the formative results of benchmark assessments, a curriculum can be redesigned, learning objectives can be reexamined, and instructional and assessment approaches can be reconsidered. Supports such as peer coaches, instructional coaches, and peer observers can provide in- and out-of-class assistance. The results of benchmark assessments can create the conditions for teams of teachers to meet and review results and to engage in analysis and action—what to do next. According to Herman *et al.* (2010), benchmark assessments help to:

1. Communicate expectations
2. Plan curricula and instruction

3. Monitor and evaluate learning

4. Predict future performance. (pp. 3–4)

At the end of this chapter, a Case from the Field presents how one high school uses benchmark assessments as a way to open the discussion with department chairs and teachers to support their efforts at using the results of these assessments to refine teaching and to support student learning.

Learning Circles Go Online

Learning circles are "small communities of learners among teachers and others who come together intentionally for the purpose of supporting each other in the process of learning" (Collay, Dunlap, Enloe, & Gagnon, 1998, p. 2). Learning circles consist of any group of teachers that meet on a continual basis over a long or short period of time with the goal fixed on an area in which a deeper understanding is sought. Learning circles require six conditions to be met (Collay *et al.*, 1998):

◆ Building community

◆ Constructing knowledge

◆ Supporting learners

◆ Documenting reflection

◆ Assessing expectations

◆ Changing cultures. (p. 8)

Online Learning Circles

Technology and digital learning environments have arrived and so too have the opportunities for professional development enhanced by it. A type of online learning circle has evolved to support more global exchanges and discussions. The online learning circle has been found to be effective in promoting learning experiences for both teachers and students (Riel *et al.*, 2002). Riel *et al.* identify six phases that constitute the structure of the online learning circle (see Figure 6.1):

◆ Phase I: Getting Ready involves finding the partners, selecting and setting up the electronic structure, and setting the stage for interaction.

◆ Phase II: Opening the Circle focuses on group formation and cohesion.

◆ Phase III: Planning the Project requires each participant to describe the project or task they sponsor for the group.

◆ Phase IV: Exchanging Work on projects constitutes the major part of the process.

◆ Phase V: Organizing the Publication is time for organizing results of work on projects.

◆ Phase VI: Closing the Circle provides time for final reflections on the process. (Riel *et al.*, 2002, Project Summary section, p. 3)

Figure 6.1. **The Six Phases of the Online Learning Circle Identified by Riel *et al.* (2002)**

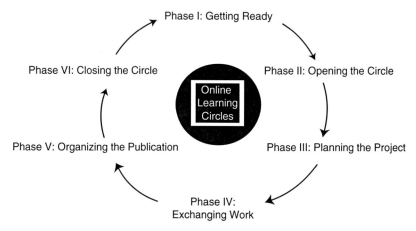

Lesson Study

The lesson study process is an iterative cycle (see Figure 6.2) involving teachers in activities across four basic steps (Lewis, Perry, & Murata, 2006):

- ♦ study curriculum and formulate goals;
- ♦ plan;
- ♦ conduct research; and
- ♦ reflect.

The processes of lesson study are briefly highlighted in Table 6.1.

Figure 6.2. **The Iterative Nature of Lesson Study**

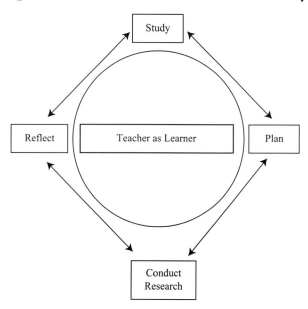

Table 6.1. **Processes of the Lesson Study Cycle**

Processes of the Lesson Study Cycle	Description
Study Curriculum and Formulate Goals	Teachers identify a topic that encompasses a learning problem related to a learning goal of the school found by studying the curriculum.
Plan	Teachers identify a specific learning problem and how this problem affects the learning goals of the students.
Conduct Research	Conducting the research involves the actual teaching of planned research lessons. These lessons involve a team of teachers observing and collecting data as one teacher teaches the lesson. This lesson may be repeated over time to allow the teacher to make adjustments and revisions.
Reflect	The team collectively reflects on the process. The team reconvenes, the lesson is discussed, and data are shared. During this reflection time, data should be used to explore and uncover concerns, new information, or celebrations.

Source: Adapted from Wiburg & Brown (2006).

Portfolios Go Electronic

The portfolio is used to chronicle growth and development, and to capture learning through artifacts that are representative of practice. There are numerous processes involved in developing a portfolio, and each process requires the application of skills. Portfolio development includes data collection (artifacts to include), analysis (the meaning of the artifacts), and then reflection on the meanings in practice that the artifacts symbolize. Danielson and Abrutyn (1997) offer a five-stage portfolio development process:

◆ Collection—save artifacts that represent the day-to-day results of teaching and learning.

◆ Selection—review and evaluate the artifacts saved, and identify those that demonstrate achievement of specific standards or goals.

◆ Reflection—reflect on the significance of the artifacts chosen for the portfolio in relationship to specific learning goals.

◆ Projection (or Direction)—compare the reflections to the standards/ goals and performance indicators, and set learning goals for the future.

◆ Presentation—share the portfolio with peers and receive feedback.

Portfolio Development is an Ongoing and Dynamic Process. The portfolio provides the opportunity for teachers to collect artifacts over an extended time period—an entire school year, even from year to year. The ongoing process of developing a portfolio makes it a natural way to extend peer coaching and the work of lesson study groups, Critical Friends Groups, action research teams, and mentoring activities. The assessment of teaching is an ongoing process, and this assessment will only hold meaning for teachers if they are active in the processes of setting goals, reflecting on practice, and decision-making.

Portfolio Development Processes: Reflection, Goal-Setting, and Decision-Making

Professional learning is enhanced through the development of a portfolio with the following processes:

- ♦ Reflection about portfolio development and design;

- ♦ Goal-setting; and

- ♦ Decision-making (the process of making decisions about what to include in the portfolio).

Figure 6.3 portrays the reciprocal nature of skill application when the portfolio is used as a complement to peer coaching, for example. Each skill works in tandem as teachers explore their practices while constructing knowledge from examining and reexamining the artifacts included in the portfolio.

Figure 6.3. Skills Inherent in Portfolio as a Form of Professional Development

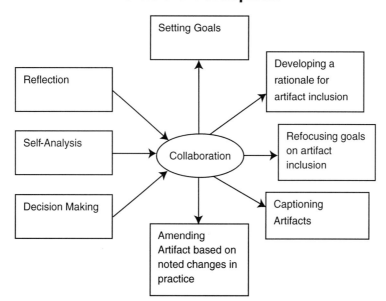

Source: Zepeda (2012a).

Electronic Portfolios (e-portfolios)

All one has to do is surf the web to see the number of digital (electronic) portfolios. System-wide storage (web space) and storage such as Cloud Technology, Google Docs, and protected sites can create protected spaces for teachers and staff to store electronic portfolios, create blogs, and use existing resources to create other spaces and tools for developing portfolios.

Study Groups

Study groups examine issues such as children and poverty, instructional practices (differentiated instruction, pacing, etc.), and bullying, for example. Study groups read and discuss books, examine latest research on selected topics, conduct and then debrief on action research, engage in cycles of peer observation or peer coaching, etc. Because most study groups provide an opportunity for teachers to focus on self-selected topics, relevance is assured. Study groups promote peer interaction by providing frequent opportunities for the sharing of ideas. Table 6.2 illus-

Table 6.2. **Range of Study Group Configurations**

Cayuso *et al.* (2004)	Birchak *et al.* (1998)
◆ *Topic Study Group*—members select a book to study and discuss what meets their interest and needs.	◆ *Issues Discussion Groups*—formed around questions and concerns on a shared issue.
◆ *Practice Study Groups*— meta-cognitive learning tool where members focus on a strategy. This may involve videotaping, peer observation, etc., with the group discussing what took place in a particular event.	◆ *Job-Alike Study Groups*—educators that have the same type of position in different schools.
◆ *Online Study Groups*—members join online chats that are about specific areas of interest.	◆ *Professional Book Discussion Groups*— initiated by a common interest to read a professional book or set of articles.
	◆ *Readers and Writers Groups*— formed to discuss literary works or pieces of writing.
	◆ *School-Based Groups*—composed of educators within a particular school.
	◆ *Teacher Research Groups*—educators who come together to discuss their systematic, intentional, classroom inquiries.
	◆ *Topic-Centered Groups*—educators from different schools who are interested in the same topic or issue.

trates the work of Cayuso, Fegan, and McAlister (2004) and Birchak *et al.* (1998), who describe the ways teacher study groups could be arranged.

Whole-Faculty Study Groups

Whole-faculty study groups are a structure through which all teachers on a faculty meet in small groups for deliberate conversations about a targeted area linked to school improvement centering on student needs and classroom instruction. Murphy and Lick (2005) state:

> The Whole-Faculty Study Group system is a job-embedded, self-directed, student-driven approach to professional development. It is a professional development system designed to build communities of learners in which professionals continuously strive to increase student learning. This is accomplished by practitioners (a) deepening their own knowledge and understanding of what is taught, (b) reflecting on their practices, (c) sharpening their skills, and (d) taking joint responsibility for the students they teach. (p. 2)

A targeted area in the school improvement plan becomes the document that drives the whole-faculty study group process, focus, and content. The guiding principles identified by Murphy and Lick (2005) include:

♦ students are first;

♦ everybody participates;

♦ leadership is shared;

♦ responsibility is equal; and,

♦ the work is public.

Whole-faculty study groups have an organizational focus on the primary goal of increasing student learning (Lick & Murphy, 2007).

Book Studies

Book studies promote conversations, reflection, and an examination of practice in the small group of teachers who meet to discuss a book that gives insight about an area of professional interest. Typically, book studies are organized around an area related to a school-wide improvement-targeted goal, an issue of practice at a grade level, or a practice with a subject-specific group of teachers. However, it is not uncommon for an entire school to read a common book of interest and for a certain amount of time at general faculty, grade-level, or department meetings to be dedicated to discussing the applicability of the contents of the book. Effective book studies have the overall goal of supporting the reading of professional materials that will support the development of thinking or refined instructional practice.

The following Case from the Field examines the use of benchmark assessments with a focus on how adults learn from the process of examining the results.

Case from the Field

Benchmarks Analysis as a Pathway to Student and Teacher Growth: A High School Engages in Pervasive Conversations

Dr. Anthony Price, Principal; Dr. Rick Tatum, Associate Principal; Mr. Gavin Matesich, Social Studies Teacher, Social Studies Department Co-Chair, and Economics Teacher; Ms. Erica Fletcher, 9th Grade Coordinate Algebra Teacher and Freshman Academy Team Leader; Mr. Marc Ginsberg, 9th Grade Literature and Composition Teacher; Cedar Shoals High School, GA

Case Organizer

Through examining models, trial and error, feedback, perseverance, and collecting data on what works, Cedar Shoals High School has refined a process for using benchmark assessments to support student learning. But the process has also served a dual role in that the conversations built into it support teachers in growing and expanding their tool box of instructional strategies, deepening their content knowledge, and finding ways to engage students in learning, and being accountable. This case is narrated by Dr. Anthony Price, Principal of Shoals High School, and holds interest for many reasons.

First, our authors offer several points of view. We hear from teachers in three subject areas; they share their perspectives about how they have grown as teachers from their work with benchmarks. Second, these examples show how very different benchmarks are for three different subject areas—mathematics, social studies, and English—but how, nevertheless, the process of using the benchmarks for making mid-course changes in instruction and clarifying student misconceptions remains constant. Third, we hear how leaders engage teachers in conversations about teaching and learning, and how these conversations lead to mutual understandings about the urgency of student engagement in the learning process. Fourth, we see a "home-grown" benchmark assessment process model for using the results to improve instruction that appears to be of such a universal design that it fits across the subject areas. Fifth, we also see how a large administrative team coordinates its efforts to monitor results.

Figure 6.4 illustrates the Cedar Shoals High School Benchmark Formative Assessment Cycle and serves as an advanced organizer to the case that follows.

The Context of Cedar Shoals High School

Cedar Shoals High School (CSHS) is an urban school with nearly 1,400 students. The school serves a predominately minority population, which represents 82 percent of the total student body. The breakdown is as follows: 57 percent African-American, 19 percent Hispanic, 17 percent White, 4 percent Multiracial, and 2 percent Asian. Seventy-seven percent of the teachers have advanced degrees. Teachers at CSHS have an average of 12 years of experience. The graduation rate at CSHS has grown from 68 percent in 2012 to 74 percent in 2013, and 15 percent of students receive gifted services.

Figure 6.4. **Cedar Shoals High School Benchmark Formative Assessment Cycle**

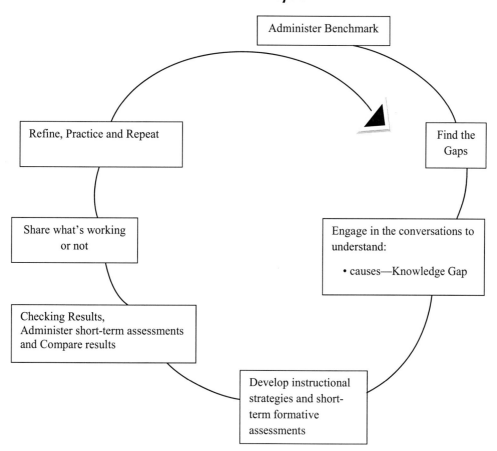

Data Help Frame a Story

Cedar Shoals High School has made significant strides in raising student achievement and increasing the graduation rate by focusing on data-driven instruction, analyzing data through grade and content areas data teams, and building a master schedule so that data teams meet and so that collaborative planning time is available for all teachers in all core content areas. Along with quarterly benchmark assessments, these practices have provided the forum for teachers to have critical conversations about teaching and learning and to engage in reflective practice, inquiry, and quasi-action research. These practices have also engaged the school leadership in the discussions and allowed the team to monitor more carefully how students are faring with learning. "It's not just about passing, it's about learning," according to Dr. Anthony Price, principal of Cedar Shoals High School.

What are Benchmark Assessments?

Our definition of benchmark assessments describes a process by which content tests based on the current standards are developed by our teachers and are administered periodically throughout the year. This process is used as a formative, not a summative approach. The Assessment and Accountability Center (Herman *et al.*, 2010) definition of benchmark assessments serves as our guiding post for the uses of formative assessments:

> Benchmark assessments are assessments administered periodically through-out the school year, at specified times during a curriculum sequence, to evaluate students' knowledge and skills relative to longer-term learning goals. Benchmark assessments can inform policy, instructional planning, and decision making at the classroom, school and or district levels. (Herman *et al.*, 2010, p. 1)

How Do We Use Benchmark Data at Cedar Shoals High School?

A three-pronged approach is used to guide the benchmark data process at Cedar Shoals High School.

Prong I: Accountability: The first aspect of this process is accountability. Without accountability by all instructional stakeholders (i.e., teachers, grade-level administrators, and principal), meaningful reflection and dialogue about improving content-specific student achievement will not occur. That is why once the results of the benchmark results are back, it is up to the teacher who gives the benchmarks to his/her students to scan the results and then send those results to the grade-level administrator and principal.

Once administrators receive the results, they analyze those results, look for strengths and weaknesses, and look for comparative trends such as comparing last year's scores, subgroup data improvement, certain standards that exhibited mastery or lack of mastery, and reviewing conclusive data such as class averages, school average, and district average of that particular benchmark. In this sense, the benchmark acts as a summative assessment letting the teacher know what the student has learned, but it is also a formative assessment showing weaknesses that must be addressed in future instruction before the end-of-year state assessment.

Prong II: Reflect and Meet: Once the preliminary analysis is concluded, it is time for teachers to reflect on their practice to determine the strengths and weaknesses of their students. This goal is accomplished by meeting with each individual content teacher to determine the plan for addressing remediation and enrichment in needed standards and to reflect on strategies to raise achievement on the assessment. During a meeting of approximately one hour, content area administrators review results with teachers. Teachers are asked to examine each standard to determine the instructional needs of their students. The administrator's role is to ask probing questions allowing teachers to reflect on the results. Therefore, in an instructional and clinical way, the principal or the assistant principal may ask the teacher several probing questions (see Figure 6.5).

Figure 6.5. **Probing Questions to Foster Dialogue—Benchmark Results**

1. How are you using formative assessment results? What are your formative assessment results telling you?

2. Because these particular standards had poor results, are you having problems with pacing?

3. How do you keep your pacing on schedule and yet provide remediation to those students in need?

4. In what instructional format will the remediation take place?

5. Are you using priority standards? How do you decide what standards are priority?

6. When you are teaching, how do you know students are showing mastery? How do you check for understanding?

These and other related questions help us get to common understandings and move us along in the development of actionable plans to improve the areas of student academic weakness or to lead to ways to enrich instruction for students who have mastered content and need to accelerate.

Prong III: Develop a Plan: By asking probing questions, the administrator allows each teacher to reflect on their individual practices. As individuals respond to these questions, team members learn from each other in forming common ways to improve teaching and learning by sharing content knowledge and strategies. Teachers are then required to develop a plan to address low standards. This plan and reflective conversation are carried back to individual data teams where common formative assessments are then written to address student weaknesses. Data teams play an important role in benchmark assessments and what happens once the results are back.

Data Teams

At Cedar Shoals High School, each content teacher serves on an area data team that meets twice a week. During these meetings, teachers analyze data and reflect on the achievement of their students. Benchmarks are just one data point used to drive instruction. Teachers also triangulate different types of data to develop common formative assessments for individual units of instruction usually lasting no more than four weeks. As these assessments are developed, teachers reflect on the students' prior knowledge and deficiencies within the standards. During this time, the team takes responsibility for their own learning and *teaching* as they reflect on the achievement of their students in their own individual classes. Feedback is solicited as the group engages in ongoing collaborative inquiry. Each member of the team remains open to alternative perspectives as a plan is made to address group and individual student needs. The administrator's role in data teams is to guide the teachers into deep conversation and reflection to make adjustments to classroom instructional practices. The administrator becomes part of the team and an instructional leader as his/her instructional background and content knowledge are equally shared with the team.

Benchmark Implementation in Mathematics Classes

School improvement planning and implementation are complex, and there are a variety of strategies for change. However, at Cedar Shoals High School, we have learned that connecting standards-based instruction and assessments—formative or summative—are essential in improving student achievement. When used in performance with school data, research-based practices, and comprehensive planning and monitoring processes, school-level benchmarks can help contribute to a successful high school improvement process designed to increase student outcomes. Benchmark assessments check for understanding along the way, guide teacher decision-making about future instruction, and provide feedback to students so they can improve their performance.

At first, math teachers were looking at benchmarks as a summative assessment closing out multiple units and viewing students' grades. Now since we have been implementing data teams with fidelity, we look at our school-level benchmarks as a formative assessment in preparation for the big assessment at the end of the course, called the End of Course Test (EOCT) for each content area. While analyzing our benchmark data as a team, math teachers have learned that benchmarks should be viewed as an opportunity to peek inside our students' heads while they are still in the process of learning. The process helps teachers and learners answer questions such as "What do I do next? Are our students mastering the standards?"

Time for Dialogue, Collaboration, and Reflection—A Must!

For mathematics classes, benchmark data also provide opportunities for reflection for both teachers and students. We are strong believers that there MUST be time for professional dialogue, collaboration, and reflection. What do we hope to gain from our reflections? Primarily, the whole objective of the benchmark assessments is to give teachers an overall forecast of our students' achievement levels, enabling us to pinpoint specific areas of learning gaps, growth areas, and areas of strength. After we give our benchmark assessments for math, we know exactly what our information gaps are and collaboratively establish "best practices" to close them.

Collaborating with other math teachers from different areas of specialization allows teachers to contribute to and benefit from the collective wisdom of everyone involved. For teachers, it deepens our understanding and effectiveness of our teaching practices and researched-based instructional strategies such as Marzano's Nine and Math in the Fast Lane Strategies. We like to ask questions—What worked? What did not work? What was effective? Did your students do better on a particular standard that my students did not do well on? What could we do differently?

Then as a follow-up to what was not successful, we begin to tweak and make adjustments so we can remediate and re-teach, if necessary. Through this process, teachers have learned to not always make "moving on quickly" the first impulse; now we allow time to reflect on and interact meaningfully with the data obtained. Another benefit for teachers has been a more focused effort to actually teach the standards with fidelity.

Benchmarks—Students Benefit

We have been using benchmark data now to monitor student learning and to provide ongoing feedback. Benchmarks help students identify their strengths and weaknesses and target areas that need work. The process helps teachers recognize where students are struggling and which standards students show lack of understanding. From there we address problems immediately. As a result, students can only benefit from these collaborative reflections because we are tailoring our instruction to meet each individual's learning style as well as academic levels.

Students also benefit when teachers learn what the student expectations for the standards are. In other words, when we know what students need to know, understand, and do, we provide better instructional approaches to meet their needs and differentiate instruction. In addition, this wisdom transforms students' learning abilities and moves them out of the failure cycle and into success, therefore building self-efficacy. As a result, students become more engaged and excited about learning.

Reflection is the Ticket

After the test has been administered, all mathematics teachers begin the reflection process by carrying out a benchmark item analysis by disaggregating their data. Item analysis helps guide remediation and acceleration. As we begin analyzing our benchmark data, we look at the domains that are identified as weak and strong areas. First, each teacher must obtain their data on Achievement Series and view the data aggregated by each class, grade, school, district, or subject. Next, each teacher can observe how each class or each individual student performed on all content standards as illustrated in Table 6.3.

We are able to identify which standards we need to remediate and to provide more practice for immediately. Also, we can do an item analysis that will let us see

Table 6.3. Benchmark Analysis—Mathematics

Test Score	CCSS Math Content CHSN-QA1	CCSS Math Content CHSN-QA2	CCSS Math Content CHSN-QA3
73%	100%	100%	100%
43%	100%	50%	50%
63%	50%	100%	100%
73%	100%	100%	100%
80%	100%	100%	100%
57%	100%	100%	50%
53%	100%	100%	100%
77%	100%	100%	0%
50%	100%	100%	100%
60%	100%	100%	0%
67%	100%	100%	100%

Table 6.4. Item Analysis to Examine Student Misconceptions in Mathematics

1-MC	2-MC	3-MC	4-MC	5-MC	6-MC
A	C	D	B	C	B
A	A	D	B	A	B
A	C	A	B	D	B
B	B	B	B	A	C
A	B	B	B	D	B
A	C	A	B	D	B
A	C	B	B	D	B
A	C	C	B	A	B
A	C	B	B	C	B
C	C	B	B	D	B

what percentage of students missed item #1, item #2, and so on. Then we can dig even deeper to see the responses each student selected so we can identify common misconceptions. For example, see Table 6.4.

Coordinate algebra teachers can easily see that students understand how to create equations in one variable from contextual situations because no one missed #4. However, #3 was a question on rearranging formulas in context, and there are several misconceptions with this question. Performing an item analysis is crucial in identifying strengths and weaknesses for each student and each content area. Accordingly, during data team meetings, we are able to diagnose more specifically student learning needs. Then, we focus on classroom instruction and strategies and teaching adjustments that could improve student achievement on those particular standards.

We select the most effective instructional strategies (experience-based and research-based) to improve student achievement on standards shown on the benchmark as not yet mastered. Finally, as a team we make a professional decision whether or not revisions should be made to the benchmark assessment. It is rare, but sometimes we may need to revise questions to ensure each question satisfies the quality check of rigor, validity, reliability, and fairness. These activities will then be adapted into existing units next year, and we will already have this prior data in mind as we develop new focuses for new students. Nevertheless, in light of the benchmark results coupled with the upcoming EOCT, the following instructional strategies have been added or modified by all mathematics teachers at Cedar Shoals High School to enhance our current practices while continuing to use three or four Math in the Fast Lane strategies daily:

♦ Using cyclic methods to review concepts: this allows students to review, relearn, or to finally grasp content that has been challenging to understand.

♦ Increased the length of time spent on individual and group practice in work sessions (making lessons student-centered).

♦ Twice a week, with the aid of Netbooks and through online internet interactive/engaging activities, students are given further exposure to content, time, individual practice on concepts learned to reinforce/strengthen understanding.

♦ We have used the current Extended Learning Time during advisement, Pathways to Success Tutoring Program, and 21st Century afterschool as an opportunity to target the students in the bubble and far-to-go categories (students performing below 70%). Students are assigned different tasks based on performance level to increase their understanding and achievement levels.

In conclusion, giving benchmark assessments is a great initiative for monitoring student progress. However, we can't stop here. We must align our school-based common formative assessments, pre- and post-tests, with district benchmarks and large-scale summative assessments to gauge student success in each content area.

Benchmark Implementation in Social Studies Classes

On the surface, our system of giving benchmarks seems quite simple. Teachers in the various subject areas teaching in Clarke County School District's two high schools meet and write common formative assessments, also known as unit pre-tests. We also collaboratively design common unit summative assessments or benchmarks. While it is the goal of these tests to effectively gauge student achievement throughout the year as classes prepare for EOCT and graduation testing, the deeper more powerful aspect of implementing benchmark testing has manifested itself in the collaborative efforts of the teachers designing, implementing, and reflecting on the meaning of the benchmark test results.

Bridging Two Schools—One Purpose—Intra-School Collaboration—The Hallmark of Benchmarks

For starters, the design and revision of the benchmarks require a heavy amount of intra-school collaboration. Teachers from both schools are given a professional development day to meet and write the benchmark tests. In our experience, these usually consist of four to five summative unit exams. Typically, you have five to seven teachers along with a district coach working on the design phase of the benchmarks. Even in the first phase of design, meaningful collaboration takes place as teachers work together to make sure that unit tests reflect what is being taught in the units aligned to the standards.

Pieces of the Conversations

Questions of sequencing, scope, language of standards, and depth of knowledge are all very prominent pieces of the conversations. Teachers break down the standards and their language to determine what is being asked and what skills the students need to display to be proficient in each standard that is assessed. Teachers then work to construct questions that adequately address each of these factors. Again, it seems like a relatively simple process, but the collaboration and discussions that emerge from these meetings have become increasingly complex but rich.

Complexity in the Design Phase of Benchmarks

In economics, the need to align benchmarks more accurately with the language of the standards led to a complete revision of all unit materials to reflect the language used in the standards, benchmarks, and presumably the EOCTs. This discussion, in turn, led to further talk among teachers regarding the best way to teach certain standards. Activities, current event articles, simulations, and multimedia clips were all exchanged and teachers came away with much more structured unit plans. Indeed, much of the important collaboration happens in the design phase of benchmark testing. At Cedar Shoals High School, we've noticed that the design phase of benchmark testing offers a chance for teachers to collaborate, not just on the tests, but also on lesson and unit design.

Collaboration, Reflection, and Re-teaching = Re-teach, Redesign, and Reassess

The other powerful opportunity for collaboration comes after the administration of the benchmark assessment. After the test has been administered, teachers meet in data teams and use the data provided and sorted through an online assessment system to determine students' strengths and weaknesses. Once weaknesses are determined and linked to standards, unit activities are scrutinized to determine effectiveness. If one teacher's data are stronger in a particular area than another teacher's, methods are compared and shared and re-teaching takes place using effective practices that are determined during the data team meeting.

The administration requires teachers to write a unit reflection summary that contains strengths and weaknesses and re-teaching plans for low standards. With low areas, teachers re-teach, redesign if necessary, and reassess. Some of the outcomes yielded by our collaborative reflection practices have included: 1) more streamlined units, 2) identification of effective and high-impact teaching strategies, and 3) more standardized and effective teaching methods across various instructors.

Benchmark Implementation in English Classes

For English classes, benchmark data provide opportunities for reflection for both teachers and students. Our teachers use item analysis data to discover both what concepts need review and why students misinterpret correct responses.

It's All About Student Learning

Simultaneously, showing students how they perform—both individually and as entire groups—on individual items provides opportunities for discussions about the nature of language beyond just discussing "the right answer." When students make an effort to understand why their errors are errors, they grow more empowered to succeed on future tests and critical tasks. Often, test-taking habits are called into question, and students understand that such reading tests necessitate more attention to detail.

Context Around Common Texts—A Double Whammy for English

Because selected response tests require basic comprehension of long passages for the purpose of answering a handful of multiple choice questions, many students get lost in both the text as well as the questions, some of which do not even require a close read of the entire text. When students perform poorly on test sections with longer reading, we have found that low reading comprehension is more often the culprit than content deficiencies. In other words, low scores do not necessarily result from students failing to understand literary concepts or organizational patterns in non-fiction.

When we teach and assess these concepts in isolation (or in context), students are generally successful. Yet students can find it difficult to synthesize isolated content knowledge and transfer it to long reading passages in the testing environment because of the nature of the test itself: long passages, a few questions, and a high-stakes, high-pressure environment that demands comprehension of the text in the context of the questions being asked. Therefore, students need to develop active reading strategies to approach cold reading of unfamiliar texts, and benchmark data provide English classes the opportunity to re-teach these skills.

English classrooms establish so much context around common texts, but in testing situations, students get no guidance or context for multiple texts, both fiction and non-fiction. Thus, engagement and comprehension strategies such as re-reading, paragraph annotation, using context clues, and even simple underlining need to be rehearsed both for and during testing situations. When students perform poorly on reading tests, they often fail to employ active reading strategies, so pointing out errors provides an opportunity to review exactly how such strategies can be used to promote greater understanding.

Item Analysis, Previous Conversations, and Actions Up Against Results

Item analysis also guides content remediation and acceleration as can be found in other subject areas. First each teacher locates his own data via Achievement Series and examines results broadly by content standard for both strengths and weaknesses. Next, within these sets, we reflect on instruction toward each content standard. We ask a few basic questions of ourselves: What were our previous conversations in data team meetings? How did each teacher engage students in the content standard thereafter? What activities and lessons were used? What were the results?

Benchmarking is a Recursive Process of Teaching and Learning

From there in data team meetings, we address how individual teachers attacked each content standard, and teachers share any new materials and resources that were successful. In our English classes, our data generally do not vary much from teacher to teacher, so we usually find ourselves choosing a renewed focus on specific content standards based on shared needs. For example, in our last benchmark cycle, students performed poorly with informational reading as related to interpreting author's purpose. As a result, we are currently incorporating more argumentative non-fiction reading into current units, regardless of the unit's overall focus. These activities will then be relayered into existing units next year, and we'll already have this prior data in mind as we develop new focuses for new students. Thus, benchmark data are not simply an end unto themselves, but rather another organic process embedded in the ongoing, recursive process of teaching and learning.

Case Summary

This case is important as it illustrates the complexities of benchmark assessments at the high school level across multiple subject areas, the different types of content considerations including instruction and assessment, against the backdrop of multiple administrators monitoring the overall progress of students and the complex structures found within the departments. The voices of teachers were heard as they shared their growth through the processes of monitoring student progress within a supportive culture that promotes professional learning for adults.

Chapter Summary

There are numerous models of professional learning that promote collaboration and reflection and which can be embedded within the work mirroring what teachers do every day—they teach children and work alongside peers. For any model of professional development to be collaborative and to promote reflection, key features are present—conversations, critical analysis of teaching, a focus on student learning, and all of these, and more, are embedded within the work day. A few models were presented in this chapter and there are more models presented in other chapters in much more detail. The next chapter examines action research.

Suggested Readings

Blankenstein, A. M., Houston, P. D., & Cole, R. W. (2008). *Sustaining professional development*. Thousand Oaks, CA: Corwin Press.

Venables, D. R. (2011). *The practice of authentic PLCs: A guide to effective teacher teams*. Thousand Oaks, CA: Corwin Press.

Zepeda, S. J. (2012). *Professional development: What works* (2nd ed.). New York, NY: Routledge.

7 Authentic Action Research

In This Chapter . . .

- The Benefits of Action Research
- Action Research is Learning
- Collaborative and Individual Action Research
- The Cyclical Nature of Action Research
- Steps Within the Action Research Model
- Cases from the Field
- Chapter Summary
- Suggested Readings

Action research is a collaborative form of job-embedded professional development, and, in most instances, it unfolds in the context of a classroom, a building, or a school system. Reflection is foundational to the action research process. With the prevalence of professional learning networks and other social media, action research evolves to the needs of the community membership. Goodnough adopted the metaphor, "learning spaces" to

> examine how collaborative action research can be used to create different types of spaces: problem-posing spaces, problem-solving spaces, meaning-making spaces, and spaces for communicating and disseminating the outcomes of collaborative action research. Action researchers pose problems and examine issues that are relevant to their own practice; they create meaning as they adopt new pedagogies and reflect on how their actions are impacting students and themselves; and they simultaneously create new knowledge while sharing it both locally and publicly. The spaces created through collaborative action research are constantly shifting as teachers uncover, examine, and scrutinize their own beliefs, the beliefs of others, and the research of others. Collaborative action research provides a venue for establishing learning spaces that promote collaboration, reflection, and classroom- and school-based change. (2011, p. xi)

Professional development embedded in practice creates the "space" to engage in action research.

The Benefits of Action Research

Action research is relevant because the area under study is one that is of interest and applicable to the adult learner. Regardless if action research is conducted solo or with others, it has many benefits that can:

◆ Motivate teachers to pursue an area of interest—people are more motivated to learn about what interests them.

◆ Focus on an issue on some aspect of practice that has you wondering, "what if" or "how about," or "why" about the possibilities if tweaks were made to a particular practice related to instruction, student groupings, assessment, etc.

◆ Lead to modification in practices (instruction, assessment, classroom routines, grading, etc.).

◆ Support self-directed learning, a powerful form of adult learning.

◆ Encourage collaboration with colleagues at the team, grade, district levels—and through technology, audiences across larger geographic regions.

◆ Enhance, supplement, and/or extend formal professional development offered at the site, within the system, or even off site at conferences.

◆ Provide sustained opportunities to reflect on practice.

◆ Provide a forum to share the results of what has been learned with colleagues—helping to create a knowledge-building community of learners.

Action Research is Learning

Action research is about learning in the context of teaching. Action research ranges from studying instructional practices to questioning patterns. Teachers engage in action research to improve practice, to refine a skill, to further develop a practice, or to gain a deeper understanding about an aspect of teaching, learning, or the students that they teach.

It's All About the Action: Action research engages teachers in their own intentional actions of collecting, analyzing, reflecting, and, then, *acting* on what has been learned (e.g., perhaps modifying practice). The processes involved in conducting action research propel movement toward change. In many ways, action research enables teachers to become "architects of change" (Vetter, 2012). The evidence collected, the sense-making during conversations with peers, and the critical reflections can support teachers in making informed decisions about changes in practices. Essentially, learning, acting, and doing are all part of the action research process.

Collaborative and Individual Action Research

Action research can be conducted solo or in the company of others, which Cunningham (2011) positions as *collaborative action research* in which teachers would together plan, implement, analyze, and then reflect on the lessons learned through their mutual inquiry. Calhoun (1994) identified three approaches to action research that held the same processes but whose participant configurations changed. The approaches included individual teacher action research, collaborative action research, and school-wide action research.

Collaborative Action Research

Collaborative action research connotes a smaller number of participants (e.g., peers on the same team or a small group of teachers, or a teacher and a coach) who study their everyday practices (Bold, 2011). Through structured examination, teachers keenly identify areas that are puzzling them with a triple intent: 1) discovery—understanding what is puzzling, 2) collaboration—learning from each other, and 3) reflection—thinking deeply with critical and constructive feedback and probing questions from peers.

Discovery—Understanding What is Puzzling

To discover what is puzzling—Teachers wrap their thinking around what is puzzling them about their practices through probing questions:

♦ What data do we have that leads us to believe there is a problem?

♦ Is the problem pervasive?

♦ How is student learning affected?

♦ Could there be a solution "out there" if we studied "this practice" that could help students learn better because we can teach in different ways to reach students? Are we using the right assessments to measure learning?

Collaboration—Learning from Each Other

When teachers work with others, they can a) improve instruction, b) increase collaboration, c) gain expertise in an area of interest, and d) lead school improvement efforts (Calhoun, 1994; Vetter, 2012).

Part of the value of conducting action research with colleagues is that lessons learned can be shared—knowledge can be co-constructed.

Reflection

A major thread in all action research models has been described by Fairbanks and LaGrone (2006) as a "reflective spiral" that occurs throughout the process (p. 8). Reflection encourages teachers to:

♦ Return to experience—by recalling or detailing salient events.

♦ Attend to or connect with feelings—this has two aspects: using helpful feelings and removing or containing obstructive ones.

♦ Evaluate experience—this involves reexamining experiences in the light of new knowledge.

Teachers who reflect gain new perspectives on the dilemmas and contradictions inherent in classroom practices, improve judgment, and increase their capacity to take purposeful action based on the knowledge they discover.

The Cyclical Nature of Action Research

The action research models advocated by Bold (2011), Glanz (2005), Sagor (2011), and Sullivan and Glanz (2013) follow very similar processes. Each model stresses a cyclical process that supports planning, action, collecting, observing, analyzing, reacting, and evaluating data collected by the teacher. Each of these processes is punctuated by reflection—on action and in action (Schön, 1983). Figure 7.1 is an iteration of the cyclical nature of action research.

Steps Within the Action Research Model

Within each of the cycles of action research are steps as illustrated in Figure 7.2. The following Case from the Field examines "three in one" action research projects in as many schools.

Figure 7.1. The Cyclical Nature of Action Research

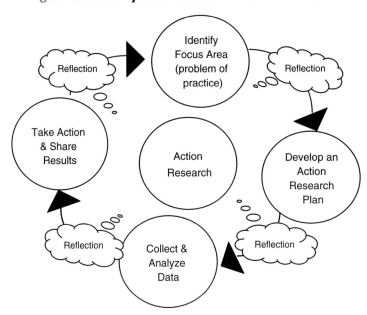

Source: Adapted from the works of Glanz (2003, 2005) and then by Sullivan and Glanz (2013).

Figure 7.2. Action Research Steps

Action Research Steps	Processes Involved in the Steps
Step 1: Selecting a focus	a. Know what you want to investigate b. Develop some initial questions c. Establish a plan to answer or better understand these questions

Action Research Steps	Processes Involved in the Steps

Step 2: Collecting data	a. Primary
	  i. Questionnaires
	  ii. Observations
	  iii. Interviews
	  iv. Tests
	  v. Focus groups
	b. Secondary
	  i. School profile sheets
	  ii. Multimedia
	  iii. Portfolios
	  iv. Records
	  v. Other

Step 3: Analyzing and interpreting data	a. Examining data b. Reflecting with colleagues about the data and the meanings of the data
Step 4: Taking action	a. Making decisions and taking action (changes and/or modifications in practice) based on the results of data and the meanings of the data

Source: Adapted from Glanz (2003, 2005), Sullivan and Glanz (2013).

Cases from the Field

Building Action Research Capacity in Teachers and Aspiring School Leaders

Judith A. Ponticell, Ph.D., Professor; Ms. Shauna Bergwall, M.Ed.; Ms. Marissa Story, M.Ed.; Ms. Sherida Weaver, M.Ed.; Educational Leadership and Policy Studies, University of South Florida, FL

Case Introduction

This Case from the Field offers views of professional development in the form of action research across three school systems in Florida. Dr. Judith A. Ponticell teaches a required course in the M.Ed. Program in Educational Leadership at the University of South Florida that includes action research. This course emphasizes building the capacity of teachers and aspiring school leaders to develop professional communities capable of improving schools. Each of the "projects," or Cases from the Field, presents poignant portrayals of building capacity—for teachers who teach migrant children, for teachers who engage in lesson study, and for teachers who teach in a charter school where professional development resides at the discretion of the site.

Part of the course requirement is for students to conduct action research to examine a school or district professional development initiative. The intent is to examine practices, expose unsuccessful as well as successful actions and outcomes, make decisions about changes needed in practice, and to identify barriers in policy and organizational supports.

These *action research projects* were guided by an inquiry protocol (see Table 7.1 at the end of the case) developed by Dr. Judith Ponticell based on components of effective professional development evaluation as presented in Thomas Guskey's book, *Evaluating professional development* (2000). The protocol provides a systematic way to guide participants in asking questions about and looking at practices in professional development programs, initiatives, and activities in their schools or districts.

Dr. Ponticell has found that the questions provide guidance for seeking information, understanding what is found, and making arguments and plans for change. The questions also help in the identification of successful practices as well as omissions, missed opportunities, or points to be challenged in practice or policy. Ponticell concluded,

> Essentially, the guiding questions help teachers and aspiring school leaders completing the action research projects to understand themselves better; to increase their awareness of their own school or district practices; to challenge what should be rather than accept what is; and to build their commitment to and confidence in their own change agency.

Building the Capacity of Teachers Who Work With Migrant Students

Ms. Sherida Weaver

Context

District A serves approximately 200,500 students grades Pre-K through 12. The student population is diverse with 38 percent of students identified as White, 31 percent Hispanic, 21 percent Black, 5 percent Multiracial, 4 percent Asian, and less than 1 percent American Indian. In 2012/13 12 percent of the district student population were identified as English Language Learners (higher than the state average of 9%). In addition, 56 percent of the district student population were identified as qualified for free and reduced lunch (a little less than the state average of 58%).

Children and youth are served in K–5 elementary schools, K–8 elementary schools, 6–8 middle schools, high schools, career centers, technology schools, magnet schools, and charter schools. The district has 15,600 certified teachers, 235 principals, and 400 assistant principals. In 2013, the district received a C grade with 55 percent of students performing at satisfactory or higher in reading, 58 percent in mathematics, 67 percent in writing, and 55 percent in science on the state's FCAT assessments.

Migrant Student Services

Migrant Student Services provides supplemental academic, social, health, and advocacy support services. Funding is provided by federal financial assistance through Part C of PL107–334, the No Child Left Behind Act of 2001. Funding is used for the benefit of identified migrant children exclusively and supports advocacy and outreach for migratory children and their families, professional development programs for migrant teachers and other personnel, family literacy programs, integration of information technology in education, and transition facilitation for secondary students into post-secondary education or employment.

Migrant program teachers are supplemental staff, meaning that they do not replace district or school staff. Migrant program services are meant to enhance the migrant student experience with additional supports that will improve their academic achievement as well as the quality of their lives. The migrant teachers serve 34 schools, including elementary schools, high schools, and career centers.

Migrant Education Program

The Migrant Education Program targets improvement of FCAT reading achievement by migrant students. Data collected on migrant students indicate that 95.8 percent of our students are Hispanic with 70 percent enrolled in classes specifically designed for English Language Learners. Currently, only 25 percent of migrant students from Grades 3 to 12 are scoring at the proficient level in reading.

Professional Development

Professional development for migrant teachers in the area of reading has been the focus for the last and current school year. Professional learning opportunities have been provided in previous years, but not in a focused or consistent manner. Professional development for the reading initiative focuses on the 30-minute tutoring, pull-out periods the migrant teachers have to supplement classroom teachers' reading instruction. Recalling that migrant program services cannot replace the classroom teacher's instruction, this provides unique challenges as migrant teachers not only have limited time with students, but also migrant teachers have to use materials that are not what the classroom teacher would use. To provide consistency of professional learning and support, monthly meetings are held.

Book Study Opens More Than Pages

Inside words by Janet Allen was selected for book study. The book provides multiple simple strategies to teach vocabulary and increase comprehension skills. Several products were given to each school for migrant teachers to incorporate in tutoring to facilitate vocabulary acquisition. These included the Sunshine State Young Reader Award books for the school level so that migrant students might borrow, read, and respond; main idea card games; animal idiom card games; Kineos (a tablet with core concept practice already installed); and prefix and suffix games. This year 500 Rosetta Stone licenses were purchased and distributed according to school needs. Training was provided by the company, and migrant teachers were sent email instructions for enrolling and managing students at their sites.

Monthly meetings include several activities: book discussion on new methods to tutor reading; peer sharing of what works; updates on district initiatives; and presentations on district services for migrant students. Meetings are aimed at increasing migrant teachers' knowledge, practices, and efficiency. Teachers work in small groups to analyze the vocabulary and comprehension content they are reading about and to identify tutoring practices that could be used at the schools, either in small groups or individually. Before the end of the meetings, teachers share with the whole group the ideas and practical applications they have discovered and discussed. The meetings were a new experience for the group.

Benefits for Teachers

Consistent monthly meetings provide a set time and place to share what is occurring with migrant students and in tutoring sessions, as well as different techniques or ideas that are working with migrant students. Teachers feel they are getting both knowledge and support specific and important to their population of students.

The group study within the meetings also appeals to the teachers as adult learners because they focus on specific content, experiment with different methods, look at the results, and adjust their craft to keep improving their tutoring delivery until the students get the concept. It empowers these teachers. They know they can make effective changes to their work that, in turn, will benefit the students in their charge. It is also safe for them to work in small groups to share information and use each other as resources. Working in groups removes some of the fear of failure that they so often have, particularly in their unique instructional setting of a once-a-week, 30-minute, pull-out period.

Benefits for Students

The migrant teachers have more, and common, tools to address issues they face with their migrant students. Teachers also have common materials, tutoring strategies, and reference information, together with a network of small group resources that they can consult when specific issues occur with their students or in their tutoring sessions. Small group study discussions and whole group report-outs at monthly meetings, together with end-of-meeting evaluations, suggest that the teachers take the knowledge they have gained from the meetings and group study and use that knowledge to improve student interaction in tutoring sessions.

Teachers also report that the students are excited about using the technology and are happy to work on the Kineos and with laptops (using online programs) and Nook readers. In my own experience it is amazing to see how students are immediately engaged and ready to work once I have the Kineos ready to go. Many of our students do not have this technology in their homes, and this gives them opportunity to use and learn from something new and different.

FCAT data are received annually, and 2011/12 data indicate that the gap between migrant and non-migrant achievement in reading is decreasing, but only by a small increment.

Lessons Learned

As the person responsible for professional development for the Migrant Education Program, it is my responsibility to 1) develop a professional learning plan and budget that are approved by my supervisor; 2) select professional learning materials; 3) deliver professional development content; 4) facilitate the monthly meetings; 5) provide primary support to the migrant teachers when they need help; 6) develop physical and online resources for the migrant teachers; and 7) archive information about the work our program does to demonstrate its value to the district.

The questions in the action research inquiry protocol (see Table 7.1) led me to examine our program's professional development efforts in the reading initiative. In reflecting on our activities and gathering information through the action research process, the following areas for improvement can lead to changes that might enhance our overall practices and effectiveness:

- *Goal Clarity*. While I and my supervisor have verbally stated our goals for this professional development initiative, we have never articulated them in writing. Doing so would provide not only a reference for our migrant teachers but also a constant check point to keep our meetings and professional learning activities consistent with our goals.

- *Content and Process of Activities*. I feel confident that teachers received a solid overview of the content of the book we read. In each group study session, we covered three strategies. Teachers were divided into groups where they worked on a strategy together to understand it and created examples to share back with the whole group. They were encouraged to discuss and share ways they could use the new strategies with their students. Each group was given a chance to share, and guidance was given each time in the form of a rubric or a response sheet of some kind.

The book was specifically chosen because the short chapters had great bang for the buck. They were easy to read and to understand, and each chapter came with a graphic organizer. A CD accompanied the book for easy reproduction of the graphic organizers. Other activities were also easy to use and incorporate into tutoring. All of the activities were designed to enhance student learning in a different yet appealing way.

What needs to be done as we continue this year and move into next year is follow-up and checking with the teachers to determine how they are using the information they gained. I can use a survey or feedback form. I can use guiding questions in the monthly meeting sharing sessions specifically targeting strategies from the book. This might encourage teachers to reflect more specifically on the book, try some of the strategies, and share their experiences.

- *Organizational Supports*. At the state level, we are required to provide professional development that supports our staff work at the school level. We also must have at least two sessions that pertain to identification and recruitment of migrant families. At the district level, we garner professional development points for each session that our staff attends.

While this is a requirement, our ability to give migrant teachers professional development is limited by the time we are allowed to take the migrant staff from their school sites. Principals can be understanding or restrictive with our staff, and the latter poses issues at times. When we started the monthly professional development meetings last year, we had to struggle a bit to get principals on board. This year there is less resistance to releasing the migrant staff to attend meetings, but we still have to be cognizant of the problems that our staff face in being released by their principals. I have set up the meetings to alternate from Friday to Monday every month.

My supervisor supports the meetings, and she has even led them at times so the teachers are aware of their value. She verbally shares her recognition after the meetings that she attends. She also circulates when the staff are working in small groups and comments positively to the groups.

- ◆ *Teacher Outcomes.* I could tell by usage reports that the teachers were not using the Kineos and its programs with fidelity. I am providing extra training, and I will incorporate follow-up and troubleshooting. Teachers will be given a trial period after training and an expected time for utilization of the Kineos to their full capacity.

While the monthly meetings worked for engaging the migrant teachers in discussions of applications and ideas for implementation, there was no follow-up monitoring at the school site. I will discuss going out to the sites more with my supervisor so we can monitor what is being done with the information we are learning and sharing at the meetings. We need to develop a formal assessment of how program content and processes are being used to gain better evidence of teacher outcomes.

- ◆ *Student Outcomes.* I need to connect the work we do at the monthly meetings to student achievement so the migrant teachers can also see my vision for the professional development and its intended eventual effect on student achievement. I have not been effective enough in this regard.

Building Capacity through Lesson Study

Ms. Shauna Bergwall

Context

District B serves approximately 94,000 students grades Pre-K through 12. The student population is diverse with 46 percent of students identified as White, 27 percent Hispanic, 21 percent Black, 3 percent Multiracial, 2 percent Asian and less than 1 percent American Indian. There are more than 15,000 students whose primary language is other than English. In 2012/13 10 percent of the district student population were identified as English Language Learners (higher than the state average of 9%). In addition, 66 percent of the district student population was identified as qualified for free and reduced lunch (more than the state average of 58%).

Children and youth are served in elementary schools, elementary/middle schools, elementary/middle/high schools, middle schools, middle/high schools, high schools, technical career centers, alternative education schools, charter schools, Department of Juvenile Justice sites, and Head Start sites. The district has 5,350 certified teachers, 140 principals, and 177 assistant principals. In 2013 the district received a C grade with 50 percent of students performing at satisfactory or higher in reading, 50 percent in mathematics, 52 percent in writing, and 46 percent in science on the state's FCAT assessments. The district has a unique challenge of serving a wide geographic area of more than 1,850 miles.

In the last few years, the district has undertaken a project to implement lesson study at many school sites in an effort to improve teaching and learning. School representatives were chosen and trained by district personnel to be facilitators and lead the lesson study initiative in their own schools. In the first cycle of lesson study, the district contact was available to lead the facilitation, with the school representative learning by observation. Subsequent cycles were led by the school-based facilitators.

The district promotes four lesson study cycles per year at each school; however, there are no plans in place to provide funding for substitutes or other plans for classroom coverage. Schools are just encouraged to be "creative" in how they arrange schedules for the two days each cycle requires.

School Site

The elementary school that is the focus of this action research project is a midsize school situated in an urban environment. Students come from the surrounding neighborhood with few being bussed in from outlying areas. Of the 500 students, 95 percent qualify for free or reduced lunch, designating the school Title I. The school has historically struggled with students reaching proficiency on state tests and undertook lesson study during the 2012/13 school year as a means to increase student engagement, build collegiality among a team of teachers, and ultimately increase student achievement.

Professional learning at the school has historically been perceived as just another thing to do. The value of professional learning has not been considered by teachers. Trainings are thought of as something they are forced to do, with little perceived relevance to teachers' day-to-day job duties.

Lesson Study at the Elementary School

Lesson study was introduced to the school's teachers as a voluntary opportunity. Teachers were asked if they would like to participate—one of the first times they had been asked to volunteer. Background information was provided to teachers on the concept of lesson study, and the parameters for teacher participation were outlined by the school facilitator. Six teachers volunteered, out of about 35. Reasons for not volunteering were not wanting to spend two days out of their classrooms, apathy for yet another district initiative, and not wanting to go above and beyond their basic job duties.

Process

Teachers who participate in lesson study are expected to be masters of their content areas, but if they are not, the team members are there to strengthen each other's content skills in weak areas. Teachers are provided time to discuss, for example, goals; predicted outcomes; teaching strategies; student thinking, responses, and behaviors; what works and helps to produce positive outcomes; and what doesn't work and needs to be changed. Teachers, after developing a trustful relationship with the other team members, are able to explore their personal teaching styles, while being offered data based on student performance to consider. Teachers are free to take what they learn in lesson study and implement it on their own in their own classrooms. Teachers are also free to take what they learn about the lesson study cycle process and implement it on a more informal basis in their own grade levels, or on a personal level.

The lesson study cycle used by the district is provided in guidelines established by the Florida Department of Education Bureau of Curriculum and Instruction. The cycle includes the following phases:

1. Form a lesson study team that includes an external expert(s) in content and/or pedagogy.

2. Schedule a common planning time.

3. Identify a common research theme (sometimes a school-wide theme) based upon student performance data and the Teacher Evaluation Model adopted by the school district.

4. Collaboratively plan a standards-based lesson aligned to course description that clearly defines the expected outcomes in terms of student learning and addresses common student misconceptions.

5. Implement the planned lesson and observe the lesson being sure to record data pertaining to what students were thinking and doing throughout the lesson.

6. Reflect upon, analyze, and discuss the lesson and student data that have been collected; then synthesize findings.

7. Define the next steps based upon what the team has learned.

8. Repeat the process using a new or revised lesson plan with the same research theme.

The time required to fully implement a cycle is two days (although that time is anticipated to get shorter the more familiar the group is with the cycle). The lesson study materials were easily obtained from the district, and the district training was run very well. There were enough materials for the teachers who participated. The materials were neatly packaged, and teachers wanted to open and read what was available. The materials were clearly laid out for teachers to follow and for the facilitator to move through the cycle(s) with ease.

Teacher Benefits

Lesson study is intended to empower teachers through discussion and analysis of the data they are provided. Literature on lesson study indicates that teachers often form bonds of trust and collegiality that reach further than the lesson study group. In a Professional Learning Community where lesson study is common, teachers choose to participate, choose the topic to focus on, and choose the content of the lesson. Teachers who participate often report feeling refreshed and ready to apply the strategies they learned as part of lesson study in their daily teaching.

Student Benefits

Informal student-attitude surveys indicate that teachers are not engaging their students but are, for the most part, providing dull, lifeless, irrelevant learning opportunities for students, which result in poor learning and low proficiency on assessments. Data available from state assessments (as well as data that are supported in formative assessments, ongoing assessments, and district-level assessments) support this conclusion.

Lesson study has the potential of increasing teachers' ability to consistently deliver high-quality/high-engagement lessons for students. If this occurs, it is my feeling that student achievement will increase. For lesson study to be successful, teachers need to be committed to the process and internalize lesson study cycle components.

Lessons Learned

I was the school facilitator for lesson study at the elementary school, as well as program facilitator for Title I. As school facilitator I guided the lesson study team through the lesson study cycle and the reflection and debriefing processes. I was expected to be savvy, knowledgeable, and tactful; able to model an analytical approach to the debriefing; and able to set a clear tone of respectful inquiry based on data presented (Florida Department of Education, Division of K–12 Public Schools, Bureau of School Improvement, 2010).

In reflecting on our activities and gathering information through the guiding questions in the action research inquiry protocol, I found both areas of concern and for improvement:

◆ *Goal Clarity.* The goals of lesson study are to bring like-minded teachers together in a common effort to examine teaching and learning by thoroughly planning, delivering, and evaluating a lesson. The facilitator's role is to guide the teachers through the process, asking probing questions along the way and facilitating the data collection process as well as allowing teachers to discover the data trends and make adjustments based on that data. Guidelines and resources provided to school facilitators and school administrators for implementation of lesson study, as well as district training for the school facilitators, made these goals clear.

However, not much information was provided to teachers. One administrator and one representative from each school attended a half-day training at the district to implement lesson study. In doing this, the district relied on the motivation and ability of the school representatives to implement lesson study at the school site. At the elementary school, teachers were leery of the concept, of the district asking them to be out of their classrooms for two days at a time, and of how this initiative would benefit them in the classroom. Some teachers participated to "get out" of their classrooms for a couple days, some participated because they truly wanted to learn more about their craft, and at least one participated to see if what was being asked of teachers violated the union contract.

◆ *Content and Process of Activities.* The elementary school only implemented one lesson study cycle. There was a noticeable change for a short amount of time. However, without administrative support of the follow-up cycle(s), change quickly died down, and momentum was lost. The team members all taught reading, so there was potential for their continuing some of what they learned through their grade-level teams.

However, there was no funding for substitute teachers nor was there the cooperation of other teachers to take on additional students for two days at a time, so the team's continued self-direction did not happen.

Furthermore, in the lesson study process teachers are trained in the cycle to help them better understand the facets of good lesson planning, delivery, and evaluation. They are not specifically trained, however, in how to implement what they learn on a daily basis. Rather, it is assumed that the astute teacher will take what he or she learns in the lesson study cycle and apply it. The downfall of lesson study may be its focus on group process rather than individual use of the process to plan, deliver, and assess instruction. Not specifically building teachers' skills to connect the lesson study cycle to self-directed learning and exploration of one's own teaching is a missed opportunity.

   ◆ *Organizational Supports.* Lesson study is a district initiative, with train-
     ing led by one of the most recognized and prominent professional
     development trainers in the district. District personnel seem to sup-
     port the initiative, allowing the trainer to use district resources to sup-
     port the effort and purchasing materials that provide step-by-step
     procedures for successful implementation of lesson study for all levels
     of schools.

While lesson study is mentioned many times in district- and school-based improvement plans as a way for teachers to effectively plan, deliver, and evaluate lessons, there is no mention of the time or resources required to effectively imple-ment lesson study. To fully implement lesson study, a school must be able to release a team of teachers from their classroom duties for two full, consecutive days per les-son study cycle. This is a challenge for some schools related to funding, and many schools don't feel they can spare the time for the teachers to be out of their class-rooms. Some schools have split classes, expecting other certified teachers to teach classrooms with many additional children in them for two days, while others have allowed substitute teachers (who may or may not be qualified) to teach classrooms full of students for two days.

The policies and procedures currently in place do not support the implementa-tion and sustainability of lesson study as it is meant to be implemented. And, there are no plans in place to address the logistical challenges and budgetary shortfalls. Rather, schools are encouraged to "be creative" in order to release teachers from their classrooms. Facilitators are encouraged to solicit donations from local compa-nies in order to provide incentives for teachers to be a part of the team. Many facilita-tors paid for lunches and small incentives out of their own pockets in order to make the first (or later) cycle(s) of lesson study happen successfully at their school sites.

Beyond logistics and budgets, it is difficult to convince administrators to allow teachers two days out of their classrooms in order to develop themselves profes-sionally. What administrators don't often see is that if they do invest those two days, the teachers can then, with guidance, take what they learn and apply it for better teaching and learning results on a daily basis. In other words, it is time well spent or well invested.

The tenets of lesson study adopted by the district say little about the principal's role in support of lesson study. At the elementary school, the principal was open to new ideas from the district and a believer in the concept of lesson study, but, according to the tenets of the adopted lesson study model, he was not encouraged to attend a cycle or ask about how teachers participated. The principal was quick to recognize efforts and successes of implementers of professional development. He thanked those responsible and teachers for their participation—often publicly—and encouraged others to join the effort. He did not, however, have a lot of insight to offer when talking with teachers about the experience. Perhaps engaging principals in a lesson study cycle would give them the experiences necessary to effectively encourage teachers. Since the principal was not privy to the content of the lesson study, he was not able to alleviate fears or anxiety among other teachers apt to join or thinking about it.

◆ *Teacher Outcomes.* Lesson study is very much a professional development opportunity teachers have to want to be a part of. This is by no means a "sit-and-get" type of training. Teachers are pushed to think outside the box, open up personally and professionally, and be fully engaged for two days. There is encouragement and guidance to do these things, but teachers must be willing to commit.

Lesson delivery is done in the classroom of one of the participating teachers, allowing a team of teachers a rare opportunity to visit the classroom of a colleague. This is the pivot piece of lesson study, observing a lesson as a team and evaluating the degree of student engagement and authentic learning that is occurring as a result of the lesson plan and delivery. This is something that is rarely done as an individual teacher, much less as a team.

For the six teachers who volunteered, lesson study turned out to be a great opportunity to enhance their teaching and students' learning in individual classrooms. Although the effects were not quantitatively measured, participating teachers' feedback about the lesson study cycle revealed they felt an increased sense of collegiality among the participating teachers and were better able to plan lessons with an increased awareness of students' reactions. Teachers also reported learning a lot about one another as well as about teaching and learning strategies. One teacher, who surprisingly volunteered at the last minute, reported the lesson study cycle was rewarding for her as she learned a lot about her own teaching practice. Some teachers who chose not to participate in the lesson study cycle were curious as to what happened, and the participants were encouraged to informally share their experiences.

◆ *Student Outcomes.* My experiences as a lesson study facilitator contribute to my belief that lesson study is a viable option for the improvement of lesson planning, delivery, and evaluation. However, lesson study is not something that can happen once or twice a school year and be expected to show high-yield results. It is something that needs to be provided and supported on an ongoing basis. For teachers to engage in continuous development of their craft, it has to be shown to provide avenues for increases in student achievement.

Students are not able to benefit from one lesson study cycle and won't benefit if teachers are not willing to put in the extra time and effort it requires to plan effective high-engagement lessons for students. Similarly, students won't benefit from lesson study if schools and districts do not provide supports necessary to enable teachers to engage in regular lesson study cycles embedded as part of their professional work, rather than just as occasional professional development opportunities.

Building Capacity for Professional Learning in an Elementary Charter School

Ms. Marissa Story

Context

The 2002 Florida School Code adopted by the Florida Legislature provided numerous statutory rights for educational choice for parents and students. Section 1002.33 established charter schools as part of the state's public education program. All charter schools in Florida are public schools. A charter school may be formed by creating a new school or converting an existing public school to charter status. In 2012/13 there were 570 charter schools serving 200,000 students.

Charter schools are intended to improve student learning and academic achievement by increasing learning opportunities for all students, with special emphasis on low-performing students and reading. Charter schools can use innovative learning strategies, create innovative measurement tools, and create new professional opportunities for teachers, including ownership of the learning program at the school site. All charter schools are required to measure learning outcomes.

Charter Elementary School was once a traditional school in District B and converted to charter status. The system came about when a group of concerned local citizens—lawyers, bank presidents, business owners, administrators, and teachers—wanted to explore new approaches to the education system. In 2004, the Education Committee of the local town's Area Chamber of Commerce had a Feasibility Study done for improvement of the area schools. The study was based on interviews and resulted in a report that identified a community consensus that a) education was the community's Achilles' heel; b) the community is responsible for the quality of its schools; c) a solution to the community's education weaknesses should benefit all students in all schools; d) all students should have the basics in reading, writing, and mathematics; and e) the curriculum should be more practical and provide real-world educational choices relevant to local families and the local economy. In response to these needs, the Charter Schools System was formed, which today consists of four elementary schools, one middle school, and one high school.

School Site

The school's enrolment for the 2013/14 school year is 484 students in Grades K through 5. The student population is composed of 257 males, 227 females, 35.1 percent White students, 32.6 percent Black students, 26.4 percent Hispanic students, and 2.3 percent students of other ethnic descent. Limited English Proficiency students were 15 percent of the student population. The majority of the student population (95%) are classified as economically disadvantaged, thus qualifying the school to receive Federal Title I funds, determined by the number of students that receive free or reduced-price meals.

The school employs 36 teachers and two administrators. In 2013 the school received a C grade. FCAT test results reported in the 2012/13 No Child Left Behind (NCLB) School Public Accountability Report (SPAR) indicated 37 percent of students performing at satisfactory or higher in reading, 43 percent in mathematics, 43 percent in writing, and 24 percent in science.

Professional Learning Context

Even though the Charter Schools System works as a whole, each school is left to determine what Professional Learning opportunities they need as an individual school. In talking to staff from other schools, they seem to want more opportunities and high-quality professional development than our current experiences at Charter Elementary School.

When administration decides that Professional Learning should occur, they notify staff members through email letting them know that there will be a meeting during their grade-level planning time. These meetings last between 30 and 40 minutes depending on the topic of discussion and follow a proposed schedule:

♦ First Wednesday of the month—reading and writing

♦ Second Wednesday of the month—math and science

♦ Third Wednesday of the month—administration

♦ Fourth Wednesday of the month—intervention and RTI (Response to Intervention).

The meetings are called Professional Learning Communities (PLCs). In these meetings the coaches, administration, or the guidance counselor meet with the teachers and present information that usually pertains to the Common Core State Standards and how it looks in reading, writing, math, and science, or information received at the latest Leadership Meeting with the Charter Schools' superintendent.

After the PLC meeting, teachers are charged with the task of trying a new strategy or incorporating one "new" thing learned during these meetings. Many times, teachers leave these meetings feeling overwhelmed. If you are learning a new strategy once a week, but are never really given time to implement it, or gather and interpret data from the results, or even discuss it with your team, then you feel as if you are being weighed down, but not supported. Teachers also expect that administration would want to see implemented initiatives in action by conducting walk-throughs and observations. At Charter Elementary School this does not happen. No follow-up occurs.

Teachers at the school generally want to learn new things, and they remember opportunities they have had in previous years—time to visit other schools, other classrooms, and other grade levels—which encouraged teachers to think and teach "outside of the box" and to create learning opportunities for students to demonstrate deeper levels of understanding. Just being told to do something in a PLC meeting is not perceived as a professional learning experience. So, many times, during the meetings teachers vent frustrations while little work or learning gets done. If staff want to acquire new knowledge of things outside of these discussions, then they must attend off-campus training. The cost for this is usually paid for by the teachers themselves.

iObservation® Initiative

Based on Robert Marzano's teaching model, iObservation® is a computer-based evaluation system with which administration can track teachers' instruction and growth. Through iObservation®, staff are able to upload artifacts to show what is being taught, document lesson plans, and demonstrate learning goals and achievements for both students and teachers.

iObservation® is based on *The art and science of teaching framework* (Marzano, 2007). The iObservation® framework is divided into three broad categories that are then divided into subcategories called Design Questions (DQ). These are as follows:

- ♦ Lesson Segments Involving Routine Events

    - ♦ DQ1: Communication Learning Goals and Feedback
    - ♦ DQ6: Establishing Rules and Procedures

- ♦ Lesson Segments Addressing Content

    - ♦ DQ2: Helping Students Interact with New Knowledge
    - ♦ DQ3: Helping Students Practice and Deepen New Knowledge
    - ♦ DQ4: Helping Students Generate and Test Hypotheses

- ♦ Lesson Segments Enacted on the Spot

    - ♦ DQ5: Engaging Students
    - ♦ DQ7: Recognizing Adherence to Rules and Procedures
    - ♦ DQ8: Establishing and Maintaining Effective Relationships with Students
    - ♦ DQ9: Communicating High Expectations for All Students

Within these categories are 41 competencies that are connected to student achievement and learning gains.

Administrators in each school in the Charter School System were tasked to select staff members to serve on the Teacher Evaluation Advisory Committee to discuss strategies, provide input, and model iObservation® in their schools. The idea behind the committee is for teachers to be the point persons to answer questions and to provide support for their school staff in iObservation® implementation. At Charter Elementary School, the administration has identified three point persons, but staff are told to contact other schools for help with iObservation® implementation. This is extremely frustrating for staff. To date no professional development has been done to support the staff in this new initiative.

Lessons Learned

As an iObservation® point person for Charter Elementary School, I believe that it is in our school's best interest to provide necessary professional development opportunities to support teacher learning and implementation of iObservation®. This would include the following, at a minimum:

- ♦ *Book Study.* According to Zepeda in *Professional development: What works* (2012a), "Book studies support smaller groups of teachers to meet at a regularly scheduled time to engage in discussions, to reflect on what has been read, and then to envision how a new practice might be implemented once back in the classroom" (p. 191). Since the Charter System has adopted Robert Marzano's book, *The art and science of teaching framework*, having a book study in place for teachers would help develop their thinking, ability to reflect on and refine their instructional practice, and better understanding of the variables on which they will be observed and rated in iObservation®.

♦ *Lesson Plan Study.* "In studying the curriculum, teachers identify a topic that encompasses a learning problem they would like to pursue. The learning problem is related to the learning goals of the school, and is initially found by studying the curriculum as it relates to the overarching goals of the school" (Zepeda, 2012a, p. 226). Lesson plan study can support the iObservation® process and teachers' learning from that process, particularly with lesson study emphasis on effects on student thinking, behavior, response, and learning in the lesson being studied. One way to help staff is to remember that the teacher is also the learner, and dedicate time for teachers to study, plan, conduct research and reflect on what they uncover in their practices.

♦ *Portfolios.* "A portfolio is a work in progress that allows teachers to chronicle (a) teaching practices, including changes made over time; (b) attaining of long- and short-term goals; and (c) the building of knowledge through constructing artifacts" (Zepeda, 2012a, p. 263). In the new iObservation® initiative this is exactly what is expected of the staff—the ability to create goals, build on these goals over time, and reflect on them through various artifacts in order to determine the effectiveness of one's teaching practice.

♦ *Interactive Website Help.* Since iObservation® is done online, it would be very useful to have professional development opportunities in which staff members can go on an "interactive walk-through" on the website in order to learn more about the various aspects that iObservation® entails and how to use the system.

♦ *Establish a Grass Roots Teacher Leadership Team* to learn about, experiment with, and develop these professional learning strategies for Charter Elementary School, and lead the school in adopting and implementing these strategies. Like-minded colleagues can work together to support one another, improve teaching and gain valuable insight into iObservation®. Working toward a change can offer teachers more stability in their roles as educators, thus benefiting those who are directly affected by this influence.

Potential Benefits for Teachers

Currently, many teachers at Charter Elementary School feel that there is not a lot of time to partner with their peers in order to assess strategies and their effectiveness in increasing student learning, thus they are not truly implementing new strategies that they have learned. Grade-level teams hold weekly meetings to discuss upcoming schedule changes and to plan for the week or month ahead. However, this is done during one of the planning periods, and, to be honest, the meetings are not very beneficial when one reflects on what professional learning could be. Implementation of iObservation® can be better supported by engaging teachers in real Professional Learning Communities.

Although the system is an overall large entity, individual schools differ in the information they get and in the ways they do things. We could probably learn much from each other, but we don't have regular opportunities to communicate across schools. By talking daily about things that are happening in our classrooms, teachers and administration can gain better understanding of student and teacher needs and their feelings toward issues that are important to them. This is especially significant in establishing professional trust between teachers and administrators in a Professional Learning Community.

There are so many ways in which teachers can be engaged in professional learning, including action research and research on current best practices through the internet, professional journals or books, and initiatives other schools have taken that can be adapted to our school situation. We could learn much together by taking time to ask important basic questions like:

- ◆ What is the goal of our PLC meetings—presenting information or engaging teachers in learning and change?
- ◆ If the goal is presenting information, does all information pertain to all staff or just a select few?
- ◆ Would information be best received by staff in small groups (such as grade levels) or as a whole?
- ◆ What are the best ways to provide information?
- ◆ If the goal is engaging teachers in learning and change, what are pressing needs to increase student learning?
- ◆ What are the best ways to engage teachers in professional learning?
- ◆ What is the best time to conduct professional learning opportunities?
- ◆ What resources are needed—personnel, materials, technology?
- ◆ What follow-up is needed?
- ◆ How can we build and sustain a Professional Learning Community?

Potential Benefits for Students

Through the PLC meetings, teachers are provided information on a new teaching strategy each week. Teachers feel they have not been given adequate time to implement new knowledge and skills that have been learned. Relevant student data based on this newly acquired information have not been gathered to see if what the teachers are learning in the professional development and then implementing in their classrooms is effective or not. While students seem to understand what is being taught and are reacting in a positive manner to classroom instruction, assessments have not been linked specifically to strategies implemented from PLC meetings. Students would benefit more from fewer targeted strategies implemented over time and assessed with measurement tools linked to the intended outcomes of the strategies.

Case Summary

Our authors leave us with compelling messages about what's possible. They have learned their lessons well, leveraging the results of their action research to make sound judgments about what is working, or what's not, and they proactively make suggestions that can and should be considered, based on the data that were collected. From these rich descriptions, schools have solid models of how to go about thinking about action research, and the Professional Development Action Research Protocol developed by Ponticell (2013) provides a solid guide for framing the discussions about not only action research but also professional development.

Table 7.1. Professional Development Action Research Inquiry Protocol

Component	Guiding Questions
Target Improvement Area	1. What is the target area? Why is professional development being focused in this area? What needs are being addressed? How is the target area aligned with the school's mission and goals? 2. What professional development program/activities are being used to address the target area? 3. What data are used to determine the target area? What data are used to select the professional development program/activities? 4. What are the goals of the program/activities? How are the goals being assessed?
Professional Development Content and Process	1. To what degree is the professional development content relevant to teachers' and students' needs? Do teachers feel they "learned" something useful and usable for their professional practice? 2. What depth of understanding of content is expected? Is content provided at an overview level, or are teachers provided adequate opportunity to explore more deeply together theory, research, and best practices? 3. Are teachers able to examine new roles, expectations, responsibilities, and/or attitudes that would be required to implement new knowledge and skills gained from the professional development content? 4. Are teachers helped to understand the magnitude, scope, credibility, and/or practicality of change required to implement new knowledge and skills gained from the professional development content? 5. Are learning experiences varied, carefully planned and organized, time-efficient, and effective? 6. Are materials provided easily accessible and used to enhance learning?

(continued)

Table 7.1. **(Continued)**

Component	Guiding Questions
Organizational Supports	Policies/Procedures

1. What organizational policies/procedures relate directly to the professional development program/activities (e.g., state-level, district-level, school-level)?
2. Are there any policies/procedures that directly or indirectly support the potential success of the professional development program/activities?
3. Are there any policies/procedures that directly or indirectly hinder the potential success of the professional development program/activities?
4. Have the professional development program/activities effected change in any organizational policies/procedures?

Resources

1. What information has been provided to teachers regarding the need for, purpose of, or goals of the professional development program/activities?
2. What information has been provided to teachers for implementation and follow-up?
3. What funding has been provided for implementation and follow-up?
4. What technology has been provided for implementation and follow-up?
5. What facilities have been made available for implementation and follow-up?
6. What personnel have been made available to support implementation and follow-up?

Collegial Support

1. To what degree are teachers in the school active learners who share enthusiasm for experimenting with new knowledge, skills, and strategies?
2. To what degree do teachers encourage and support learning and change among their colleagues?
3. To what degree do teachers belittle or attempt to sabotage learning and change among their colleagues?
4. To what degree can teachers visit the classrooms of their colleagues in school or in other schools to a) observe their efforts to implement new learning and skills gained from professional development, b) discuss ideas and strategies, c) problem-solve and plan collaboratively, and d) engage in conversation about success, failures, and ways to improve?

Component	Guiding Questions
	Principal Leadership and Support

Principal Leadership and Support

1. To what degree does the principal involve teachers in selecting, planning, organizing, delivering, and assessing the effectiveness of the professional development program/activities?
2. To what degree is the principal an active, attentive, and enthusiastic learner in the professional development program/activities?
3. To what degree does the principal encourage learning and experimentation among teachers? To what degree does the principal alleviate teachers' fears or anxiety regarding criticism or sanction if positive results are not readily apparent?
4. To what degree is the principal open to new ideas and suggestions? To what degree does the principal publicly advocate for, honor, and value teachers' perspectives?
5. To what degree does the principal facilitate and support regular follow-up sessions and activities to support implementation and assessment of the professional development program/activities?
6. To what degree does the principal recognize efforts and successes in implementation and assessment of the professional development program/activities?

District Leadership and Support

1. To what degree are district administrators involved in planning the professional development program/activities? To what degree do district administrators take part in the professional development program/activities?
2. To what degree do district administrators openly support the implementation of the professional development program/ activities (e.g., providing time for collaboration among schools; meeting requests for information, materials, or other resources in a timely manner; providing support for follow-up activities)?
3. To what degree do district administrators encourage learning and experimentation among teachers? To what degree do district administrators alleviate teachers' fears or anxiety regarding criticism or sanction if positive results are not readily apparent?
4. To what degree are district administrators open to new ideas and suggestions? To what degree do district administrators publicly advocate for, honor, and value teachers' perspectives?
5. To what degree do district administrators recognize efforts and successes in implementation and assessment of the professional development program/activities?

(continued)

Table 7.1. **(Continued)**

Component	Guiding Questions
Teacher Outcomes	1. Have critical indicators of effective use of new knowledge and skills gained from the professional development program/activities been established, described, and clarified for teachers? 2. How are these indicators assessed during implementation of the new knowledge and skills? 3. To what degree are teachers involved in assessing implementation and discussing results of the assessments? 4. To what degree do teachers implement new knowledge and skills as intended? To what degree do teachers make modifications and why?
Student Outcomes	1. Is teachers' implementation of new knowledge and skills positively affecting student learning and achievement? How do you know? What evidence have you collected? 2. Is teachers' implementation of new knowledge and skills positively affecting student attitudes or perceptions of learning and their confidence in themselves as learners? How do you know? What evidence have you collected? 3. Were specific student learning goals identified when the professional development program/activities were planned, and were these goals met? Were modifications made during implementation and what are the modifications? Why were the modifications made? If goals were not met, what follow-up actions need to be taken? 4. What data were collected to determine student success? How are data specifically related to the purpose and goals of the professional development program/activities?

Source: Developed by Judith A. Ponticell, Ph.D., University of South Florida, based on components of effective professional development evaluation as presented in Thomas R. Guskey's *Evaluating professional development* (2000).

Chapter Summary

Either as a collaborative effort with peers or as a solo venture, action research is a job-embedded professional development model that can be supported by other processes such as peer coaching, enhanced through book study, and graduate-level courses. Chapter 8 examines another job-embedded form of professional development—learning from student work and common formative assessments.

Suggested Readings

Dana, N. F. (2013). *Digging deeper into action research: A teacher inquirer's field guide*. Thousand Oaks, CA: Corwin Press.

Hendricks, C. C. (2012). *Improving schools through action research: A reflective practice approach* (3rd ed.). Boston, MA: Pearson.

Mills, G. E. (2014). *Action research: A guide for the teacher researcher* (5th ed.). Boston, MA: Pearson.

Sagor, R. D. (2011). *The action research guidebook: A four-stage process for educators and school teams* (2nd ed.). Thousand Oaks, CA: Corwin Press.

8 Studying Student Work and Assessments— Teachers as Change Agents

In This Chapter . . .

- ◆ Embedding the Study of Student Work as a Learning Opportunity
- ◆ Studying Student Work Is Professional Development
- ◆ Case from the Field
- ◆ Common Formative Assessments as Job-Embedded Learning
- ◆ Case from the Field
- ◆ Chapter Summary
- ◆ Suggested Readings

Studying student work can lead teachers to learning more about the results of their efforts based on the very work that students do as the end-products of teaching. Student work can help us understand better if they are learning. Darling-Hammond and Falk (2013) remind us of the importance of studying student work and that:

> Examining and assessing student's work helps teachers learn more about what their students know and can do, as well as what they think. Doing this in the context of standards and well-designed performance tasks stimulates teachers to consider their own curriculum and teaching. Together, teachers can then share specific instructional approaches that can be used to support the strengths and needs of their students. (p. 6)

Embedding the Study of Student Work as a Learning Opportunity

When we study student work, we are really looking in the mirror at our own practices. Through student work, we can think back to the instructional practices used and make linkages about what our students can do based on how and what we have taught, the experiences and guided practice associated with the content, and the feedback given to students.

Although this chapter is not about formative assessment, per se, a few ideas are offered to ground our thinking about studying student work to inform both teacher and student growth—simultaneously. Working as peers, teachers might want to switch to a mind- and practice-set of assessment *for* learning. Chappuis and Chappuis (2007) advocated for a system of assessment for learning that would occur as instruction unfolds in the classroom with students; however, the same principles can be applied with teachers as they use student work to assess their own practices and what they are learning. Chappuis and Chappuis share:

1. The timeliness of results enables teachers to adjust instruction quickly, while learning is in progress.

2. The students who are assessed are the ones who benefit from the adjustments.

3. The students can use the results to adjust and improve their own learning. (2007, p. 19)

Advantages for Students and Teachers

When teachers examine student work alone or with others, they can reflect on how and why students are or are not learning. If students have misconceptions, teachers are able to assess and provide clarity to strengthen student understanding of concepts (Burton, 2012). Examining student work can help teachers make better decisions related to the curriculum and its development, refinements to instructional strategies, and what assessments to use (Sadler, Sonnert, Coyle, Cook-Smith, & Miller, 2013).

Studying Student Work Is Professional Development

Studying and examining student work promotes key constructs that are at the heart of professional development—inquiry, site-based research, and collaboration—situating the teacher as an active learner. Nidus and Sadder (2011) provide "ways to weave student work into the fabric" of professional development (p. 34), and the following suggestions are adapted from their work:

◆ Blog about assessments and keep the discussion going in between team meetings.

◆ Develop an action research project that examines some type of assessment slant related to student understanding as exhibited in work samples.

◆ Dedicate at least one or two meetings a month to assessing student work on common assessments.

◆ Bring student work to professional development activities to serve as a basis for discussion. (p. 34)

Getting Started with Examining Student Work

For some, engaging in collaborative work around common formative assessments and student work can be daunting because what students do can be "tracked back" to teachers. Some might find this connection threatening; others, however, find comfort in the opportunities to work with peers to unpack how standards are being learned and assessed along with the results of these efforts. At the end of the day, the most important thing is the development of strategies to walk into the classroom the very next day with new perspectives, new strategies, modified strategies, or plans for mid-course changes in the flow of the content, based on the needs of students. Some ideas are offered to start the process of studying student work.

Norms. Norms are the ways in which people behave and interact with one another. For example, in a setting that supports teachers in studying student work, the following norms would encourage collaboration:

◆ We value and respect the contributions of our peers.

◆ Our peers have important perspectives to share.

◆ The evidence in the artifacts or the results (e.g., item analysis) are used to frame discussions.

◆ No value judgments are made about students and their abilities "to get it."

◆ If we disagree, we disagree with the idea(s) or the perspective(s) and not the person.

Be Purposeful and Start Small. Teachers, who are at the beginning stages of examining student work, should begin with a single standard (curricular/learning) and then examine student work samples that reflect that standard.

What Types of Student Work to Study? The answer to this question is, "It depends," on the learning objectives, standards, elements, where students are in the process of the lesson, the unit, etc. The objective is to study not only the artifacts but also the learning objectives, the standards, and the instructional approaches to see how students perform, what they have mastered, and what shifts in instructional practices need to be made.

Keep the Discussion Going. Conversations about student work and assessments are focused on student learning, and McDonald (2001) offers that conversations should be "highly structured," use some type of "protocol," and offer a "buffer against quick judgments and harsh words" to "make the process safe" (p. 121).

Studying student work is complex and occurs on many levels at the site and across the system levels. In a perfectly aligned world, both site- and system-levels would intersect seeking coherence in assessment practices. In this chapter, two Cases from the Field are offered. The first examines one school's sustained efforts studying student work, the processes used, and the results of their efforts.

Case from the Field

Lilburn Middle School's Student Achievement Turnaround: A Building-Level Effort to Study Student Work to Improve Writing

Stefanie W. Steele, Ph.D., Assistant Principal; Mr. Michael Richie, 8th Grade Language Arts Teacher; Ms. Carla D. Clark, Assistant Principal; Wisteria Williams, Ed.D., 7th Grade Social Studies Teacher and Content Leader; Mr. Christopher Carter, Assistant Principal; Lilburn Middle School, GA

Case Organizer

Professional development is coupled with dedicated time during the day and week, and the teachers at Lilburn Middle School collaborate studying not only student work but also their instructional practices. Through this type of inquiry, teachers strive to understand student misconceptions and what students know, understand, and can do.

The Context of Lilburn Middle School

Gwinnett County Public Schools, located in the North-Metro Atlanta area, is the largest school system in Georgia, and, in 2013, served 169,150 students in 132 schools. Lilburn Middle School (LMS) was built in 1932. The student enrolment is diverse with 1,677 students of which approximately 65 percent are Hispanic, 22 percent are Black, and 3 percent are White. Approximately 93 percent of LMS students receive free and reduced lunch, 24 percent of the students receive Limited English Proficiency (LEP) or English Language (EL) Services, 13 percent Special Education Services, and 8 percent are Gifted.

Between 2000 and 2008, the LMS leadership changed five times. In 2008, Dr. Gene Taylor was appointed principal, and under his leadership the school began an aggressive approach to teacher professional development that focused on job-embedded learning along with a strong component of examining student work to inform instructional practices. During the 2010 school year, Dr. Taylor brought on board an entirely new leadership team that included a former literacy coach, Ms. Carla Clark, and two teachers—a seasoned social studies leader, Mr. Christopher Carter, and Mr. Michael Richie, an 8th Grade language arts teacher.

There Was a Need for Focused Approaches and Monitoring Expectations

Writing was a targeted area because only 70 percent of the students passed the system test at the 8th grade. The first step was for teachers to return to the basics of instruction and to build instructional consistency. Consistency and implementation of the writing curriculum from class to class were monitored through daily walk-throughs by the administrative team. Teachers were given timely and frequent feedback about the writing process. The expectation was that writing skills would be implemented school-wide through the examination of student work across disciplines.

Professional Learning

The state rubric had changed and professional development on grading student papers with the rubric was paramount for success. The teachers found the state rubric too ambiguous, so they added detailed descriptions that aligned with the writing curriculum in the Gwinnett County Public Schools. The teachers were given several collaborative opportunities to grade students' papers with the rubric. The intense approach to teacher professional development was in place to ensure that teachers and students alike were prepared to implement the adjustments needed to ensure gains on the 8th Grade writing test.

The ambitious plan included writing instruction two days a week, quarterly mock writing tests, weekly examination of student writing, and a new rubric based on the four essential domains of writing. Teachers across grade levels and content areas attended several professional development sessions to learn about ways to infuse writing into the academic culture at LMS.

Extended Learning Time (ELT) Writing Plan

The Writing Plan was solidified and included key components and non-negotiables aimed to improve student writing across the 8th Grade. For teachers, the plan detailed such information as the number of days of writing instruction per week (four days), specific details about expectation for writing days (every Thursday), and sustained writing days (Fridays). Time dedicated to writing increased exponentially and specific types of writing were required (mini-lessons, writing prompts); direction on the uses of examples was explored, and sustained feedback to students was required.

Student Expectations

Students were held responsible for becoming writers, and there were expectations related to the Friday Writing Structure during which they engaged in 60 minutes of sustained writing in the classroom (see Figure 8.1).

Figure 8.1. **Friday Writing Structure**

Friday Writing Structure

1. Pick up your lined sheet and prompt sheet.

2. Sharpen pencils if needed. You must have your own pencils with erasers!

No Talking
BELL TO BELL on Fridays!

3. Open your binder to the WRITING section and take out *help sheets* such as TRANSITION handouts, 5-paragraph ESSAY REQUIREMENTS, elements of a THESIS, examples of HOOKS, any notes or handouts we have discussed.

4. Begin pre-writing on Your Prompt Page. Pre-writing is REQUIRED!

   – Pre-writing ....10 minutes

   – Drafting ....35 minutes

   – Revising/Editing Draft ....10 minutes

5. You will TURN IN: (WHEN I CALL FOR PAPERS!! Work on your essay for the entire period!)

   1. Lined paper with essay.

   2. Prompt sheet with pre-writing.

YOUR FULL NAME and TODAY'S
DATE MUST BE ON BOTH SHEETS!

Manage YOUR TIME carefully!

If you do not successfully complete your Friday Writing assignment, you will be escorted to the 8th grade Academy to complete your assignment with Ms. Clark during Connections.

Tools to Support Studying Student Work

A structured conferencing feedback form was developed to provide feedback to students through the dialogue it generates with their teachers throughout the writing process. The use of conferencing forms also provides teachers with a concise format to quickly examine work and to focus collaborative discussions among their peers during content planning. This data informed planning and assessment conversations and development (see Figure 8.2).

Figure 8.2. **Sample Writing Prompt and Student Conferencing Form**

Expository Writing Prompt

Writing Situation

The world is filled with many wonderful places to visit. It could be a country far away like China, a beautiful beach in Georgia, or a quiet place close to your home. You may or may not have visited this place before. What is your most favorite place?

Directions for Writing

Write an essay explaining why this is your most favorite place in the world. Be sure to include plenty of details and examples.

F: _____	Introduction	Feedback:
A: _____	☐ Hook ☐ Bridge (General Statement) ☐ Thesis Body (3 paragraphs)	_____ _____ _____ _____
T: _____	☐ Topic Sentence ☐ Transition Words ☐ FRESQA	_____ _____
P: _____	Conclusion ☐ Transition words	_____ _____

A half sheet is provided for brainstorming

Progress Continues

Our teachers are continually learning from student writing and crafting instruction that meets their learning needs. During 2011 after examining student work, an additional strategy emerged for the 8th Grade language arts teachers to use. Target Time instruction began to focus on identified weak grammar and mechanical skills. The need to create "writing frames" (see Figure 8.3) emerged from the common content planning designed to support writing for English for Speakers of Other Languages (ESOL) and Students With Disabilities (SWD).

Additionally, at the beginning of the 2011 school year, the 8th Grade teachers met as a team to reflect collectively on what they had learned over the past few years as they used student work to inform their instruction. The outcome of that meeting resulted in a "Top 15 List" of writing rules (see Figure 8.4) that all teachers use to teach important reminders and writing rules to all students.

Through a partnership with the Georgia State University Network for Enhancing Teacher-Quality (NET-Q) several LMS Teachers from all content areas were trained from year to year to facilitate Cross-Career Learning Communities (CCLCs) to support building capacity. Training included a 30-hour professional learning program in which teachers were trained to work as a collaborative team to examine student work to improve instruction. CCLCs are dedicated to collaborative analysis of teaching, learning, and assessment practices especially supporting beginning-year teachers. The Cross-Career Learning Communities training helped us fine-tune our skills using the ATLAS Protocol (see Figure 8.5) to examine student work. Through this process, more consistent feedback is possible (see Figures 8.6 and 8.7) to help students improve their writing and for teachers to learn more about their instructional practices.

Figure 8.3. **Sample Expository Frame**

Sample Expository Frame:

Dear _____, (Only if it is in letter format)

Did you know that_____?

Imagine_____

I remember when_____.

There are many wonderful_____;

however, _____ for the following reasons.

     To begin with, _____.

When_____. Consequently, _____,

and _____. For instance, _____,

but _____.

There_____ because _____.

This is just one reason why _____.

In addition, _____. Would you believe that only ___% of

_____? For example,_____.

because _____. Thus, _____.

Furthermore, _____.

I recently read in an article if _____,

then _____.

To illustrate, _____.

A leading researcher commented, "_____".

Clearly, _____.

Without a doubt, _____.

I remember when _____.

Although _____.

     Finally, _____.

Like my _____ always says, "_____."

Figure 8.4. **Important Rules for Great Essays at Lilburn Middle School**

Important Rules for Great Essays at Lilburn Middle School

(not listed in any particular order of importance)

1. No 2 sentences [N2SSWSW—no 2 sentences starting with the same word] in the same paragraph.

2. The first sentence of an essay must HOOK the reader by grabbing his attention.

3. Each paragraph must contain at least SIX SENTENCES.

4. Paragraphs 2, 3, and 4 must begin with effective TOPIC SENTENCES.

5. Your essay must be a FULL 1½ pages long.

6. The THESIS statement should be the last sentence in the introductory paragraph.

7. INDENT every paragraph.

8. Do NOT skip spaces between paragraphs.

9. Use appropriate TRANSITION WORDS to begin paragraphs 2–5.

10. NEVER REPEAT ideas or thoughts.

11. NO USE OF THE WORD "I" IN EXPOSITORY WRITING.

12. Paragraphs 2–4 MUST INCLUDE some form of ELABORATION.

13. The front side of your paper should contain 3 paragraphs only! Put the 3rd body and the conclusion on the back side. Make this a habit!

14. Include QUESTIONS in your writing to engage the reader.

15. Don't TELL . . . but SHOW the reader about your topic.

TEACHERS: Use a big flip pad for good questions. Have students go up and write their own tips to expand our list!

Figure 8.5. ATLAS—Learning from Student Work

Selecting Student Work to Share

Student work is the centerpiece of the group discussion. The following guidelines can help in selecting student work that will promote the most interesting and productive group discussions:

Choose assignments that involve lots of thinking and that give students some freedom in how they approach the task. Avoid work that consists primarily of answers with little explanation or that involves the application of a well-defined procedure. At times it may be useful to share several pieces of student work that show different approaches to the same assignment.

Ambiguous or puzzling work tends to stimulate the best discussions. Since it does not readily match expectations, it encourages close attention to details and affords multiple interpretations. If this feels uncomfortable, it may be useful to start by examining anonymous samples of student work collected from within the group or gathered from other sources.

Another approach for selecting student work is for the group to plan a class-room activity jointly, teach it independently, then bring the student work back to the group for discussion. This approach is a good way to begin examining teaching or assessment practices based on what the group has learned from looking at student work.

Sharing and Discussion of Student Work

Discussions of student work sometimes make people feel "on the spot" or exposed, either for themselves or for their students. The use of a structured dialogue format provides an effective technique for managing the discussion and maintaining its focus.

A structured dialogue format is a way of organizing a group conversation by clearly defining who should be talking when and about what. While at first it may seem rigid and artificial, a clearly defined structure frees the group to focus its attention on what is most important. In general, structured dialogue formats allot specified times for the group to discuss various aspects of the work.

Consider the student whose work is being examined to be a silent member of the group. Assume, as for any member, that the student is acting in good faith and has put forth his or her best effort.

Reflecting on the Process

Looking for evidence of student thinking . . .

• What did you see in this student's work that was interesting or surprising?

• What did you learn about how this student thinks and learns?

• What about the process helped you to see and learn these things?

Listening to colleagues thinking . . .

• What did you learn from listening to your colleagues that was interesting or surprising?

• What new perspectives did your colleagues provide?

• How can you make use of your colleagues' perspectives?

Reflecting on one's own thinking . . .

• What questions about teaching and assessment did looking at the students' work raise for you?

• How can you pursue these questions further?

• Are there things you would like to try in your classroom as a result of looking at this student's work?

Source: © National School Reform Faculty/NSRF. (n.d.). *ATLAS Learning from Student Work*. Used with Permission. This protocol was originally developed by Eric Buchovecky, based on the work of the Leadership for Urban Mathematics Project, the Assessment Communities of Teachers Projects, and Steve Seidel, and Evangeline Harris-Stefanakis of Project Zero of Harvard University, and then was edited further by Gene Thompson-Grove for the NSRF. NSRF website is http://www.nsrfharmony.org.

Figure 8.6. **Teacher Feedback**

Figure 8.7. **ATLAS Protocol-Learning from Student Work**

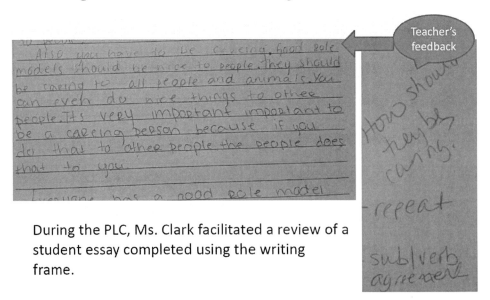

During the PLC, Ms. Clark facilitated a review of a student essay completed using the writing frame.

Responsibility for Writing Goes Beyond English Teachers—Authentic Literacy in Social Studies

At LMS the responsibility for writing goes beyond the realm of English teachers. Our social studies teachers used an aggressive approach to examine student work to inform practice through the use of the Authentic Literacy Template (ALT) in fall 2011. Through a joint partnership with an initiative at Georgia State University, we formed as a collaborative teacher learning group and used the ATLAS Protocol in Social Studies with ALT to examine student work. The goal for ALT is to encourage students to write academically in content areas.

Using the ATLAS Protocol, student work is the primary source of the group discussion. The protocol is an organized and facilitated discussion, in which the process transfers from the description of samples of student work, to the interpretation of the student work, and to the discussion of implications for classroom practice. As a group, the social studies teachers formally examine student writing three times a semester. One lesson we learned was to modify the writing template and give more simplistic instructions of writing prompts. In between cycles of reviewing student writing, the social studies teachers review journal articles collaboratively to stay current with trends in the field and to learn more about providing additional supports for our diverse group of learners. Using differentiated instruction, culturally diverse students can explore a topic through a teaching approach that best meets their learning styles, while exploring the values, beliefs, and ideas that have shaped their experiences.

Differentiating the instruction emerged as a need, so we used more short video clips, music, visual aids, emphasized academic vocabulary, and had students engage in weekly journaling to enhance and supplement our instructional strategies.

Our Results

The data tell the next part of our journey. Our results match our beliefs that students can learn to write, but there need to be structures in place for both students and teachers.

Lessons Learned

We share the lessons learned during our journey:

1. Plan professional development to ensure the adult learners have numerous opportunities to collaborate and to establish common goals with set outcomes.

2. The greatest gains have come from working as a collaborative team during weekly content meetings. We dedicated this time to examining student work.

3. By understanding our students' weaknesses, we were able to develop appropriate strategies, to differentiate our instruction, and to pinpoint more accurately where students were "stuck" in the writing process.

Figure 8.8. Lilburn Middle's 8th Grade Georgia Writing Assessment Seven-Year Trend

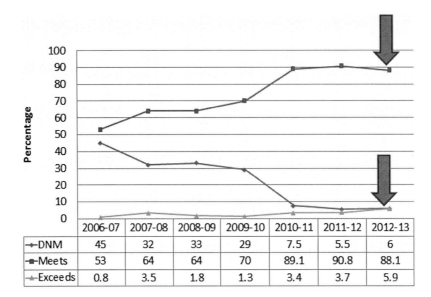

	2006-07	2007-08	2008-09	2009-10	2010-11	2011-12	2012-13
DNM	45	32	33	29	7.5	5.5	6
Meets	53	64	64	70	89.1	90.8	88.1
Exceeds	0.8	3.5	1.8	1.3	3.4	3.7	5.9

4. Job-embedded learning has become a significant part of the culture in the Professional Learning Communities at LMS, becoming second nature for teachers because we infused these practices in weekly planning sessions.

5. Teachers are transferring skills learned through examining student work in writing to other subject areas.

6. The teachers at LMS have benefited from professional development with the ATLAS Protocol where student work and collaboration are key components to exchanging knowledge and informing professional practice.

We have come to trust the judgments of our colleagues, and we have embraced divergent points of view as pressure points for learning.

Case Summary

The teachers persevered with the necessary detail, the protracted discussions, and the dedication to "stick with" examining student work as a means to support student writing. Many discoveries about instructional pacing, differentiation, and the emerging needs of students surfaced through these efforts. This effort was job-embedded, relied on formal professional development (summer training), follow-up, and was supported by the school administration, and a partnership with a local university.

Common Formative Assessments as Job-Embedded Learning

Working with common formative assessments is a form of job-embedded learning that holds benefits for both students and teachers as identified in Table 8.1.

A second is presented—this one focusing on what a system-wide effort at embedding professional learning around common formative assessments looks like in practice.

Table 8.1. **Benefits of Common Formative Assessments**

Benefits for Students and Teachers	Illustrative Sources
Results from common formative assessments enable teachers to give students feedback more quickly so they modify instructional plans	Ainsworth & Viegut (2006); Stiggins, Arter, Chappuis, & Chappuis (2006)
Identify more quickly struggling students and point to when to differentiate	Ainsworth & Viegut (2006); Stiggins & DuFour (2009)
Share effective instructional practices, monitor progress, and celebrate growth	Ainsworth & Viegut (2006); Stiggins *et al.* (2006); Stiggins & DuFour (2009)
Support purposeful planning, pacing, and better alignment with instruction and methods	Ainsworth & Viegut (2006); Darling-Hammond & Falk (2013)
Promote teacher reflection	Burton (2012)
Increased collaboration	Ainsworth & Viegut (2006)

Case from the Field

The Big Questions Around Common Core Standards for Mathematics—A System-Wide Approach to Learning from Common Formative Assessments

Ms. Glenda Huff, Mathematics Coordinator, 6–12; Dr. Mark Tavernier, Director of Teaching and Learning, Division of Instructional Services and School Performance; Dr. Noris F. Price, Deputy Superintendent, Clarke County School District, GA

Case Organizer

The following Case from the Field examines what one school system did with the Common Core Standards for Mathematics and building a culture for Common Core Formative Assessments and how these efforts led to deeper levels of teacher engagement, learning, reflection, and collaboration throughout the process. This case is important because it examines a "system" perspective and how teachers collaborated and learned as a "larger learning community."

The Context of the Clarke County School District

Located in the college town of Athens, Georgia, the Clarke County School District offers its 12,000 diverse students a variety of unique programs due to strong community support and partnerships. A state-level model technology school district, the district prides itself on being at the forefront of digital learning and nearly every student has a district-provided device. Also a leader in global learning, all students in Grades 6–10 benefit from the International Baccalaureate Middle Years Programme, which is not implemented as a gifted program because of the district core belief that all students can achieve. The district also has a strong arts program, and was recently named one of the top 100 communities in music education, as awarded by the NAMM (National Association of Music Merchants) Foundation.

By partnering with the University of Georgia to create a nationally innovative Professional Development School District partnership, there are several professors-in-residence from the university, as well as a variety of methods courses taught onsite. Another partnership example is the Athens Community Career Academy— noted by the lieutenant governor as one of Georgia's top five career academies— where students have the opportunity to earn free college credit from courses taught by Athens Technical College faculty members.

Both of the district's traditional high schools are in the *Washington Post*'s top 8 percent, as well as both being Advanced Placement Honor Schools. The district is home to Georgia Principal of the Year, a MetLife/NASSP (National Association of Secondary School Principals) Breakthrough School, a National Blue Ribbon School and a National Title I Distinguished School. For more information, visit www.proudtobeccsd.com.

Rethinking Cognitive Demands and Common Core State Standards

Since their release, the Common Core State Standards (National Governors Association Center for Best Practices, & Council of Chief State School Officers, 2010a) have been the catalysts in helping the teachers of mathematics rethink the cognitive demands required of students as they move toward mastery of the rigorous mathematics that these new standards demand, requiring a balanced combination of both mathematical understanding and procedures. The Common Core State Standards for Mathematical Practice (2010b) (see Figure 8.9) were written to describe how students should interact with mathematics to be successful.

Experts in the area of mathematics suggest that professional learning activities related to implementing these new standards strongly connect the practice standards with the Common Core State Standards for Mathematical Practice. As an example, the Common Core State Standards Match Practice # 4 Model with Mathematics is presented in Figure 8.10.

Figure 8.9. **The Common Core State Standards for Mathematical Practice**

The Common Core State Standards for Mathematical Practice
1. Make sense of problems and persevere in solving them. 2. Reason abstractly and quantitatively. 3. Construct viable arguments and critique the reasoning of others. 4. Model with mathematics. 5. Use appropriate tools strategically. 6. Attend to precision. 7. Look for and make use of structure. 8. Look for and express regularity in repeated reasoning.

Source: www.corestandards.org/math/practice (National Governors Association Center for Best Practices, & Council of Chief State School Officers, 2010b).

Figure 8.10. **Mathematics Core Standard Practice # 4**

Mathematics—Standards for Mathematical Practice—Model with Mathematics: Core Standard Practice # 4
Mathematically proficient students can apply the mathematics they know to solve problems arising in everyday life, society, and the workplace. In early grades, this might be as simple as writing an addition equation to describe a situation. In middle grades, a student might apply proportional reasoning to plan a school event or analyze a problem in the community. By high school, a student might use geometry to solve a design problem or use a function to describe how one quantity of interest depends on another. Mathematically proficient students who can apply what they know are comfortable making assumptions and approximations to simplify a complicated situation, realizing that these may need revision later. They are able to identify important quantities in a practical situation and map their relationships using such tools as diagrams, two-way tables, graphs, flowcharts, and formulas. They can analyze those relationships mathematically to draw conclusions. They routinely interpret their mathematical results in the context of the situation and reflect on whether the results make sense, possibly improving the model if it has not served its purpose.

Source: www.corestandards.org/Math/Practice/MP4 (National Governors Association Center for Best Practices, & Council of Chief State School Officers, 2010b)

Levels of Thinking Needed

A closer look at a mathematics practice standard reveals more about the level of thinking and kind of thinking that is required of students. Classroom instruction and assessment will need to mirror this same type of thinking. Consider the level of thinking required to find the solution to the problem below:

$$5 \div \frac{1}{2} = n$$

For many students, recalling and applying the algorithm for dividing fractions will yield the correct solution. If a student remembers the mechanics of multiplying by the reciprocal when dividing fractions a correct solution can be obtained.

$$\frac{5}{1} \times \frac{2}{1} = 10$$

For many, finding how many groups of ½ are included in 5 will yield the correct solution. Through an understanding that the quantity 5 can be represented on a number line and that each 1-unit segment of the number line can be divided in half, the solution can be obtained.

There are 10 groups of ½ in 5.

The new standards require that students apply the mathematics they know to solve problems arising in everyday life. Students should be able to identify important quantities in a practical situation, and map these quantities using tools such as diagrams, tables, equations, and other visual models. Consider the level of thinking that would be required to solve the problem below:

Jasmine has 5 cups of frosting. She wants to put ½ cup of frosting on each cupcake she makes. About how many cupcakes can she frost?

---

   a. Solve the problem.

   b. Draw a model to help explain your reasoning.

   c. Write a number sentence that shows your reasoning.

Big Questions for Teacher Learning From Understanding Student Tasks

Content standards across grade bands and content areas demand a more sophisticated level of thinking to meet minimum proficiency levels on national, state, and local assessments. With an increase in the level of cognitive demand required to be successful on high-stakes assessments, teachers are faced with the question: How do I meaningfully connect standards, assessment, and instruction so that my students are successful?

A Roadmap Emerges

Originally, the Clarke County School District Director of Teaching and Learning challenged district-level content coaches to work with subject and grade-level teacher teams to construct engaging units of study based on a common unit planner. As a district math coach, Ms. Glenda Huff was eager and excited to help teachers create units of study that were clear, targeted, and focused on teaching for understanding. Units were to include a list of content standards, a year-long scope and sequence, big ideas, essential questions, learning experiences, assessments, and authentic performance tasks. Units were created during the summer months, and teachers began implementation in the fall.

Essentially, we had two mission-critical objectives. First, we needed to look at the big picture—what are our desired results? What evidence will show us we have achieved the intended results, and what experiences and instruction will align with these efforts to assess student success? (See Figure 8.11.)

Figure 8.11. **The Roadmap**

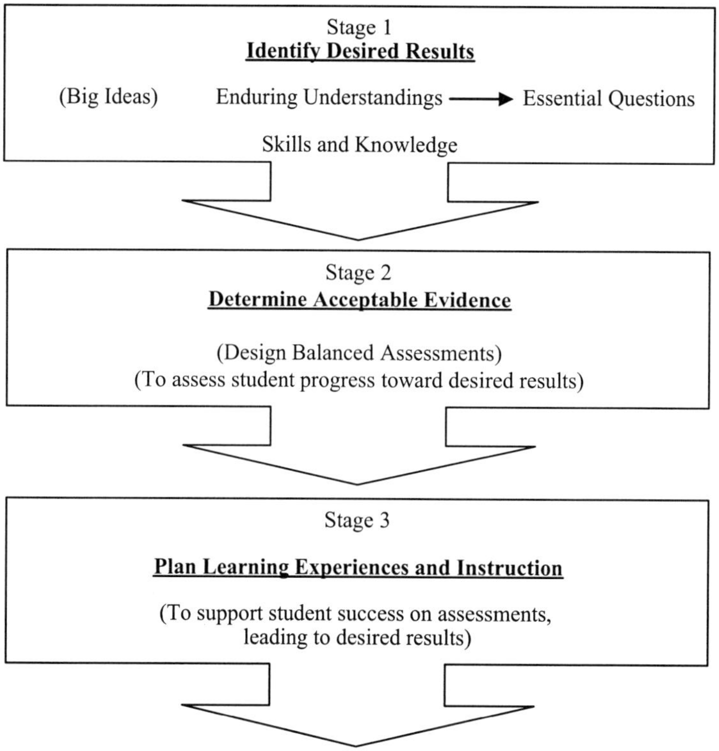

Teams and Collaborative Norms Replace Isolation

The second objective was to examine, develop, and/or refine units of study. Teacher teams, representing schools across the district, reflected on each unit of study and collaboratively completed a unit review form (see Figure 8.12). Through

Figure 8.12. Unit Review Form

Unit Review Form Grade Level _____ Unit Number/Name _____

Content Area: _____ Evaluation Team: _____

Use this form to evaluate each unit by indicating whether or not Unit Design Standards have been met and providing feedback on any improvements needed. Feedback should be very specific so that it can guide curriculum work as it takes place.

	Unit Design Standards	Y/N	Unit Feedback
Stage 1: Where are we going?	Standards/Elements/Related Standards —Standards and Elements are clearly identified. —Process Standards are included in <u>Related Standards</u>.		
	Understandings —are generalizations derived from inquiry. Specific insights that should be inferred from study of topic —are what we want students to realize and remember —may "transfer" across content areas —are ideas that help make sense of past lessons, conduct current inquiry, and create new knowledge.		
	Essential Questions —have no simple "right" answer; thought provoking —are in student-friendly language —help organize instruction; sequenced to lead from one to the next.		
	Skills and Knowledge —Skills and knowledge students need to complete unit performance/learning tasks are included.		

collaborative efforts, conversations focused on students and the standards, and what we needed to ensure student success, learning from one another became the norm, and isolation became obsolete. We had a common goal. We had a process, and our teachers had relationships with teachers in their own buildings; and through this joint work, our team grew to include all teachers of mathematics within the system.

Based on this feedback, we revised our work and began afresh with edited units the following fall. We continued this cycle for several years. As a group, we learned to pace curriculum and share our understanding of the standards via tasks, assessment items, activities, and standards-based resources.

The Norms of Learning Changed Practices for Teachers and Students

With a better understanding of the big ideas and the expectations of the standards, a middle school group of math teachers collaboratively decided to adopt the National Science Foundation problem-based curriculum. The notion of working collaboratively soon transformed itself into regular classroom practices. In other words, what teachers were doing spilled over into the classrooms.

Our students began to work together to solve problems, complete assignments and projects, share ideas, and critique the reasoning of others. More and more, classrooms with straight rows began to vanish, and learning circles and small groupings emerged across our district.

Currently, teacher teams house curricular resources in an electronic format via Google Docs. Teacher teams learned to create folders as well as share, edit, link, and upload documents. Teachers currently collaborate and share their ideas in real time as they grapple with curriculum and instructional issues. Students learn from teachers, and they too use Google Docs as tools to collaborate.

Deepening the Content, Deepening the Learning for Students and Teachers

Subsequently, district-level content coaches were tasked with supporting teachers in updating current units based on the work of Ainsworth (2003). In the process of "unwrapping" key priority standards, teacher teams matched the skills in the standards to one of the six cognitive processes in the revised Bloom's Taxonomy. Teams then designed assessment questions to reflect the approximate level of the corresponding thinking skills. This was a good starting place for making connections between standards, assessment, and instruction. Through the use of a very simple template, the teams recorded their work in prioritizing and labeling standards and elements (see Figure 8.13).

Connecting Standards, Assessment, and Instruction

In the summer of 2013, a group of middle and high school mathematics teacher teams looked carefully at the concepts and skills in the key priority standards for each unit of instruction.

Figure 8.13. Prioritization Template—Clarke County School District

6th Grade Unit 4 6 EE 5 Unwrapping

Insert a standard below (include code). CIRCLE (or capitalize) the SKILLS that students need to be able to do and UNDERLINE the CONCEPTS that students need to know
◆ MCC6 EE 5 UNDERSTAND solving an equation or inequality as a process of answering a question: Which values from a specified set, if any, make the equation or inequality true?

CONCEPTS (what students must know)	SKILLS (what students must be able to do)	DOK
Solving an equation as a process of answering the question: Which values make the equation true?		
	UNDERSTAND	3
Solving an inequality as a process of answering the question: Which values make the inequality true?	UNDERSTAND	2
	USE	2
Substitution to determine whether a number in a specified set makes an equation true.		

Every Architect Has the Right Tools to Use

Teams used Bloom's Taxonomy and Webb's DOK to review levels of thinking and cognitive demand. The Hess Cognitive Rigor Matrix (2013) combines the two models and allowed teams to categorize uniquely selected learning activities and assessment items for related standards. Using the content standards, teams identified verbs and the noun phrases that follow each level on either on Bloom's Taxonomy or the Hess Cognitive Rigor Matrix (see Figure 8.14).

The Hess Cognitive Rigor Matrix (2013) helped the teams identify a Depth of Knowledge (DOK) for each of the unwrapped and prioritized standards. Teams learned to create matching assessment items and related learning activities.

Every Architect Knows What to Do with the Right Tools

At the beginning of each unit of instruction, teachers administered the common assessment and then analyzed the data. Teams examined student work and made

Figure 8.14. Hess Cognitive Rigor Matrix

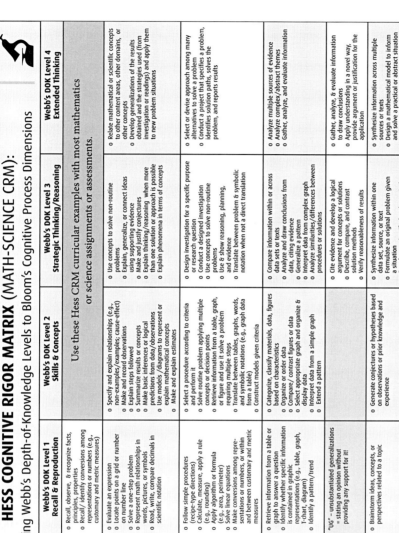

TOOL 2

HESS COGNITIVE RIGOR MATRIX (MATH-SCIENCE CRM):
Applying Webb's Depth-of-Knowledge Levels to Bloom's Cognitive Process Dimensions

Revised Bloom's Taxonomy	Webb's DOK Level 1 Recall & Reproduction	Webb's DOK Level 2 Skills & Concepts	Webb's DOK Level 3 Strategic Thinking/Reasoning	Webb's DOK Level 4 Extended Thinking
		Use these Hess CRM curricular examples with most mathematics or science assignments or assessments.		
Remember Retrieve knowledge from long-term memory, recognize, recall, locate, identify	o Recall, observe, & recognize facts, principles, properties o Recall/ identify conversions among representations or numbers (e.g., customary and metric measures)			
Understand Construct meaning, clarify, paraphrase, represent, translate, illustrate, give examples, classify, categorize, summarize, generalize, infer a logical conclusion), predict, compare/contrast, match like ideas, explain, construct models	o Evaluate an expression o Locate points on a grid or number on number line o Solve a one-step problem o Represent math relationships in words, pictures, or symbols o Read, write, compare decimals in scientific notation	o Specify and explain relationships (e.g., non-examples/examples; cause-effect) o Make and record observations o Explain steps followed o Summarize results or concepts o Make basic inferences or logical predictions from data/observations o Use models /diagrams to represent or explain mathematical concepts o Make and explain estimates	o Use concepts to solve non-routine problems o Explain, generalize, or connect ideas using supporting evidence o Make and justify conjectures o Explain thinking/reasoning when more than one solution or approach is possible o Explain phenomena in terms of concepts	o Relate mathematical or scientific concepts to other content areas, other domains, or other concepts o Develop generalizations of the results obtained and the strategies used (from investigation or readings) and apply them to new problem situations
Apply Carry out or use a procedure in a given situation; carry out (apply to) a familiar task), or use (apply) to an unfamiliar task	o Follow simple procedures (recipe-type directions) o Calculate, measure, apply a rule (e.g., rounding) o Apply algorithm or formula (e.g., area, perimeter) o Solve linear equations o Make conversions among representations or numbers, or within and between customary and metric measures	o Select a procedure according to criteria and perform it o Solve routine problem applying multiple concepts or decision points o Retrieve information from a table, graph, or figure and use it solve a problem requiring multiple steps o Translate between tables, graphs, words, and symbolic notations (e.g., graph data from a table) o Construct models given criteria	o Design investigation for a specific purpose or research question o Conduct a designed investigation o Use concepts to solve non-routine problems o Use & show reasoning, planning, and evidence o Translate between problem & symbolic notation when not a direct translation	o Select or devise approach among many alternatives to solve a problem o Conduct a project that specifies a problem, identifies solution paths, solves the problem, and reports results
Analyze Break into constituent parts, determine how parts relate, differentiate between relevant-irrelevant, distinguish, focus, select, organize, outline, find coherence, deconstruct	o Retrieve information from a table or graph to answer a question o Identify whether specific information is contained in graphic representations (e.g., table, graph, T-chart, diagram) o Identify a pattern/trend	o Categorize, classify materials, data, figures based on characteristics o Organize or order data o Compare / contrast figures or data o Select appropriate graph and organize & display data o Interpret data from a simple graph o Extend a pattern	o Compare information within or across data sets or texts o Analyze and draw conclusions from data, citing evidence o Generalize a pattern o Interpret data from complex graph o Analyze similarities/differences between procedures or solutions	o Analyze multiple sources of evidence o Analyze complex/abstract themes o Gather, analyze, and evaluate information
Evaluate Make judgments based on criteria, check, detect inconsistencies or fallacies, judge, critique	o "UG" – unsubstantiated generalizations = stating an opinion without providing any support for it!		o Cite evidence and develop a logical argument for concepts or solutions o Describe, compare, and contrast solution methods o Verify reasonableness of results	o Gather, analyze, & evaluate information to draw conclusions o Apply understanding in a novel way, provide argument or justification for the application
Create Reorganize elements into new patterns/structures, generate, hypothesize, design, plan, produce	o Brainstorm ideas, concepts, or perspectives related to a topic	o Generate conjectures or hypotheses based on observations or prior knowledge and experience	o Synthesize information within one data set, source, or text o Formulate an original problem given a situation o Develop a scientific/mathematical model for a complex situation	o Synthesize information across multiple sources or texts o Design a mathematical model to inform and solve a practical or abstract situation

© Karin K. Hess (2009, updated 2013). Hess Cognitive Rigor Matrix (CRM) in Local Assessment Toolkit. Permission to use only with full citation. khess@nciea.org or kar_hes@msn.com

Source: © Hess, Karin K. (2009, updated 2013). Hess Cognitive Rigor Matrix in *Linking Research with Practice: A Local Assessment Toolkit to Guide School Leaders.* Used with author's permission.

inferences about student answers. The inferences helped teachers identify common instructional strategies that would address student needs.

It All Leads Back to Student Learning

Teacher teams often model the instructional strategies for one another to ensure that they create similar learning experiences for all of their students. During the unit, teams paid careful attention to their questioning strategies. Teacher teams used DOK question stems across the Hess Cognitive Rigor Matrix (2013). At the end of the unit, the teacher teams administered the same common assessment. Again, they analyzed the data and looked for strengths and weaknesses to create a plan of action for their students. Teacher teams celebrated successes. Students as well as teachers were able to identify their strengths and weaknesses in relation to the unit of instruction. Unwrapping standards, identifying DOK levels, and creating common assessments helped teachers connect standards, assessment, and instruction.

But just as important, this curricular and assessment work helped our system teachers come together and learn from one another. With the advent of the Common Core State Standards, we were all starting from "scratch," and we had to build our confidence level with new content, with new assessments, and with working with one another in more collaborative ways.

The uses of electronic tools helped keep our ideas moving forward and helped us track what was working and what was not. As a smaller community of learners, we were able to come together focusing on student work, our understanding of our own teaching and the standards that guided this work, and the impact that our instruction was having on students.

Bringing Leaders Deeper into the Fold of Teaching and Learning

We presented our work with common assessments and the Hess Cognitive Rigor Matrix (2013) to the principals and assistant principals in our school district as part of their professional learning. It was important for the leaders to know about the Hess Cognitive Matrix (2013) because they conduct numerous announced and unannounced classroom observations, they participate in system-wide walk-through observations, and they engage in grade-level and school improvement efforts. We wanted to ensure they were aware of how teachers in mathematics were using common assessments, framing questions, and engaging students in thinking mathematically.

Today, our discussions and the collaboration continues, our teachers are coaching one another, engaging in conversations, and keeping our collective focus on students and their learning.

Case Summary

Through a coherent plan across the system, the teachers in the Clarke County School District have a common understanding of the language of the standards, what the standards look like in practice, and they have colleagues to collaborate with as they develop lessons, develop common formative assessments, assess student results, and rework instructional materials and strategies. School leaders who do classroom observations were engaged in learning about common assessments and the Hess Cognitive Rigor Matrix (2013) so they could support teachers in this ongoing work. The professional learning was pervasive, ongoing, and was adapted to the needs of teachers based on the needs of students.

Chapter Summary

Examining student work is the type of professional development that is directly related to student and teacher learning and is, perhaps, one of the strongest forms of job-embedded learning opportunities that teachers can engage. Coupled with coaching, peer observations, action research, and other forms of collaborative and reflective learning activities, examining student works holds great promise for making a difference in student and teacher learning. Looking ahead, Chapter 9 examines the windows of opportunity that digital learning environments have opened for professional development.

Suggested Readings

Brady, L., & McColl, L. (2010). *Test less assess more: A K–8 guide to formative assessments*. New York, NY: Routledge.

Venables, D. R. (2011). *The practice of authentic PLCs: A guide to effective teacher teams*. Thousand Oaks, CA: Corwin Press.

Wylie, E. C., Gullickson, A. R., Cummings, K. E., Egelson, P. E., Noakes, L. A., Norman, K.M., & Veeder, S.A. (2012). *Improving formative assessment practice to empower student learning*. Thousand Oaks, CA: Corwin Press.

9 Innovative Digital Learning Opportunities Support Professional Development

In This Chapter . . .

♦ Digital Learning Environments

♦ Synchronous and Asynchronous Environments

♦ Professional Learning Networks (PLNs)

♦ Case from the Field

♦ Cultivate Online Learning Environments

♦ Digital Tools to Support Collaborative Professional Development

♦ Case from the Field

♦ Chapter Summary

♦ Suggested Readings

Throughout this book, purposeful connections to digital learning environments have been made to help adults make the same leaps in learning as their students. We have examined some ways that digital tools, applications, and platforms support innovative approaches to extend teacher development. Job-embedded learning and what constitutes effective professional development do not change because of technology.

There are fully online professional development offerings, self-paced courses, and massive open online courses (MOOCs), and these types of professional learning opportunities certainly have a space in a digital learning community. There are other more immediate and accessible tools and platforms encapsulated within the school's broadband width, resources such as digital applications and hand-held devices, and hardware that support in-house professional development as well as daily, job-embedded learning opportunities for teachers.

Digital Learning Environments—A National Plan, Influence, Recommendations, Standards

In many ways, technology is pushing the learning boundaries for teachers related to when and how they learn from their work. On a national stage, technology has been a topic of high interest related to student and teacher learning. For teachers, the interest centers on professional development so that they can model learning to their students, and the key reports, recommendations, and standards align in their suggestions about professional development and the uses of technology to support teacher learning (Beglau *et al.*, 2011; Killion, 2013b; ISTE/NETS-S, 2008; US Department of Education, 2010).

The National Educational Technology Plan (2010)

In 2010, the US Department of Education, Office of Educational Technology, released the report, *Transforming American education: Learning powered by technology*, which contained the National Educational Technology Plan and its recommendations. Three important points were made about the interconnected relationship between learning, teaching, and experiences in a digital environment:

♦ Learning depends on effective teaching, and we need to focus on extended teams of connected educators with different roles who collaborate within schools and across time and distance and who use technology resources and tools to augment human talent.

♦ Effective teaching is an outcome of preparing and continually training teachers and leaders to guide the type of learning we want in our schools.

♦ Making engaging learning experiences and resources available to all learners anytime and anywhere requires state-of-the-art infrastructure, which includes technology, people, and processes that ensure continuous access. (p. 5)

Making the connection to professional learning in a digital learning environment, the US Office of Educational Technology (2010), strongly urges:

Episodic and ineffective professional development is replaced by professional learning that is collaborative, coherent, and continuous and that blends more effective in-person courses and workshops with the expanded opportunities, immediacy, and convenience enabled by online environments full of resources and opportunities for collaboration. (p. xii)

Goal 3.0, Teaching: Prepare and Connect, is presented with two of its five goals related to technology given their relative importance to professional development (see Figure 9.1).

Teachers who connect learning, teaching, and experiences in digital ways enhance their own learning while being able to communicate, interact, and LEARN

**Figure 9.1. Goal 3.0 Teaching: Prepare and Connect—
National Educational Technology Plan**

3.0 Teaching: Prepare and Connect

Professional educators will be supported individually and in teams by technology that connects them to data, content, resources, expertise, and learning experiences that enable and inspire more effective teaching for all learners.

To meet this goal, we recommend the following actions:

3.1 Expand opportunities for educators to have access to technology-based content, resources, and tools where and when they need them.

Today's technology enables educators to tap into resources and orchestrate expertise across a school district or university, a state, the nation, and even around the world. Educators can discuss solutions to problems and exchange information about best practices in minutes, not weeks or months. Today's educators should have access to technology-based resources that inspire them to provide more engaging and effective learning opportunities for each and every student.

3.2 Leverage social networking technologies and platforms to create communities of practice that provide career-long personal learning opportunities for educators within and across schools, preservice preparation and in-service education institutions, and professional organizations.

Social networks can be used to provide educators with career-long personal learning tools and resources that make professional learning timely and relevant as well as an ongoing activity that continually improves practice and evolves their skills over time. Online communities should enable educators to take online courses, tap into experts and best practices for just-in-time problem solving, and provide platforms and tools for educators to design and develop resources with and for their colleagues.

Source: US Department of Education, Office of Educational Technology. The National Education Technology Plan. (2010, pp. 49–50).

(emphasis added by author) in different ways with their immediate colleagues, their students, and others in professional learning networks as depicted in Figure 9.2.

Influence—Policy to Aspirations in Practice

Killion (2013b) poignantly speaks of the need for high-quality professional development complemented by technology, but note the caveat in the last line:

> Technology creates significant opportunities for more focused professional learning, especially when it is effectively integrated into a comprehensive system for professional learning; provides easy access to content that is relevant to individual, team, school, district, and state goals; and includes high-quality content, application of learning within the work setting, and

Figure 9.2. Connecting Learning, Teaching, and Experiences to LEARN in Digital Ways

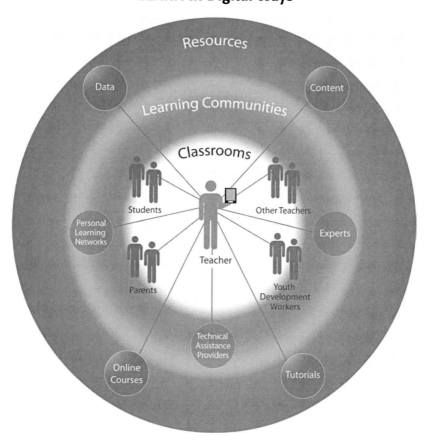

Source: US Department of Education, Office of Educational Technology. The National Education Technology Plan. (2010, p. 40).

constructive feedback and support over time to refine implementation of learning. It is evident that not all technology-enhanced professional learning meets these criteria. (p. 4)

Recommendations—Getting to Job-Embedded Professional Learning in a Digital Environment

In their 2011 report, the International Society for Technology in Education (ISTE) brought forward several issues related to professional development and the uses of technology (Beglau *et al.*, 2011). ISTE recommend a three-pronged methodology for professional development for a digital learning environment that embraces:

◆ an effective coaching model;

◆ online communities for greater collaborative idea sharing; and

◆ a fully embedded use of technology. (p. 4)

From a school and system perspective, this three-pronged methodology is important for two very important reasons related to professional development:

1. This methodology, if integrated in its totality as a support, becomes a digital peer coaching model that if feedback loops were made more explicit would potentially emerge as a promising practice to implement in its totality.

2. Teachers need to model digital citizenship skills and have the same degree of fluency across multiple mediums to advance digital-age learning in the very same ways as students are expected to as explicated in the ISTE National Educational Technology Standards for Students (NETS-S). The ISTE/NETS-S call for students to have a high degree of fluency, communication, and application of technology across multiple mediums to advance digital-age learning as illustrated in Figure 9.3.

ISTE/NETS-S Standards

Figure 9.3. ISTE-National Educational Technology Standards for Students (NETS-S)

1. Creativity and Innovation: Students demonstrate creative thinking, construct knowledge, and develop innovative products and processes using technology.
2. Communication and Collaboration: Students use digital media and environments to communicate and work collaboratively, including at a distance, to support individual learning and contribute to the learning of others.
3. Research and Information Fluency: Students apply digital tools to gather, evaluate, and use information.
4. Critical Thinking, Problem Solving, and Decision Making: Students use critical thinking skills to plan and conduct research, manage projects, solve problems, and make informed decisions using appropriate digital tools and resources.
5. Digital Citizenship: Students understand human, cultural, and societal issues related to technology and practice legal and ethical behavior.
6. Technology Operations and Concepts: Students demonstrate a sound understanding of technology concepts, systems, and operations.

Source: ISTE-National Educational Technology Standards for Students (NETS-S) www.iste.org/standards/standards-for-students/nets-student-standards-2007

Synchronous and Asynchronous Environments

Although examined in Chapter 2 in relation to the adult learner, there are two types of learning environments: 1) synchronous and 2) asynchronous. Both synchronous and asynchronous environments serve a purpose and add value to job-embedded learning opportunities.

Synchronous learning environments allow people to work together at the same time ("real time"). For example, teachers in the state could gather to hear a guest speaker give a presentation. Slides could be shown or a videoclip. Opportunity for open chat over the web (web-conferencing) could be available. Locally, 3rd-Grade teachers across the district meet to discuss common formative assessments in mathematics related to the Common Core with the district mathematics coach moderating with the assistance of grade-level leaders at each site.

In *asynchronous learning environments*, people do not participate with one another at the same time. Interaction occurs when it is convenient using social networks to post comments, responses, ideas (e.g., Facebook, Twitter), email individually or by list-serv (group), and use discussion boards, for example. Often, teachers will work on group documents in between team meetings using a common storage space such as Google Docs. This type of collaborative work often trickles to off hours.

Professional Learning Networks (PLNs)

The strength of online Professional Learning Networks is that they allow any-time communication, decrease isolation, support the exchange of ideas, and accommodate teacher availability (Duncan-Howell, 2010). A PLN includes the people we learn from and share with using a digital platform such as Facebook, Twitter, a blog, discussion forums, chat rooms, resource rooms and repositories, etc. PLNs provide a safety net for teachers, and Meyers and colleagues (2009) report:

1. Networks connect teachers to one another, removing them from the isolation inherent in their work.

2. Networks help teachers rediscover the value of their work, increasing their self-esteem and self-efficacy.

3. Networks provide teachers with the skills they need outside the classroom to advocate for what they need inside their classrooms.

4. Networks help teachers deal productively with the many frustrations inherent in teaching.

5. Networks inspire teachers to action. (p. 14)

Professional learning networks promote *social and collaborative learning*.

PLNs Promote Knowledge-Building and Sharing through Communities of Practice

Through the free exchange of ideas, members in a community of practice share knowledge, promote learning, and build expertise in a particular area (Lave & Wenger, 1991; Wenger, 1998). How to transfer and apply this new knowledge builds capacity for the individual and the group (Chesbro & Boxler, 2010). Cambridge, Kaplan, and Suter (2006) share communities of practice that fill professional learning needs as explained in Figure 9.4.

The following Case from the Field illustrates how Professional Learning Networks can support teacher professional development in the early years of teaching.

Figure 9.4. The Importance of Communities of Practice

Communities of Practice are important because they. . .

- **Connect people** who might not otherwise have the opportunity to interact, either as frequently or at all.

- **Provide a shared context** for people to communicate and exchange information, stories, and personal experiences in a way that builds understanding and insight.

- **Enable dialogue** between people who come together to explore new possibilities, solve challenging problems, and create new, mutually beneficial opportunities.

- **Stimulate learning** by serving as a vehicle for authentic communication, mentoring, coaching, and self-reflection.

- **Capture and diffuse existing knowledge** to help people improve their practice by providing a forum to identify solutions to common problems and a process to collect and evaluate best practices.

- **Introduce collaborative processes** to groups and organizations as well as between organizations to encourage the free flow of ideas and exchange of information.

- **Help people organize** around purposeful actions that deliver tangible results.

- **Generate new knowledge** to help people transform their practice to accommodate changes in needs and technologies.

Source: Cambridge, Kaplan, & Suter (2006, p. 1) (emphasis added).

Case from the Field

Professional Learning Networks Support Teachers

Miss Christina Spears, Science Teacher, North Oconee High School; Dr. Philip Brown, Principal, Oconee County School District, GA

Case Organizer

The following Case from the Field illustrates how digital tools and platforms can support new teachers through the reflections of Miss Christina Spears, now a seventh-year veteran science teacher at North Oconee High School.

The Context of North Oconee High School

North Oconee High School (NOHS) is a growing rural high school in Northeast Georgia. The school started in the 2013/14 school year with over 1,100 students. The faculty consists of over 60 teachers, 3 counselors, 3 assistant principals, and 1 principal. Our motto at North Oconee is "Teach, Inspire, Transform, And Nurture Students (Titans)." North Oconee is one of two high schools in Oconee County. The school district is located outside of Athens, Georgia and a large percentage of community members in Oconee County are employed by the University of Georgia. The school lacks diversity, with over 80 percent of the school being White. The next largest subgroup is Hispanic, making up almost 10 percent of the student population. The free and reduced lunch student population has risen from 16 to 22 percent over the past three years.

Based on Georgia's College and Career Readiness Performance Index (CCRPI), in 2013 NOHS was recognized as the top comprehensive high school in the state of Georgia. The school's Advanced Placement program has grown by over 300 percent over the past three years with over 50 percent of last year's seniors taking and passing an AP exam with a score of 3 or higher. The graduation rate at North Oconee High School is consistently over 90 percent with more than 80 percent of the graduating seniors attending a four-year institution.

External "Safety Net"

As one of many "millennial" teachers, Miss Spears shared that the connection to digital Professional Learning Networks supported the development of her outlook on teaching in a positive way. Miss Spears recalled:

> During my first year of teaching, I remember feeling so alone with the content and trying to do everything myself.

Miss Spears read posts by other teachers to learn what worked and what did not work with a particular lab activity or to glean advice and troubleshooting techniques for her own teaching practices. Miss Spears expressed that online chats and professional learning communities were akin to a "safety net" to help her solve problems as they arose in the classroom. Miss Spears reported that she typically viewed and posted to the discussion boards from the online community at least once a week and even on weekends at her convenience. She expressed an appreciation for the opportunity to share fears and concerns, problem-solve, and to receive or share support and positive feedback from colleagues and experts.

Fast-Forward—Moving along the Career Continuum

Now as a more experienced teacher, Miss Spears continues to express her excitement at having the opportunity to connect with a diverse base of experts from New England to Hawaii and the opportunity to interact with the "best teachers in New York" to discuss AP Biology curriculum development and assessment issues by simply logging on to a free web resource. "I can use technology to share documents, test questions, activities, and troubleshoot issues with a group of my colleagues. This group can be local to the surrounding area or in different states, which is what makes the uses of social networks so appealing," according to Miss Spears.

Case Summary

Miss Spears was resolute that her use of technology helped to remind her that teaching is about engaging in a lifetime of learning. Miss Spears explained that she felt that belonging to a PLN supported her endeavor to learn how to teach the students in the best way possible, and she shared wisdom gained from her experiences, "If we look at things the same way every time and never change what we do, then we are not going to reach our students."

Cultivate Online Learning Environments

Schools are filled with incredibly talented teachers who are creative, specialize in learning, and they have the *talent*, the *resources* (even the most rudimentary technology will suffice), *internet connectivity*, *servers*, and other devices to bring forward online learning environments to:

◆ support and extend face-to-face meetings;

◆ increase efficiency (start the process of reviewing student work samples);

◆ give feedback to draft formative assessments;

◆ store work to create a public source of knowledge and artifacts;

◆ blog about a common curricular issue to share ideas, reflect about student work; and

◆ post results about action research.

The Opportunities Are Endless

My thinking about digital learning environments has been influenced greatly by Dr. Philip Lanoue, Superintendent of the Clarke County School District. Dr. Lanoue, recently recognized as one of the Top 50 Technological Innovators in Education by the Center for Digital Education and in the journal, *Converge*, shared that with the level of sophistication with which our students enter schools, "we need to get the kids to the starting line, and let them go." In the same breath, Dr. Lanoue noted seriously the need to support teacher development in using digital learning tools so that "they and their students will grow through the experiences of using technology to learn, together."

Keep All Teachers Engaged

Given overall demographic data, teachers span the career stages (beginning teacher to teachers readying to retire). It's safe to surmise, our schools are filled with "Millennials," defined as people born after 1982, whom Lancaster (2010) reports are a highly collaborative generation, and:

♦ They've worked on team projects from middle school through college.

♦ They see technology not simply as a tool for getting things done, but as the basis for conducting their lives.

♦ They can share ideas and opinions, conduct research, learn best practices and connect with colleagues. To be cut off from these opportunities in a profession that is already somewhat isolating might seem too high a price to pay.

♦ They are accustomed to accessing a much wider world.

♦ Websites like Facebook, MySpace, and LinkedIn provide Millennials with more than just ways to chat with friends and post photos. (p. 14)

The message is clear, technology can support professional development for teachers, teams, and schools to learn from their individual and collective work. More information about adult learners can be examined in Chapter 2.

Digital Tools to Support Collaborative Professional Development

There are numerous digital tools to support teacher professional development through co-planning, studying student work, analyzing the results of benchmarks and common formative assessments, etc. No digital tool will ever replace the value of face-to-face communication with peers. No tool can magically make a person a "reflective practitioner," and no tool can be just picked up and used with fidelity the first time. However, Beglau *et al.* (2011) spoke persuasively about the power of social media tools and the supports that can be offered to job-embedded learning.

Trends in using social media tools, Internet transmitted voice and video communication, and blogging support informal learning and strengthen human connections. These same forms of learning and community building lend themselves well to focused, job- embedded, professional learning. By combining what we know about effective professional learning with trends for using technology for informal community building and learning, a sustainable ecosystem will form: highly effective, engaging, and relevant environments for professional learning that were not possible before the rise of readily available access to information and communication technology. (p. 4)

Coaching and other types of follow-up support, either face-to-face or online in a professional learning network, are highly desirable.

In a perfect world, teachers would embrace digital tools to keep discussions going in between meetings, keep private blogs to reflect on practice, construct a professional e-portfolio, and reach out to a larger audience of experts to augment learning at the site from the work of teaching. These learning opportunities, when amassed, can draw from some of the richest and most recent resources from within the site and beyond.

Start Slow and Be Deliberate

The tools that are described here are illustrative of the many digital tools that are available to support teachers. For digital natives, they might appear simplistic, but simple is sometimes better! Blogs, wikis, Twitter, Facebook, and other electronic tools and platforms have common features that support professional learning, some in different ways. In general, the platforms promote social learning, the co-construction of knowledge, break the patterns of isolation, and connect like-minded people.

Blog

A blog can be used to reflect on experiences, to keep discussions going, to connect with others to ask questions, to seek counsel, to get feedback, etc. The power of the blog is that one can go back and reflect on posts made by others. Hyperlinks, audio podcasts, and videostreams can also be added to blogs. Tips for starting a blog, joining a Professional Learning Network (PLN), and other digital professional learning materials can be found at EduBlogs at http://teacherchallenge.edublogs.org/2013/08/13/step-1-set-up-your-blog/

Wiki

A wiki is a multifaceted web-based tool that can host text that may be edited (if a person has permission). Text may contain hyperlinks to documents, videos, and other items. The discussion feature allows participants to share comments and to engage in discussion about the document, leaving a history of commentary. Wikis can be used as a follow-up to professional development where participants can view materials, engage in discussion, and create new materials (Sandifer, 2011).

Twitter

Users can Tweet messages up to 140 characters; they must be registered to reply to a Tweet but can read-only if not registered. Teachers follow thought leaders and other experts in the field to gain insights about teaching, seek information, and establish working relationships.

Podcasts

Podcasts are digital files posted on a website that are downloaded on portable media (computer) as rich site summary (RSS) feeds that can be subscribed to for future podcasts. Teachers can make podcasts of their reflections and share them to the members of their Professional Learning Networks, subscribers to their blogs, etc.

Facebook

Individuals or groups join to interact with others, and exchange information, posts, photos, videos, etc.

Pinterest

Massive storage area to "pin" articles, photos, lesson plans, videos, or any other items of interest. What is stored can be shared with others, and re-posted on other social media sites such as Facebook.

There are certainly more digital tools and platforms, but for the purposes of this book, the social and online tools that foster collaboration and reflection have already been examined (e.g., see Chapter 2). The final Case from the Field examines how one principal not only uses technology to "flip" faculty meetings but also other digital tools to support teacher development.

Case from the Field

Flipping Professional Development—Modeling Learning on Demand

Dr. Philip Brown, Principal, North Oconee High School, Oconee County School District, GA

Case Organizer

The case shows the power of modeling against the backdrop of how "flipping" can support the delivery of professional development that is more responsive to time, the need for adult learners to be more engaged in active work that holds relevance, and job-embedded opportunities with immediate applicability to the work of teaching.

In the Beginning. . .

"Do you not find our faculty meetings boring?" This was a question posed as I completed the first semester of being principal at NOHS. Administrative team members shared that our teachers were not engaged and nearing resentment having to attend faculty meetings. To gather data on their perceptions of faculty meetings, a survey was developed to seek input to rectify this situation.

Figure 9.5. **Six-Question Survey Administered to Teachers at North Oconee High School**

1. On a scale of 1 to 5, with 1 being not engaged and 5 being highly engaged, how engaged are you in our faculty meetings?

2. On a scale of 1 to 5, with 1 being not differentiated and 5 being extremely differentiated, how differentiated do you find the content in our faculty meetings?

3. If you were the principal, would you change our faculty meetings? If so, how would you change them?

4. Do we need faculty meetings?

5. If the administration emailed you the information covered in a faculty meeting, would you read the email?

6. Should faculty meetings be geared toward professional learning or dissemination of information?

Message Heard, Loud and Clear

The faculty members spoke clearly, and the overall sentiment was that if the information could be communicated through email, allow email to be the modality of communication. Teachers wanted faculty meetings that had 1) a purpose, 2) a focus on professional development, 3) input about the content of the meetings, and 4) a consistent mechanism to give content input.

The Start of Something New

From the survey results and the open-ended responses, a Professional Learning Leadership Team was formed and consisted of an assistant principal and a few teacher-leaders, with the goal of creating a *professional learning plan* for the next semester that would carry through to the next year. We wanted to have a short- and long-term view of what was needed to build a sense of *coherence*.

The objectives of the Professional Learning Leadership Team were 1) to look at our strengths and weaknesses, 2) to develop a professional learning plan that would address areas where we needed to improve, and 3) to review the pedagogical practices within the professional learning plan. In other words, what types of activities and what learning modalities did our teachers want to ensure their engagement in professional learning were the inseparable questions.

The group gathered and reviewed data from walk-throughs, discipline, standardized assessments, and school climate surveys. The team contacted faculty about their individual professional learning needs. We wanted teachers to tell us how they wanted the content delivered and the times that worked best for them.

Needed—Differentiated Content and Approaches for EACH Teacher

Based on the data, the Professional Learning Leadership Team communicated the need for a mix of morning and afternoon faculty meetings, lunch-and-learn seminars, professional learning during faculty meetings. The teachers needed and wanted a differentiated look at providing learning experiences. For the differentiated approach, the goal was to look at each teacher as an individual and work with the individual to determine his or her needs based on content areas, interests, strengths, weaknesses, and short- and long-term goals. For example, if a teacher wanted to explore iPad use in mathematics, we worked with this teacher to design professional development that would help him/her grow in this area. If another teacher wanted help with classroom management, we looked for seminars, resources, and mentors in the building and district that would help the teacher in this area.

Needed—Faculty Meetings as Learning Opportunities

The Professional Learning Leadership Team worked collaboratively to develop a plan for organizing faculty meetings for the next semester. The big discussion began with the question, "What are the learning objectives we would like to accomplish during the next semester?" After identifying the objectives and the content, we discussed activities, readings, technologies, and overall communication necessary to plan faculty meetings. Discussions were based on the faculty survey, the summaries of the Professional Learning Leadership Team, and the informal exchanges between teachers and the principal.

Learning, Not Time, IS the Driver of Faculty Meetings

The primary objective was to create an environment where the focus was on adult learning and not a calendar of faculty meetings. We made a commitment that the learning needs of our teachers needed to drive our decisions instead of time and convenience being the leading factor in the decision-making process related to what we did at faculty meetings. This shift was a departure from the norm associated with the convenience to provide teachers with a list of faculty meeting dates at the beginning of the year. However, we wanted to move away from this model by thinking through what the adults needed to learn, what we could do to support this type of individualized and collective learning as the motivation for our monthly meeting schedule.

It's Flipping Time

We needed to change our approach, but, more importantly, we needed to *model* our instructional expectations with teachers. The result was what we would describe as flipped faculty meetings. At the time, we had three teachers who we had encouraged to try flipping their classrooms by providing a lecture through a video and using class time to work through problems or discuss the content. By flipping the class, teachers provide students with a video to watch outside of the classroom, while using class time to facilitate discussions and assist students in solving problems and issues. Teachers experimented with various programs for developing the videos based on their comfort levels.

The transition provided our school with the opportunity to redesign what and how we defined professional learning. For the first faculty meeting of the semester, our assistant principal recorded a voiceover PowerPoint presentation describing the newly adopted evaluation system from the state. The goal was for our assistant principal to provide teachers with an in-depth review of all documents included in the process. She was able to display these documents, as well as direct the teachers to certain highlights within the document, using a program named Screen Cast-o-matic. This program is one of a number of different programs that educators can use to create videos.

After completing the video, the administrative team emailed the video along with a list of guiding questions and asked faculty to review materials before the next meeting. The videos could be viewed by the faculty at their convenience. Our administrative team did not need to produce a video for some meetings because a video from the state department of education or an educational association was available to meet our needs. The length of the videos depends on the topic or topics being covered. Our goal is for the videos to be no longer than 20 minutes.

Faculty Meetings Are About Discussions

By allowing teachers to review the content before the faculty meeting, our meetings quickly developed into discussions focused on important concepts covered in the pre-viewed videos and associated materials. Faculty meetings are now interactive opportunities for teachers to discuss relevant issues related to the school and their classrooms. The feedback has been positive, noting that the conversations are rewarding. Flipping faculty meetings also allowed faculty meetings to be more fluid. We met some weeks; other weeks did not require a meeting.

The topics covered in the past semester included: student feedback, best practices in lesson hooks and closings, effectively integrating technology into the classroom, Common Core, and data teams. To review the Common Core, we asked teachers to review a video about how the Common Core State Standards were created. Then, teachers were asked to review their specific content areas and be ready to discuss at the next faculty meeting. During the faculty meeting, we provided each content area with an assignment and asked the group to determine if the assignment provided the rigor expected within the Common Core State Standards.

We overheard teachers arguing about the types of questions being asked of the students; others examined the relevance of the assignment to the lives of 15- and 16-year-olds. It was clear that we had flipped our faculty meetings from a time of "sit-and-get" to a time of questioning and discussing.

Video-Capture of Teaching Exemplars

We also used video to highlight effective practices within classrooms at NOHS. For example, our administrative team used our electronic devices to capture moments during classroom observations that could serve as examples for other faculty members to watch. This process improved faculty morale and our focus on collaboration. We have a bank of teaching clips to help our new teachers or teachers who might be struggling. We also use Twitter as a communication vehicle for sharing pictures and examples of best practices within our classrooms. Twitter provided us with an opportunity to share the excellent work of our teachers with the media, community, parents, students, and other teachers.

Show Us the Data!

Professional development is an area in which we collect a large amount of quantitative and qualitative data. Our belief is, why continue with a program if it is not helpful in developing our people? We gathered data before moving to this flipped model, as well as a semester after making the change. The data underscored that our faculty and staff support and appreciate the move to this new flipped model. The teachers appreciated our willingness to be vulnerable and to work through a new pedagogical approach. As administrators, the process helped us remember what it was like to be a teacher and plan activities that hopefully would end by meeting our learning objective. This small but simple reminder continued to assist our leadership team in looking for ways in which we could support our teachers.

Unintended Benefits

By using the flip model in professional learning, we found unintended benefits of creating the videos. During our planning meeting for our teacher induction program, we discovered that we could use the videos to help teachers with concepts covered the previous semester. We became more efficient by being able to provide the new teachers with essential information that has to be shared with all teachers (e.g., teacher evaluation system). The addition of the videos helped our administrative team save time, as well as share a consistent message with our veteran faculty and new faculty members about exemplars of quality teaching.

Lessons Learned and Future Directions

Our future professional learning plans will be comprised of flipped faculty meetings. We also plan to continue the process of providing professional learning that is differentiated based on the career stage and needs of the teacher with matching learning styles and preferences in mind as well as their individual needs in content areas, interests, strengths, weaknesses, and short- and long-term goals. For example, should a math teacher receive the same professional learning as a foreign-language teacher? I could make the argument for some concepts that the delivery should be the same. Conversely, it should be different at other times. We look forward to continue pushing back against traditional forms of faculty meetings, as well as professional development and learning to meet the needs of our teachers.

Flipping Professional Development Resources

1. *7 Steps to Flipped Professional Development*

   Retrieved from http://gettingsmart.com/2013/01/7-steps-to-flipped-professional-development/

2. *Flipped PD*

   Retrieved from https://sites.google.com/a/cloud.stillwater.k12.mn.us/flipped-pd/

Case Summary

The reorganization of professional development at this high school illustrates how one school approached making fundamental changes using feedback from teachers, involvement of multiple stakeholders, and a willingness to use technology and to individualize learning objectives for each teacher.

Chapter Summary

Technology has provided a rich digital learning environment for adults to extend professional learning beyond the confines of the buildings in which they teach. However, technology and its numerous digital tools offer great promise to enhance job-embedded learning as well. In many ways, technology is stretching our current understandings of the ways in which adults learn from their work during the day. However, technology is affording opportunities to teachers to extend making sense of their work after hours through engaging in Professional Learning Network mediums such as YouTube and Pinterest, following thought leaders on Twitter, reading and posting on blogs, and participating in other social media outlets. Technology will never replace face-to-face collaboration but will certainly add deeply to the ways in which teachers collaborate and learn with their peers and, by extension, their students. Chapter 10 leads us to closure of this book.

Suggested Readings

Killion, J. (2013). *Meet the promise of content standards: Tapping technology to enhance professional learning.* Oxford, OH: Learning Forward.

Meltzer, S. T. (2012). *Step-by-step: Professional development in technology.* New York, NY: Routledge.

Ross. J. D. (2011). *Online professional development: Design, deliver, succeed!* Thousand Oaks, CA: Corwin Press.

Sandifer, S. D. (2011). *Wikis for school leaders: Using technology to improve communication and collaboration.* New York, NY: Routledge.

Swanson, K. (2013). *Professional learning in the digital age: The educator's guide to user-generated learning.* New York, NY: Routledge.

Thompson, R., Kitchie, L., & Gagnon, R. (2011). *Constructing an online professional learning network for school unity and student achievement.* Thousand Oaks, CA: Corwin Press.

10 Taking the Fast Track at Your Own Speed

Looking back on the collaborative and reflective nature of professional development, this book brings forward several ideas that can support teachers as they take the fast track attending to their learning while embracing their own speed. Millennial or not, adult learners need, want, and deserve to travel at a rate, in a space, and with colleagues who can embrace learning from each other. Although there can be initial turbulence while learning to work with others, the mutual benefits in the long-run for students and teachers' own professional lives will outweigh any mild disequilibrium.

In a professional sense, there is one thing teachers never say farewell to—and that is learning. From the day you answered that call to be a teacher, you have learned from your students. It is the hope that this book helps you walk away with some ideas about your own learning and professional development. Theory and practice converge in this book to offer what I hope is a balanced perspective of job-embedded professional development bringing forward processes such as coaching to extend and deepen learning.

It is the hope that this book encourages you to insert yourself as a learner among your peers. Everyone brings knowledge, experience, and perspective. It is the hope that the lessons from the Cases from the Field have given firsthand glimpses of powerful examples of job-embedded learning illustrating that "homegrown" methods can meet teacher and student needs. The canned, one-size approach to professional development must become extinct because it serves no purpose, and it is woefully inadequate in meeting the complex challenges of teaching.

It is my hope that you have "take-aways" from reading this book and will come back to its pages often as a resource while taking the fast track learning at your own pace. Offered in no particular order, here are my top 10 take-aways from writing this book:

1. Teachers are adult learners. Self-directed learning promotes individual learning and can simultaneously enhance a) student learning, b) the needs of the school, grade, etc. In other words, teachers must become the primary architects of their continued professional learning, and this means they need the support, resources, and arrangements to do so.

2. We are pushing the boundaries of job-embedded learning in light of the backdrop of digital learning environments, platforms, and applications that influence the ways in which we learn. We are now connected by broadband width through Skype, a wiki, a blog, Twitter, or through

membership in a PLN. We have infinite tools to make our work more efficient in between meetings, to collaborate with peers in our own schools or across the globe.

3. Closely related, digital learning platforms are further blurring our understandings of job-embedded learning because as adults, teachers are taking advantage of online opportunities to collaborate with professionals about the work of teaching that is inextricably related to what occurs during the day but which occurs off hours via digital environments. What a wonderful problem to have—teachers learning more, every day from every available resource they have, when they have time!

4. Collaboration is an absolute necessity, and the time is ripe for job-embedded learning opportunities to be embraced. Think of the powerful learning teachers engage in when they examine student work, participate in action research, or observe a peer teach. Think of the tools that teachers have to communicate, share, and store information— now connect the dots in terms of knowledge, capacity, and human capital.

Job-embedded learning continues to get richer as the "take-aways" continue.

5. Coaching is one of the most valuable job-embedded professional development strategies that can be implemented to support any effort. Coaching is inclusive, comprehensive, and one of the very few professional development strategies to show increased transfer of practice the very next day in the classroom.

6. Conversations are the key drivers of building relationships, trust, and a sense of efficacy—the belief that teachers have in themselves and that they can accomplish the complex work required of teaching. However, conversations are important for another reason. It is through conversations that we can probe thinking—ours and our colleagues' about our practices, our products, and the results we are getting or why not in the classroom.

7. We need to create safe places where teachers can engage in work together—peers need each other and the social support to learn. The new work of teaching cannot thrive in an environment where peers are separated from one another.

8. There are numerous models and configurations of professional development and each one should be examined carefully and purposefully adapted to the needs of the school.

9. Take risks with learning—we ask our students to take risks every day. Think of the powerful message by modeling risk taking in front of students.

10. Champion your own learning as much as you do the learning of your students—then look at the connections between what you and your students can do together. Even more powerful learning, I strongly suspect, would occur as a result.

Regardless of what we take away from this book, we should agree that there is a sense of urgency for us to examine teachers' professional practices and opportunities for job-embedded learning. We are in a different place today, and tomorrow will be different. That is the only constant, and that is why we need to examine closely the work of teaching so that we can capitalize on that work and learn from it. That is the sum total of job-embedded learning.

References

Acheson, K., & Gall, M. (2011). *Clinical supervision and teacher development: Preservice and inservice applications* (6th ed.). New York, NY: Wiley.

Ainsworth, L. (2003). *Unwrapping the standards: A simple process to make standards manageable.* Englewood, CO: Advanced Learning Press.

Ainsworth, L., & Viegut, D. (2006). *Common formative assessments: How to connect standards-based instruction and assessment.* Thousand Oaks, CA: Corwin Press.

Allen, J. (2007). *Inside words: Tools for teaching academic vocabulary, grades 4–12.* Portland, ME: Stenhouse Publishers.

Archambault, L., Wetzel, K., Foulger, T. S., & Williams, M. K. (2010). Professional development 2.0: Transforming teacher education pedagogy with 21st century tools. *Journal of Digital Learning in Teacher Education, 27*(1), 4–11. Retrieved from www.eric.ed.gov/contentdelivery/servlet/ERICServlet?accno=EJ898518

Arnau, L. (2013). *Rules for observing peers' strengths.* Athens, GA: University of Georgia.

Arnold, N., & Paulus, T. (2010). Using a social networking site for experiential learning: Appropriating, lurking, modeling and community building. *The Internet and Higher Education, 13*(4), 188–196. doi: 10.1016/j.iheduc.2010.04.002

ATLAS. (n.d.). *ATLAS learning from student work.* The National School Reform Faculty/NSRF. Retrieved from http://www.nsrfharmony.org

Avalos, B. (2011). Teacher professional development in "Teaching and Teacher Education" over ten years. *Teaching and Teacher Education: An International Journal of Research and Studies, 27*(1), 10–20. doi:10.1016/j.tate.2010.08.007

Bandura, A. (2006). Toward a psychology of human agency: Perspectives on psychological science. *Association for Psychological Science, 1*(2), 164–180. doi: 10.2307/40212163

Bandura, A. (1977). Self-efficacy: Toward a unifying theory of behavioral change. *Psychological Review, 84*(2), 191–215. doi:10.1037/0033–295X.84.2.191

Bangs, J., & Frost, D. (2012). *Teacher self-efficacy, voice, and leadership towards a policy framework for education international: A report on an international survey of the views of teachers and teacher union officials.* Cambridge: Cambridge University, Educational International Research Institute.

Beglau, M., Hare, J.C., Foltos, L., Gann, K., James, J., Jobe, H., . . . Smith, B. (2011). Technology, coaching, and community: Power partners for improved professional development in primary and secondary education. An ISTE White Paper, Special Conference Release. Retrieved from www.iste.org

Bhatta, T. R. (posted on Saturday, October 1, 2011). Self-directed professional development: Success mantra or a myth? Blog post at http://neltachoutari.wordpress.com/2011/10/01/self-directed-professional-development-success-mantra-or-a-myth/

Birchak, B., Connor, C., Crawford, K. M., Kahn, L., Kaser, S., Turner, S., & Short, K. G. (1998). *Teacher study groups: Building community through dialogue and reflection.* Urbana, IL: National Council of Teachers of English.

Blankenstein, A. M., Houston, P. D., & Cole, R. W. (2008). *Sustaining professional development.* Thousand Oaks, CA: Corwin Press.

Bloom, B. S. (Ed.). (1956). *Taxonomy of educational objectives: The classification of educational goals.* New York, NY: Longman.

Bold, C. (2011). Transforming practice through critical reflection. In C. Bold (Ed.) *Supporting learning and teaching* (pp. 189–202) (2nd ed.). Abingdon, Oxon: Routledge.

Borko, H. (2004). Professional development and teacher learning: Mapping the terrain. *Educational Researcher, 33*(8), 3–15. doi: 10.3102/0013189X033008003

Brady, L., & McColl, L. (2010). *Test less assess more: A K–8 guide to formative assessments.* New York, NY: Routledge.

Brookfield, S. D. (1995). *Becoming a critically reflective teacher.* San Francisco: Jossey-Bass.

Burton, E. P. (2012). Student work products as a teaching tool for nature of science pedagogical knowledge: A professional development project with in-service secondary science teachers. *Teaching and Teacher Education, 29*(2013), 156–166. doi: 10.1016/j.tate.2012.09.005

Calhoun, E. F. (1994). *How to use action research in the self-renewing school.* Alexandria, VA: Association for Supervision and Curriculum Development.

Cambridge, D., Kaplan, S., & Suter, V. (2006). *Community of practice design guide: A step-by-step guide for designing and cultivating communities of practice in higher education.* Virtual Communities of Practice Initiative. Washington, DC: EDUCAUSE Virtual Library. Retrieved from http://www.educause.edu/library/resources/community-practice-design-guide-step-step-guide-designing-cultivating-communities-practice-higher-education

Cayuso, E., Fegan, C., & McAlister, D. (2004). *Designing teacher study groups: A guide for success.* Gainesville, FL: Maupin House.

Chappuis, S., & Chappuis, J. (2007). The best value in formative assessment. *Educational Leadership, 65*(4), 14–19. Retrieved from http://www.ascd.org/publications/educational-leadership/dec07/vol65/num04/The-Best-Value-in-Formative-Assessment.aspx

Chesbro, P., & Boxler, N. (2010). Weaving the fabric of professional learning in the 21st century through technology. *Journal of Staff Development, 3*(1), 48–53. Retrieved from www.nsdc.org/news/articleDetails.cfm?articleID = 2017

Çimer, S. O., & Günay, P. (2012). Teachers' perceptions and practices of reflection. *International Journal of Educational Research and Technology, 3*(1), 52–60. Retrieved from www.soeagra.com/ijert.html

Cogan, M. (1973). *Clinical supervision.* Boston: Houghton-Mifflin.

Collay, M., Dunlap, D., Enloe, W., & Gagnon, G. W. (1998). *Learning circles: Creating conditions for professional development.* Thousand Oaks, CA: Corwin Press.

Costa, A. L., & Garmston, R. J. (2002). *Cognitive coaching: A foundation for Renaissance Schools* (2nd ed.). Norwood, MA: Christopher-Gordon.

Cranston, J. (2011). Relational trust: The glue that binds a professional learning community. *Alberta Journal of Educational Research, 57,* 59–72. Retrieved from http://ajer.synergiesprairies.ca/ajer/index.php/ajer/article/view/869

Creemers, B., Kyriakides, L., & Antoniou, P. (2013). *Teacher professional development for improving quality of teaching.* New York, NY: Springer.

Croft, A., Coggshall, J. G., Dolan, M., Powers, E., & Killion, J. (2010). *Job-embedded professional development: What it is, who is responsible, and how to get it done well.* Issue Brief Washington, DC: National Comprehensive Center for Teacher Quality.

Cross, K. P. (1992). *Adults as learners: Increasing participation and facilitating learning.* San Francisco, CA: Jossey-Bass.

Cunningham, D. (2011). *Improving teaching with collaborative action research.* Alexandria, VA: Association for Supervision and Curriculum Development.

Curry, M. W. (2008). Critical friends groups: The possibilities and limitations embedded in teacher professional communities aimed at instructional improvement and school reform. *Teachers College Record, 110*(4), 733–774. Retrieved from www. tcrecord.org/

Dalellew, T., & Martinez, Y. (1988). Andragogy and development: A search for the meaning of staff development. *Journal of Staff Development, 9*(3), 28–31. Retrieved from www.learningforward.org/publications/jsd#.UrY_BWRDuWE

Dana, N. F. (2013). *Digging deeper into action research: A teacher inquirer's field guide.* Thousand Oaks, CA: Corwin Press.

Danielson, C., & Abrutyn L. (1997). *An introduction to using portfolios in the classroom.* Alexandria, VA: Association for Supervision and Curriculum Development.

Darling-Hammond, L., & Falk, B. (2013). *Teacher learning: How student-performance assessments can support teacher learning.* Washington, DC: Center for American Progress.

Darling-Hammond, L., & McLaughlin, M. W. (2011). Policies that support professional development in an era of reform. *Phi Delta Kappan, 92*(6), 81–92. Retrieved from www.pdkintl.org/publications/kappan/

Darling-Hammond, L., & Richardson, N. (2009). Teacher learning: What matters? *Educational Leadership, 66*(5), 46–53. Retrieved from www.ascd.org/publications/educational-leadership/feb09/vol66/num05/Teacher-Learning@-What-Matters%C2%A2.aspx

Darling-Hammond, L., Wei, R. C., Andree, A., Richardson, N., & Orphanos, S. (2009). *Professional learning in the learning professional status report on teacher development in the U.S. and abroad: Technical report.* Dallas, TX: National Staff Development Council.

Derrington, M. L., & Angelle, P. S. (2013). Teacher leadership and collective efficacy: Connections and links. *International Journal of Teacher Leadership, 4*(1), 1–13. Retrieved from http://www.csupomona.edu/~education/ijtl/issues.shtml

Desimone, L. M. (2011). A primer on effective professional development. *Phi Delta Kappan, 92*(6), 68–71. doi: 10.2307/25822820

Dewey, J. (1938*). Education and experience.* New York, NY: Collier Macmillan Publishers.

Dozier, C. (2006). *Responsive literary coaching: Tools for creating and sustaining purposeful change.* Portland, ME: Stenhouse.

Drago-Severson, E. (2009). *Leading adult learning: Supporting adult development in our schools.* Thousand Oaks, CA: Corwin Press.

Duncan-Howell, J. (2010). Teachers making connections: Online communities as a source of professional learning. *British Journal of Educational Technology, 41*(2), 324–340. doi: 10.1111/j.1467–8535.2009.00953.x

Fairbanks, C. M., & LaGrone, D. (2006). Learning together: Constructing knowledge in a teacher research group. *Teacher Education Quarterly, 33*(3), 7–25. Retrieved from http://www.eric.ed.gov/contentdelivery/servlet/ERICServlet?accno=EJ795223

Florida Department of Education, Division of K–12 Public Schools, Bureau of School Improvement (2010). *A guide to implementing lesson study for district and school leadership teams in differentiated accountability schools.* Tallahassee, FL: Author.

Frost, D. (2011). *Supporting teacher leadership in 15 countries: The International Teacher Leadership project, Phase 1—A report.* Cambridge: Cambridge University—Leadership for Learning.

Fullan, M. (2008a). Leading change: A conversation with Michael Fullan. *In Conversation, 1*(1), 1–8. Ontario, CA: Ontario Ministry of Education. Retrieved from www.edu.gov. on.ca/eng/policyfunding/leadership/change.pdf

Fullan, M. (2008b). *The six secrets of change.* San Francisco, CA: Jossey-Bass.

Garmston, R. J. (1987). How administrators support peer coaching. *Educational Leadership, 44*(5), 18–26. Retrieved from http://www.ascd.org/publications/educational-leadership/feb87/vol44/num05/toc.aspx

Garmston, R. J., & von Frank, V. A. (2012). *Unlocking group potential to improve schools*. Thousand Oaks, CA: Corwin Press.

Glanz, J. (2005). Action research as instructional supervision: Suggestions for principals. *NASSP Bulletin, 89*(643), 17–27. doi: 10.1177/019263650508964303

Glanz, J. (2003). *Action research: An educational leader's guide to school improvement* (2nd ed.). Norwood, MA: Christopher-Gordon Publishers.

Goldhammer, R. (1969). *Clinical supervision: Special methods for the supervision of teachers*. New York, NY: Holt, Rinehart, & Winston.

Goodnough, K. (2011). *Taking action in science classroom through collaborative action research: A guide for educators*. Rotterdam, The Netherlands: Sense Publishers.

Gross Cheliotes L. M., & Reilly, M. A. (2012). *Opening the door to coaching conversations*. Thousand Oaks, CA: Corwin Press.

Gross Cheliotes L. M., & Reilly, M. A. (2010). *Coaching conversations: Transforming your school one conversation at a time*. Thousand Oaks, CA: Corwin Press.

Gulamhussein, A. (2013a). *Teaching the teachers: Effective professional development in an era of high stakes accountability*. Alexandria, VA: The Center for Public Education and the National School Boards Association.

Gulamhussein, A. (2013b). Professional development and the common core. July/August. *American School Board Journal*. Retrieved from http://www.asbj.com/MainMenuCategory/Archive/2013/August/Professional-Development-and-the-Common-Core.html?DID=285203

Guskey, T. R. (2000). *Evaluating professional development*. Thousand Oaks, CA: Corwin Press.

Guskey, T. R., & Yoon, K. S. (2009). What works in professional development? *Phi Delta Kappan, 90*(7), 495–500. doi: 10.2307/20446159

Hanley, M. (2009). Are you ready for informal learning? *Information Outlook, 13*(7), 12–14, 16–18. Retrieved from www.sla.org

Hendricks, C. C. (2012). *Improving schools through action research: A reflective practice approach* (3rd ed.). Boston, MA: Pearson.

Hendrickson, C. R. (2010). Preface: *The MetLife survey of the American teacher: Collaborating for student success*. New York, NY: Metropolitan Life Insurance Company.

Herman, J. L., Osmundson, E., & Dietel, R. (2010). *Benchmark assessments for improved learning* (AACC Policy Brief). Los Angeles, CA: University of California.

Hess, K. K. (2009, updated 2013). Hess cognitive rigor matrix in *Linking research with practice: A local assessment toolkit to guide school leaders*. Underhill, VT: self-published.

Ideapaint™ (2013). Millennial workplace trends survey: Corporate America begins to solve the Millennial paradox. Ashland, MA: Ideapaint™. Retrieved from ideapaint.com. Author.

iObservation® (n.d.). Supervising and supporting effective teachers in every classroom. Learning Sciences International. Retrieved from http://www.iobservation.com/

ISTE/NETS-S. (2008). *Standards for Teachers 2008*. Eugene, OR: International Society for Technology in Education. Retrieved from http://www.iste.org/standards/standards-for-teachers.

ISTE/NETS-S. (2007). *NETS-S for students 2007*. Eugene, OR: International Society for Technology in Education. Retrieved from http://www.iste.org/standards/standards-for-students/nets-student-standards-2007.

James, W. (n.d.). BrainyQuote.com. Retrieved April 5, 2014, from BrainyQuote.com website: http://www.brainyquote.com/quotes/quotes/w/williamjam107172.html

Javadi, M. H. M., Zadeh, N. D., Zandi, M., & Yavarian, J. (2012). Effect of motivation and trust on knowledge sharing and effect of knowledge sharing on employee's performance. *International Journal of Human Resource Studies, 2*(1), 210–222. doi: 10.5296/ijhrs.v2i1.1675

Joyce, B., & Showers, B. (2002). *Student achievement through staff development: Fundamentals of school renewal* (3rd ed.). Alexandria, VA: Association for Supervision and Curriculum Development.

Joyce, B., & Showers, B. (1982). The coaching of teaching. *Educational Leadership, 40*(1), 4–10. Retrieved from www.eric.ed.gov/contentdelivery/servlet/ERICServlet?accno= ED249593

Joyce, B., & Showers, B. (1981). Transfer of training: The contribution of "coaching." *Journal of Education, 163*(2), 163–172. Retrieved from www.eric.ed.gov/contentdelivery/ servlet/ERICServlet?accno=ED231035

Katzenmeyer, M., & Moller, G. (2009). *Awakening the sleeping giant: Helping teachers develop as leaders* (3rd ed.). Thousand Oaks, CA: Corwin Press.

Keay, J. K., & Lloyd, C. M. (2011). *Linking children's learning with professional learning: Impact, evidence and inclusive practices.* Rotterdam, The Netherlands. Sense Publishers.

Killion, J. (2013a). Tapping technology's potential. *Journal of Staff Development, 34*(1), 10–14. Retrieved from www.learningforward.org/publications/jsd/jsd-blog/ jsd/2013/03/08/february-2013-vol.-34-no.-1

Killion, J. (2013b). *Meet the promise of content standards: Tapping technology to enhance professional learning.* Oxford, OH: Learning Forward.

Killion, J., & Todnem, G. (1991). A process for personal theory building. *Educational Leadership, 48*(6), 14–17. Retrieved from www.ascd.org/publications/educational-leadership.aspx

Knight, J. (2007). *Instructional coaching: A partnership approach to improving instruction.* Thousand Oaks, CA: Corwin Press.

Knowles, M. S. (1975). *Self-directed learning: A guide for learners and teachers.* Englewood Cliffs, NJ: Prentice Hall.

Knowles, M. S., & Associates. (1984). *Andragogy in action: Applying modern principles of adult learning.* San Francisco, CA: Jossey-Bass.

Lancaster, L. C. (2010). Meeting millennial teachers on their own high-tech turf. *The School Administrator, 1*(67), 14–15. Retrieved from http://www.aasa.org/School AdministratorArticle.aspx?id=11036

Lave, J., & Wenger, E. (1991) *Situated learning.* Cambridge, UK: Cambridge University Press.

Law, V. (n.d.). BrainyQuote.com. Retrieved April 5, 2014, from BrainyQuote.com website: http://www.brainyquote.com/quotes/authors/v/vernon_law.html

Learning Forward (2012). *Standards for professional learning: Learning communities.* Oxford, OH: Learning Forward. Author. Retrieved from http://learningforward.org/ standards/learning-communities#.Up5Gt-Ilhrg

Learning Forward (2011). *Standards for professional learning.* Oxford, OH: Author.

Lewis, C., Perry, R., & Murata, A. (2006). How should research contribute to instructional improvement? The case of lesson study. *Educational Researcher, 35*(3), 3–14. doi:10.3102/0013189X035003003

Lick, D. W., & Murphy, C. U. (Eds.) (2007). *The whole-faculty study groups field-book: Lessons learned and best practices from classrooms, districts, and schools.* Thousand Oaks, CA: Corwin Press.

Malecki, C. K., & Demaray, M. K. (2003). What type of support do they need? Investigating student adjustment as related to emotional, informational, appraisal, and instrumental support. *School Psychology Quarterly, 18*(3), 231–252. doi:10.1521/ scpq.18.3.231.22576

Marsick, V., Watkins, K., & Lovin, B. (2012). Revisiting informal and incidental learning as a vehicle for professional learning and development. In C. Wise, P. Bradshaw, and M. Cartwright (Eds.), *Leading professional practice in education* (pp. 59–76). London: Sage Publications, The Open University.

Marzano, R. J. (2007). *The art and science of teaching: A comprehensive framework for effective instruction*. Alexandria, VA: Association for Supervision and Curriculum Development.

Marzano, R. J., Simms, J. A., Roy, T., Helflebower, T., & Warrick, P. (2013). *Coaching classroom instruction*. Bloomington, IN: Marzano Research Laboratory.

Maslow, A. H. (1954). *Motivation and personality*. New York, NY: Harper & Row.

McClelland, D.C. (1987). *Human motivation*. New York, NY: Cambridge University Press.

McDonald, J. (2001). Students' work and teachers' learning. In A. Lieberma, & L. Miller (Eds.) *Teachers caught in the action: Professional development that matters* (pp. 209–235). New York, NY: Teachers College Press.

Meltzer, S. T. (2012). *Step-by-step: Professional development in technology*. New York, NY: Routledge.

Mercer, S. H., Nellis, L. M., Martinez, R. S., & Kirk, M. (2011). Supporting the students most in need: Academic self-efficacy and perceived teacher support in relation to within-year academic growth. *Journal of School Psychology*, *49*(3), 323–338. doi: 10.1016/j.jsp.2011.03.006

Merriam, S. B., Caffarella, R. S., & Baumgartner, L. M. (2013). *Learning in adulthood: A comprehensive guide* (3rd ed.). E-Book. San Francisco, CA: Jossey-Bass.

MetLife (2010). *The MetLife survey of the American teacher: Collaborating for student success*. New York, NY: Metropolitan Life Insurance Company. Author.

Meyers, E., Paul, P. A., Kirkland, D. E., & Dana, N. F. (2009). *The power of teacher networks*. Thousand Oaks, CA: Corwin Press.

Mills, G. E. (2014). *Action research: A guide for the teacher researcher* (5th ed.). Boston, MA: Pearson.

Miranda, T. T. (2012). Lessons learned from transformational professional development. In M. Golden (Ed.), *Teaching and learning from the inside out: Revitalizing ourselves and our institutions* (pp. 77–88). New Direction for Teaching and Learning, Number 130, Summer. San Francisco, CA: Jossey-Bass.

Mizell, H. (2008). *Remarks of Hayes Mizell on July 12, 2008. Meeting of the National Staff Development Council's state affiliate leaders*. Retrieved from http://learningforward. org/publications#.U0L83lfLIXs

Murphy, C. U., & Lick, D. W. (2005). *Whole-faculty study groups: Creating professional learning communities that target student learning* (3rd ed.). Thousand Oaks, CA: Corwin Press.

National Governors Association Center for Best Practices, and Council of Chief State School Officers (2010a). Common core state standards. Washington, DC: National Governors Association Center for Best Practices and Council of Chief State School Officers. Authors. Retrieved from http://www.corestandards.org/the-standards

National Governors Association Center for Best Practices, & Council of Chief State School Officers (2010b). Common core state standards—Mathematics. Washington, DC: National Governors Association Center for Best Practices and Council of Chief State School Officers. Authors. Retrieved from http://www.corestandards.org/Math

National School Reform Faculty (2006). *Evolving glossary of NSRF terms*. Bloomington, IN: Harmony Education Center. Author. Retrieved from http://www.nsrfharmony. org/glossary.html#Critical_Friends_Groups

National School Reform Faculty at the Harmony Education Center and the Southern Maine Partnership (n.d.). *Southern Maine Partnership: Guide to good probing questions.* Retrieved from www.nsrfharmony.org/. Author.

Nidus, G., & Sadder, M. (2011). The principal as formative coach. *Educational Leadership, 69*(2), 30–35. Retrieved from http://www.ascd.org/publications/educational-leadership/oct11/vol69/num02/The-Principal-as-Formative-Coach.aspx

Nieto, S. (2009). From surviving to thriving. *Educational Leadership, 66*(5), 8–13. Retrieved from http://http://www.ascd.org/publications/educational-leadership.aspx

Nolan, J. F., Jr., & Hoover, L. A. (2011). *Teacher supervision evaluation: Theory in practice* (3rd ed.). New York, NY: John Wiley and Sons, Inc.

Northwest Regional Educational Laboratory (2005). Having another set of eyeballs: Critical friends groups. *Northwest Education, 11*(1), 7–8. Author. Retrieved from http://educationnorthwest.org/resource/1035

O'Neil, J. (1998). Constructivism—wanted: Deep understanding. In J. O'Neil & S. Willis (Eds.). *Transforming classroom practice* (pp. 49–70). Alexandria, VA: Association for Supervision and Curriculum Development.

Opfer, V. D., & Pedder, D. (2011). The lost promise of teacher professional development in England. *European Journal of Teacher Education, 34*(1), 3–24. doi: 10.1080/02619768.2010.534131

Pajares, M. F. (2002). *Overview of social cognitive theory and of self-efficacy.* Retrieved from http://www.emory.edu/EDUCATION/mfp/eff.html.

Pajares, M. F. (1992). Teachers' beliefs and educational research: Cleaning up a messy construct. *Review of Educational Research, 62*(3), 307–332. Retrieved from http://www.jstor.org/stable/1170741

Palmer, P. J. (1998). *The courage to teach: Exploring the inner landscape of a teacher's life.* San Francisco, CA: Jossey-Bass.

Pappas, P. (2010a, January, 4). A taxonomy of reflection: Critical thinking for students, teachers, and principals (Part 1). [Web Log Post] Retrieved from Copy/Paste http://www.peterpappas.com/2010/01/taxonomy-reflection-critical-thinking-students-teachers-principals.html

Pappas, P. (2010b, January, 6). The reflective teacher: A taxonomy of reflection (Part 3). [Web Log Post] Retrieved from Copy/Paste http://www.peterpappas.com/2010/01/reflective-teacher-taxonomy-reflection.html

Parise, L. M., & Spillane, J. P. (2010). Teacher learning and instructional change: How formal and on-the-job learning opportunities predict changes in elementary school teachers' instructional practice. *Elementary School Journal, 110*(3), 323–346. doi: 10.1086/648981

Patterson, K., Grenny, J., McMillan, R., & Switzler, A. (2012). *Crucial conversations: Tools for talking when stakes are high* (2nd ed.). New York, NY: McGraw Hill.

Peterson, D. S., Taylor, B. M., Burnham, B., & Schock, R. (2009). Reflective coaching conversations: A missing piece. *The Reading Teacher, 62*(6), 500–509. doi: 10.1598/RT.62.6.4

Pink, D. H. (2011). *Drive: The surprising truth about what motivates us.* New York, NY: Riverhead Books.

Riel, M., Cheng, B., Polin, L., Wiske, S., Koch, M., Harasim, . . . & Bonk, C. (2002). Research learning circle: Online learning and teaching. *Inter-Learn.* Retrieved from http://members.cox.net/mriel/circle.html.

Roberts, S. M., & Pruitt, E. Z. (2009). *Schools as professional learning communities: Collaborative activities and strategies for professional development* (2nd ed.). Thousand Oaks, CA: Corwin Press.

Rock, M. L., Zigmond, N. P., Gregg, M., & Gable, R. A. (2011). The power of virtual coaching. *Educational Leadership, 69*(2), 42–48. Retrieved from http://www.ascd.org/publications/educational-leadership/oct11/vol69/num02/The-Power-of-Virtual-Coaching.aspx

Ross. J. D. (2011). *Online professional development: Design, deliver, succeed!* Thousand Oaks, CA: Corwin Press.

Sadler, P. M., Sonnert, G., Coyle, H. P., Cook-Smith, N., Miller, J. L. (2013). The influence of teachers' knowledge on student learning in middle school physical science classrooms. *American Educational Research Journal, 20*(10), 1–30. doi: 10.3102/0002831213477680

Sagor, R. D. (2011). *The action research guidebook: A four-stage process for educators and school teams* (2nd ed.). Thousand Oaks, CA: Corwin Press.

Sandifer, S. D. (2011). *Wikis for school leaders: Using technology to improve communication and collaboration.* New York, NY: Routledge. Schön, D. (1987). *Educating the reflective practitioner: Toward a new design for teaching and learning in the professions.* San Francisco, CA: Jossey-Bass.

Schön, D. (1983). *The reflective practitioner: How professionals think in action.* New York, NY: Basic Books.

Scott, S. (2004). *Fierce conversations. Achieving success at work and in life, one conversation at a time.* New York, NY: Berkley Publishing Group.

Seimears, C. M., Graves, E., Schroyer, M. G., & Staver, J. (2012). How constructivist-based teaching influences students learning science. *Educational Forum, 76*(2), 265–271. doi: 10.1080/00131725.2011.653092

Sergiovanni, T. J., & Starratt, R. J. (2009). *Supervision: A redefinition* (9th ed.). New York, NY: McGraw Hill.

Silverstein, S. (1996). *Falling up.* New York, NY: HarperCollins.

Sparks, D. (2013, November 6). Why professional development without substantial follow-up is malpractice. Dennis Sparks on Leading and Learning. [Web Blog]. Retrieved from http://dennissparks.wordpress.com/2013/11/06/why-professional-development-without-substantial-follow-up-is-malpractice/

Stiggins, R., Arter, J., Chappuis, J., & Chappuis, S. (2006). *Classroom assessment for student learning: Doing it right—using it well.* Princeton, NJ: Educational Testing Service.

Stiggins, R., & DuFour, R. (2009). Maximizing the power of formative assessments. *Phi Delta Kappan, 90*(9), 640–644. doi: 10.2307/27652743

Sullivan, S., & Glanz, J. (2013). *Supervision that improves teaching: Strategies and techniques* (3rd ed.). Thousand Oaks, CA: Corwin Press.

Swanson, K. (2013). *Professional learning in the digital age: The educator's guide to user-generated learning.* New York, NY: Routledge.

Thompson, R., Kitchie, L., & Gagnon, R. (2011). *Constructing an online professional learning network for school unity and student achievement.* Thousand Oaks, CA: Corwin Press.

Tice, J. (2011). *Reflective teaching: Exploring our own classroom practice.* British Council TeachingEnglish. London: British Council. Retrieved from http://www.teachingenglish.org.uk/article/reflective-teaching-exploring-our-own-classroom-practice

Timperley, H. (2008). *National education findings of assess to learn (AtoL) report.* Wellington, New Zealand: Ministry of Education.

Timperley, H., Wilson, A., Barrar, H., & Fung, I. (2007). *Teacher professional learning and development. Best Evidence Synthesis Iteration.* Wellington, New Zealand: Ministry of Education.

Tkatchov, O., & Pollnow, S. K. (2011). *A practical guide to teaching and learning.* Lanham, NY: Rowman & Littlefield Publishers, Inc.

Troen, V., & Boles, K. C. (2012). *The power of teacher teams: With cases, analyses, and strategies for success*. Thousand Oaks, CA: Corwin Press.

Tuckman, B. W. (1965). Developmental sequence in small groups. *Psychological Bulletin, 63*, 384–399. doi: 10.1037/h0022100

Tuckman, B. W., & Jensen, M. A. C. (1977). Stages of small group development revisited. *Group and Organizational Studies, 2*, 419–427. doi: 10.1177/105960117700200404

US Department of Education, Office of Educational Technology. The National Education Technology Plan. (2010). *Transforming American education: Learning powered by technology*. Washington, DC: U. Department of Education. Retrieved from https://www.ed.gov/technology/netp-2010

Venables, D. R. (2011). *The practice of authentic PLCs: A guide to effective teacher teams*. Thousand Oaks, CA: Corwin Press.

Vetter, A. (2012). Teachers as architects of transformation: The change process of an elementary-school teacher in practitioner research group. *Teacher Education Quarterly, 39*(1), 27–49. Retrieved from http://www.eric.ed.gov/contentdelivery/servlet/ERICServlet?accno=EJ977355

Villa, R. A., Thousand, J. S., & Nevin, A. I. (2013). *A guide to co-teaching: New lessons and strategies to facilitate student learning* (3rd ed.) Thousand Oaks, CA: Corwin Press.

Vygotsky, L. (1978). *Mind in society: The development of higher psychological processes*. Cambridge, MA: Harvard University Press.

Waldron, N. L., & McLeskey, J. (2010). Establishing a collaborative school culture through comprehensive school reform. *Journal of Educational and Psychological Consultation, 20*(1), 58–74. doi: 10.1080/10474410903535364

Walpole, S., & McKenna, M. C. (2012). *The literacy coach's handbook: A guide to research-based practice* (2nd ed.). New York, NY: Guilford.

Wenger, E. (1998) *Communities of practice: Learning, meaning, and identity*. Cambridge, UK: Cambridge University Press.

Whitcomb, J., Borko, H., & Liston, D. (2009). Growing talent: Promising professional development models and practices. *Journal of Teacher Education, 60*(3), 207–212. doi: 10.1177/0022487109337280

Wiburg, K. M., & Brown, S. (2006). *Lesson study communities: Increasing achievement with diverse students*. Thousand Oaks, CA: Corwin Press.

Williams, I. M., & Olaniran, B. A. (2012). Professional development through web 2.0 collaborative applications. In V. P. Dennen & J. B. Myers (Eds.), *Virtual professional development and informal learning via social networks* (pp. 1–24). Hershey, PA: IGI Global.

Wood, F. H., & Killian, J. E. (1998). Job-embedded learning makes the difference in school improvement. *Journal of Staff Development, 19*(1), 52–54. Retrieved from www.ascd.org/publications/classroom_leadership/may2002/Job-Embedded_Professional_Development_and_Reflective_Coaching.aspx

Wood, F. H., & McQuarrie, F. (1999). On-the-job learning. *Journal of Staff Development, 20*(3), 10–13. Retrieved from www.learningforward.org/publications/jsd#.UrZLrGRDuWE

Woolfolk, A. E. (2014). *Educational psychology* (12th ed.). Englewood Cliffs, NJ: Prentice Hall.

Wylie, E. C., Gullickson, A. R., Cummings, K. E., Egelson, P. E., Noakes, L. A., Norman, K. M., & Veeder, S. A. (2012). *Improving formative assessment practice to empower student learning*. Thousand Oaks, CA: Corwin Press.

Wynne, S. C. (2010). Job-embedded learning: How teachers learn from one another during the workday. Unpublished doctoral dissertation. University of Georgia, Athens, GA.

Yoon, K. S., Duncan, T., Lee, S. W., Scarloss, B., & Shapley, K. L. (2007). *Reviewing the evidence on how teacher professional development affects student achievement* (Issues and Answers Report, REL 2007-No. 033). Washington, DC: US Department of Education Sciences, National Center for Education Evaluation and Regional Assistance, Regional Educational Laboratory Southwest. Retrieved from http://ies.ed.gov/ncee/edlabs

Zepeda. S. J. (2013). *The principal as instructional leader: A practical handbook* (3rd ed.). New York, NY: Routledge.

Zepeda, S. J. (2012a). *Professional development: What works* (2nd ed.). New York, NY: Routledge.

Zepeda, S. J. (2012b). *Instructional supervision: Applying tools and concepts* (3rd ed.). New York, NY: Routledge.

Zepeda, S. J. (2012c). *Informal classroom observations on the go: Feedback, discussion, and reflection* (3rd ed). New York, NY: Routledge.

Zepeda, S. J. (2011a). Instructional supervision, coherence, and job-embedded learning. In T. Townsend & J. MacBeath (Eds.), *International Handbook on Leadership for Learning*. New York, NY: Springer Publishing Company.

Zepeda, S. J. (2011b). *Job-embedded learning: A powerful, practical, and cost-effective form of professional development*. Larchmont, NY: Eye on Education. Retrieved from http://eyeoneducation.com/bookstore/client/client_pages/pdfs/Zepeda_Job_Embedded_Learning.pdf

Zweibel, B. (2005/2014a). The coaching F.R.A.M.E. of reference model. Leadership-Traction®. Retrieved from www.ldrtr.com

Zweibel, B. (2005/ 2014b). Coaching helps people F.O.C.U.S. LeadershipTraction®. Retrieved from www.ldrtr.com

Zweibel, B. (2005/2014c). Questions that gather information versus deepen the learning. LeadershipTraction®. Retrieved from www.ldrtr.com

Index

Note: page numbers in **bold** refer to tables and page numbers in *italics* refer to images